Augustin Cabanès

Curious bypaths of history

Being medico-historical studies and observations

Augustin Cabanès

Curious bypaths of history
Being medico-historical studies and observations

ISBN/EAN: 9783742827104

Manufactured in Europe, USA, Canada, Australia, Japa

Cover: Foto ©ninafisch / pixelio.de

Manufactured and distributed by brebook publishing software
(www.brebook.com)

Augustin Cabanès

Curious bypaths of history

Chas. Carrington. Editeur.

Pathological Studies of the Past.

Curious Bypaths of History

BEING

MEDICO-HISTORICAL STUDIES and OBSERVATIONS

BY Dr. Cabanès

Frontispiece by DANIEL VIERGE

Engraved on Copper by F. MASSÉ

PARIS
LIBRAIRIE DES BIBLIOPHILES
CHARLES CARRINGTON, ÉDITEUR
13, Faubourg Montmartre, 13
1898

To the Reader.

THIS BOOK FOR MEN ALONE IS MEANT,
BOOK-WORMS, OR CURIOSITIES ANENT;
OF SOUND MIND, OF SERIOUS BENT,
ON CURIOUS, HIDDEN BOOKS INTENT,
ON ODD RESEARCH AND LEARNING.

SHOULD RATHER ALL THY THOUGHTS ENGAGE
THE TRIFLES OF THE PRESENT AGE,
ITS WORDS WILL NOT THY THIRST ASSUAGE,
CLOSE IT AT ONCE, ITS ABSTRUSE PAGE
WILL NOT REPAY THY TURNING.

FOND MAIDS AND INEXPERIENCED YOUTHS
PRITHEE CONCEAL ITS BITTER TRUTHS.

PISANUS FRAXI.

FOREWORD

Carmina hæc si quis, non sunt quoque, prava fatebor:
Sed, quæ non prosunt singula, multa juvant.

Ovid.

Whoever hesitates to utter that which he thinks the highest truth, lest it should be too much in advance of the time, may reassure himself by looking at his acts from an impersonal point of view. Let him duly realize the fact that opinion is the agency through which character adapts external arrangements to itself that his opinion rightly forms part of this agency is a unit of force, constituting, with other such units, the general power which works out social changes, and he will perceive that he may properly give full utterance to his innermost conviction, leaving it to produce what effect it may.—*Herbert Spencer.*

EDITOR'S FOREWORD.

[Ten Minutes with the Reviewers].

The pathology of history is one of the most fascinating studies that can occupy the attention whether of the general reader or the professional man. It contains surprises beside which the revelations of the sensational novel dwindle into commonplace. Studies like these, moreover, derive increased interest from the fact of being based on documentary evidence. Such proofs we admit, are not of a nature always to carry conviction to minds steeped in scepticism, but they are the only kind procurable, and, it must not be overlooked that, life itself is largely made up of a more or less fair balancing of probabilities. The task of the modern historian is less to discover new truths than to strip off the lies that have grown up clustering around the old traditions. We do not pretend that new material is no longer to be found. The contents of the present work would sufficiently refute any such theory.

It is with much misgiving that we issue the present book. Its predecessor, entitled "The Secret Cabinet of History", was received with "such a shout", as a Hibernian friend called it, "of ominous Silence" by the English Press that small kindness is expected for the present venture.

Liberties of expression which in the French tongue are regarded as the common currency of conversation were in the more boisterous English toned down to the point of delicacy, while others scarcely capable of such attention were left to languish in their original garb untranslated. But even these precautions were not sufficient for what honest old Doctor Johnson would have stigmatised as, the muck- and gutter-hunters, and copies sent out for review were quietly appropriated without the slightest mention or, in one or two instances, only criticised and attacked. The latter course, we do not deny, is the right of every journal that receives a book for review; but the principle which will allow the acceptance of a work sent for a specific purpose without the least attempt or intention to carry out that purpose, belongs, it appears to our rude mind, to a code of Ethics bordering on what in thieves' slang is known as "finger-smithing".

Not until it was too late for us to withdraw, did we realise how little a fearless handling of history is relished across the Channel. And yet the work in its French dress was received with acclamation by every journalist throughout the Continent, and hundreds of flattering reviews helped to quicken the sale of what constitutes one of the most unique works of historical science. Some English journals, however, less fearful of Mother Grundy than their fellows, gave the book kindly welcome enough. Amongst these we may mention *The Star* (October 5th); *The Rochdale Observer* (October 8th); *The Boston Daily Globe* (June 12th).

"The Jamaica Post" (July 5th).

This ably edited paper devoted a long article to the book and predicted "success for it throughout the British Empire and the United States" comparing it to G. W. M. Reynold's "*Mysteries of the Court of London*", with the difference that the latter was founded on fiction whereas Dr. Cabanès' work is founded on history. "So far as our purview goes," concluded the reviewer, "there is nothing in literature with which it can be compared."

Compare this with the following splenetic utterance of
"The Academy" (Oct. 16th).

"The outward form, no less than the contents, of this book inevitably make us think of Browning's 'scrofulous French novel' with its 'grey paper and blunt type'. Dr. Cabanès' notion of secret history comprises unpleasant medical details concerning Louis Quinze and Louis Seize, Marie-Antoinette, Marat, Talleyrand, and others. There may have been some reason for writing the book: there was none for translating it, for any historian likely to use it to profit would certainly be able to read it in the original."

The "malice prepense" in this foul and mean attack is so obvious that it defeats its own end. Of course, "any historian would certainly be able to read it in the original"; always presuming three things (I) if he could read French; (II) if he had the leisure to come to Paris: and (III) if he knew where to unearth the documents. One might just as well argue that it is unnecessary to publish the news that appears in the daily newspapers, as people could find it out for themselves. So they could *Mr. dog-in-the-manger "Academy"*, if they had the time, and knew where to get it.

This semi-learned journal seems to be unaware of the fact that after all Dr. Cabanès is only following in the track of distinguished Frenchmen who have virtually created new laws for the interpretation of Modern History. The facile use of such terms as "*Scrofulous*", and the petty snapping at the *outward* form of the book, instead of fixing on the contents, show a deplorable obliquity of moral vision. It means "*No case.* Abuse plaintiff's attorney." Taine; Ste Beuve; Littré; Michelet: all applied the same principles to History as Dr. Cabanès, and "the Academy" should have known it.

Before leaving this little interesting subject, I have one other "bone to pick" with these over-clever people. I believe it is the rule, wherever English fair play is understood, to give a man due notice when any sparring is begun against him. The "Academy" did no such thing. Their senseless little "par" was printed, the paper distributed, and the "Academy's" man no doubt took a short cut to Holywell Street to sell the review-copy of the book he had so ridiculously traduced. Only through a press-cutting channel did we learn of his exploit. Godfrey Higgins, a far greater scholar than all the scialists of the "Academy" put together, wrote in the Preface to the "Celtic Druids":—"I take the liberty of saying, that I cannot conceive it possible for any person possessing honourable intentions, to write against me in any way without giving me information of it, or sending me a copy of his publication. To attack, and not to do this, is the act of the midnight assassin." We may add that we do not for a moment contest the right of these gentlemen to attack. Let them come on. But we do protest against being hit "below the belt", or knifed in the back.

The notice contributed by

'The Pall Mall Gazette' (June 5th).

was far more just, and correctly interpreted the aim of the book:

"The medicine man has of recent years been infected by the cacoëthes scribendi. Since Dr. Conan Doyle escaped, a good many of his colleagues seem to have broken away incontinently. Hence they make incursions into fiction, and generally with some success, for the doctor of to-day is, as a rule, a man of a liberal education. We now have the doctor as a historian in M. Cabanès's 'Secret Cabinet of History' (Paris: Carrington), and very interesting he is. The side-lights the man of medicine throws on certain obscure points of French history are of real, if somewhat meretricious, value. After all, the personal factor—more especially in the mediæval history—cannot be altogether eliminated. Professor Hume was fond of saying that if Charles V, at one critical period had not had such a bad attack of gout the history of the Reformation in Germany would probably have been very different. The horrors, too, of the deathbed scene in the Œil de Bœuf as painted by a doctor, surpass even Carlyle's lurid picture. Indeed all the essays in this little volume are of interest, full of quaint learning and deep research. The fate of the brain of Talleyrand, 'that brain', as Victor Hugo cried, 'which had inspired so many men, built up so many edifices, led two revolutions, deceived twenty monarchs, and had contained the world', and at the last was thrown into the drain of the Rue Richepanse, and the quest of the lost eye of Gambetta, are among the striking curiosities of history. At the same time it must be added that the volume [illegible] written *pueris virginibusque.* Although the author is anxious not to outrage what the translator sweetly calls the 'proprieties', his erudite is at times swept away by the interest of his studies. Moreover, the original was written in French. Lest it fall into the hands of a maiden uncle the 'Secret Cabinet of History' should be kept under lock and key along with Balzac's 'Contes Drolatiques': to which, by the way, it forms a sort of scientific commentary."

A pseudo-aristocratic journal.

Compare this with the following *morceau* from a weekly journal of gutter scandal; professedly devoted to the interests of truth, but, in reality, a heterogeneous collection of all the newest pornographic society small talk, and you get a clear idea of the inner workings of pettifogging journalism. The man who runs this paper at an immense profit to himself, has been proved by financial papers to be a rank fraud, and to have given his "tips" to the public with an eye to his own personal fattening. He says,

> "From a cursory examination of the work I should say that it affords a fresh proof that this particular trade is a fraudulent one."

If by "trade" he means the publishing business, he is certainly right, for nothing is more fraudulent for the unwary publisher. If he means, as far as the public is concerned, then he simply "bites off his nose to be revenged on his face" for being himself a publisher, he thereby proves himself a "fraud", as, in our opinion, he undoubtedly is, and all the worse for being an old one. We do not record the name of this individual, as for fear of being trapped, he wisely omitted to name our book, though that was the only one sent to him. We take philosophic consolation in the thought that while our book will be consulted by curious and earnest students, his prurient journal will be forgotten, long after we are all mouldering dust. The time has gone by when the saying of Rinconete y Cortadillo, *Lo que dice la lengua paga la gorja*, had any validity; and insults flung out by low-minded ruffians have now to be treated with the same contempt as snarling curs. "But now chaunce hathe soe served, that I showlde fall into thier handes, to this intente (I suppose), that I. . . . might the better understande how mich affiance I ought to have in human casualties."

The Weekly Sun (June 20th)

proved very much fairer, but commits much the same mistake as "The Academy" while proving much more gentlemanly and academic:

"*The Secret Cabinet of History*" (Paris, Charles Carrington) is in some respects a very remarkable book. It is an outcome of that specialising tendency of our age which demands that every important event, whether domestic or historical, shall be treated from the well informed standpoint of an expert. A witty judge has been heard to remark that he would unhesitatingly place expert witnesses in the foremost rank of liars; but in this book, entirely devoted to French events, our expert is careful to give chapter and verse for every statement he makes. Doctor Cabanès takes us into all the secret cabinets of history, and treats every case as if he were the medical man in charge, and were taking notes for his own benefit. These notes are given to the world, and if it were a medical man writing for medical men there could be no objection to them, but it is doubtful if the general publication of such details is necessary either for the historical student or the ordinary reader. The historian of course would have to study these matters to arrive at a right understanding of events, but then the same sources of information would be open to him as to Dr. Cabanès. As an instance of the material the book contains, a whole chapter is devoted to the accouchement of Napoleon's Queen and the anxieties of the Emperor.

The Saturday Review (6th Nov.)

devoted a few lines as follows to the book, which, although brief, are very fair and, coming from such an influential quarter, are all the more weighty.

"*The Secret Cabinet of History.*" (By Doctor Cabanès. Paris: Carrington, 1896.) This book, published in Paris and excellently translated by Mr. Costello, is one of the most interesting curiosities for the collector of strange books that has appeared of late years. The interest is purely medical, and ought to produce the most lively emotions among medical men. The several essays of which it is composed are highly accounts, compiled from secret letters and records, of the lastinous diseases of the French kings, and detailed narrations of their wives' accouchements. To the lay mind the book is interesting, because it is so obviously genuine and because it shows with singular and cynical clearness how a pain in the stomach may alter the destinies of a kingdom.

The London medical papers, although copies were sent them for review, took absolutely no notice of the book. It was reserved for a far-away American medical journal—

"**Medicine**" (Detroit, Mich. U. S. A.)

to gauge the exact aim and object of the work. In their issue of September (1897) they thus delivered themselves:

"Pathology in history is always of interest, especially since by affecting the leaders or rulers of a nation it tends to affect the nation as a whole. This volume contains thirteen separate essays on subjects involved in historical pathology. The first one relates to a youthful indiscretion of Louis XIV whereby, as Dr. Cabanès proves, Louis XIV very early contracted gonorrhoea. While it was recognised by his courtly physicians, they concealed the origin of the disorder from interested motives, although describing its clinical features very clearly. The second discusses the fistula of the same king, and mentions all the surgical procedures adopted, as well as the fees paid to surgeons. The disease became fashionable among the courtiers, and one lady of honor was disconsolate because her physician was unable to discover that she had any trace of the royal disorder. The phymosis from which Louis XVI suffered played a large part in determining certain features of the French Revolution. For a while it rendered Louis XVI impotent and this fomented intrigues by the future Louis XVIII, Charles X and the Duke of Orleans, which seriously damaged the moral character of Marie Antoinette. These intrigues undoubtedly aided the general Revolutionary movement, since all three of the intriguants hoped to profit by this movement. Another item of special interest to physicians is the proof given that Marat suffered from both mental, dermic, and other somatic symptoms of diabetes, which doubtless underlay his suspicious and jealous tendencies. The change recorded in Marat's attitude during the Revolution is readily explained by the tone given to his thoughts through the irritability produced by this disease. The work of which this is the first volume merits purchase and perusal by any physician of literary and historical tastes. The second volume will prove equally interesting, to judge from the table of subjects given in the present work."

We have to apologize to the reader for having taken up his attention so long with matters less of public than personal interest. No one can have greater respect and admiration for English journalists than have we. No other country in the world can boast so large a percentage of talented and fair-minded men as those who control the London and Provincial press. That the press should, notwithstanding, be sometimes debased by a few black sheep seeking to gratify private malice is not surprising, and the proofs of such malice, we shall, when the occasion arises, disclose in larger detail.

Not only has the "Secret Cabinet of History" been proscribed, but other works issued by us have also been placed on the index. The result is invariably to enhance the value of the book and cause it to fetch a price it would not otherwise command. In 1896, for instance, we published a work entitled "The Book of Exposition"[1] translated from the Arabic, and forming a natural Supplement to Sir Richard F. Burton's famous version of "*The Thousand Nights and a Night*". Our book was printed in an edition limited to 200 copies on hand-made paper, and issued to private subscribers only, at the prohibitive charge of two guineas per copy. No attempt was made at concealment, as the title-page bore our address (32 rue Drouot), and the work was registered at the *Ministère de l'Intérieur*, Paris, in conformity with the law of copy-right. Yet the Postal authorities, to our astonishment, pounced on all copies forwarded by mail, and our equally innocent agents in London were threatened with legal action. We did not dream such high-handed proceedings possible in a country which sanctions the free circulation amongst school children of an unexpurgated edition of the Old Testament, and the works of Shakespeare.

The moral object of our book was distinct enough, and its ethnographical significance clearly defined. It fights against sexual irregularities. Only by knowing them can danger be avoided.

[1] The full description runs as follows:—

"The Book of Exposition" literally translated from the Arabic by an English Bohemian ("Kitab Al-Izah Fi 'Ilm Al-Nikah Bi-T-Tamam W-Al-Kamal"). With Translator's Foreword, numerous important Notes illustrating the Text and several very interesting Appendices. In one large post 8vo Volume. Neatly bound in black cloth with gilt top; cover decorated with Arabic monogram of the title of the work.

The moral and physical beauties of womankind are brought into prominence, and the passions that war against her proper place in Nature are fiercely combatted. This was the aim of the Arab sheikh who wrote in Arabic some three hundred years ago; no other aim has been ours in offering an English version for the first time to scholars. Why then pursue and proscribe it? We leave those who move in certain ranks of English Society to judge whether the translation of the "Book of Exposition", has any *raison d'être* in presence of the scandals that, from time to time, recall the lurid conflagration of Sodom and Gomorrha.

The immoral Morality of England will offer a splendid field of research to the future historian. Macaulay has a passage of great power on the subject:[1]

"We know no spectacle so ridiculous as the British public in one of its periodical fits of morality. In general, elopements, divorces, and family quarrels, pass with little notice. We read the scandal, talk about it for a day, and forget it. But once in six or seven years our virtue becomes outrageous. We cannot suffer the laws of religion and decency to be violated. We must make a stand against vice. We must teach libertines that the English people appreciate the importance of domestic ties. Accordingly, some unfortunate man, in no respect more depraved than hundreds whose offences have been treated with lenity, is singled out as an expiatory sacrifice. If he has children, they are to be taken from him. If he has a profession, he is to be driven from it. He is cut by the higher orders, and hissed by the lower. He is, in truth, a sort of 'whipping-boy', by whose vicarious agonies all the other transgressors of the same class are, it is supposed, sufficiently punished. We reflect very complacently on our own severity, and compare, with great pride, the high standards of morals established in England with the Parisian laxity. At length our anger is satiated. Our victim is ruined, and heart-broken. And our virtue goes quietly to sleep for seven years more."

"La Pudique Albion" never fails to justify her hard-won name of "Hypocrite", and America competes with her strongly for the inglorious title. Our Yankee cousins stamped out Slavery; one day they will unlock the gate and disemprison Liberty. All

[1] See MACAULAY'S Review of Moore's LIFE OF BYRON, in *Essays and Reviews*", London, 1886.

books of any note have been persecuted. The "*Age of Reason*" was put down by the Police, and men gathered behind hedges to read by stealth copies they had bought with their united pence. If the Bible itself were, by some Magic turn of Fortune's wheel, to fall again under the ban, it would be eagerly read where it is now used in English parlour windows, as a conventional stand for the flower-pot.

There was talk of a Treasury prosecution of Burton's Arabian "Nights", to which our book claims to be a sequel. When the worthy Chevalier heard of the intended onslaught, he merely said "Let them come on. I shall go into open Court with the Bible in one hand and the works of Sterne, Shakespere, and the English Dramatists in the other, by way of support and reserve." The authorities wisely refrained. Probably Sir Richard, being one of their own class, knew too much for them. They prefer smaller fry. The works Burton cited may be bought in London for Sixpence apiece. His translation was issued to Private Subscribers only, and not exposed in shop-windows. So was ours. Why then make any difference? Ernest Vizitelly for Englishing and publishing the French works of Emile Zola was prosecuted by the Solicitor-general. A white-haired man of some seventy years of age, he had passed his whole life in the service of Literature, and his very judges admitted the unimpeachableness of his motives. The finding, natheless, of that profound Literary Censorship—a British Jury (the "Academy" of England) was "Guilty", and, pecuniarily ruined, away went the old Scholar to "do" eighteen months "hard"! A few years later, the Great French novelist himself crossed over to England, and was feasted at Guildhall by the Lord Mayor and the worthy Aldermen of the City of London. We quote the following from the

"Westminster Gazette" (September 21st 1893)

"No man ever received a more courteous and respectful greeting than he, in Lincoln's Inn to-day — yet it is only a few years ago since his English publisher, an old man with a name respected in English journalism, was haled to prison for publishing what, at most, was but a bowdlerised edition of one of the Sage of Medan's most harrowing dissections of the moral cancer. How changed to-day!"

The worthy "Westminster" is quite right: things *have* changed, and changed considerably to boot. For the respectable firm of Chatto and Windus are at the present moment (Nov. 6th) issuing "*The Dram Shop* (l'Assommoir) of Zola—one of the most powerful stories he wrote. While, bolder still, "*a private issue* (?) *of all* the works" of Master Emile, is announced, "*as now for the first time* completely translated into English by ARTHUR SYMONS, *and others*." We only trust that the "Lutetian Society" will not get hunted down by the infamous National (Im?)purity Associations, sworn enemies to all unbowdlerised versions. Probably in no other city in Europe could such an inconsistent state of things take place. We have personally no desire to share Vizetelly's martyrdom. Rather do we prefer to hope that London's Lord Mayor will recognise the services our pen has rendered to Literature, and invite us across to the slaying of a "fatted calf". An old book lays down the dictum that "all things are possible to him that believeth". Our private store of modesty really prevents our doing otherwise.

To people with plenty of leisure and a paucity of cerebral tissue desiring something to do, we respectfully submit the following recommendation of Sir R. F. Burton:

"These Vigilants and Purifiers, with that hypocritical severity which ever makes the worst sinner in private the most rigorous judge in public, lately had the impudent impudence to summons a publisher who had reprinted the Decameron with the "objectionable passages" in French. Mr. Alderman Faudell Phillips had the good sense contemptuously to dismiss the summons. Englishmen are no longer what they were if they continue to tolerate this ignoble espionnage of vicious and prurient virtuous "Associations". If they mean *real* work why do they commence by condemning scholar-like works, instead of cleansing the many foul cesspools of active vice which are a public disgrace to London."

A few words more, and we will bring our rambling remarks

to a close. The present work is a sequel to the "Secret Cabinet of History", already mentioned, and the forerunner of a third volume which will appear later and contain further pathological studies of the same kind.

We foolishly imagined that the earlier book would meet with an open-arm welcome and be quickly clasped to the scholar's breast. Alas, how short-lived was our fancy, how sad the disillusion. Book-sellers would not stock it; in fact seemed to take a dislike to the poor bantling.

> "I do not like thee Dr. Fell
> The reason why I cannot tell".

We were left to push the sale for ourselves and sent out the following letter: -

"Paris, August, 1897.

"Dear Sir

'The Secret Cabinet of History'.

"I may take it for granted that you have seen a mention made in the English papers concerning this work, some favourable, some otherwise. The '*Pall Mall Gazette*' whose notice is appended, led me to believe that the work would be fit to be placed in the hands of a select public. My offer of an agency to one or two large English publishers, however, met with a courteous refusal and I cite one of these as follows:-

> "*Dear Sir, We received your work and have now read*
> "*a copy of the 'Secret Cabinet of History'. Although the*
> "*work is of much interest, yet we fear that it is not one we*
> "*could take up. People in England are very prudish, and*
> "*if we were known to be publishers of this they might be*
> "*disinclined to buy the novels and classical reprints which*
> "*are the bulk of our trade. Thanking you nevertheless for*
> "*the opportunity afforded us, We are, etc.*"

"I am therefore constrained to go to my public direct, and, as I save an Agent's commission, I shall be glad to deliver to you a copy at the rate of Half-a-guinea (English postal order) carriage prepaid. The work forms a handsome volume, and apart from its contents, which cannot fail to interest you, it is a book which every Amateur and Student would like to handle.

"I am,

dear Sir,

Yours obediently"

This had good effect and the work has since commanded a steady sale, more especially amongst medical, and other professional men. Thinkers and scholars are, after all, the only people we work for, or care to serve. The searcher after scenes of lubricity to excite sensual passions will find nothing here to excite his perverted brain. Our old friend, Isidore Liseux, once said of a certain book, issued under his auspices:—

> "*Certes, nous ne voudrions pas conseiller cette lecture à la virginité ignorante, mais peut-être la recommanderions nous moins à la maturité en quête d'excitations érotiques. Les vieillards qui demandent à une littérature spéciale le* STIMULUS VENERIS, *ne trouveraient pas ici ce qu'ils cherchent.*"

We appropriate these words because admirably expressing the character of the present studies.

We owe undeserved thanks to Dr. Cabanès for his permission to add our article on *Flagellation in France* at the end of his studies; a permission of which we have not availed ourselves. It is no easy thing to deal with live authors. In fact, between the double fire of the Author and the Critics, the publisher has a pretty nice time of it. When, as a mere act of courtesy, and not because we cared a "tinker's benediction" about his precious permission, we asked our friend for consent to insert the article named, he raised a host of difficulties about his "responsibility" and made such a huge "mountain out of our molehill", that on receiving the doctor's written acquiescence the following day, we rapidly made up our mind, now that the point was gained, to send this meticulous little man to the "devil", and do without the famous "permission". Pray take no alarm, kind reader! You are not to be swindled out of your "flagellation" article. It has been printed uniform with the present volume, paged on its own account, provided with a special cover and title page, and issued *gratuitously* to every purchaser of "The Curious Bypaths of History". A word of warning to the critics; in handling these studies, put on a pair of white gloves, after the fashion of the brave *douaniers* of Spain when turning over ladies' trunks, as, should our fiery little doctor call you out, a strong wrist will be needed to beat down his guard. In any case, count upon our services.

We hardly owe any apology to the reader for the appearance of this article. Indeed, many people wrote, begging us to put forth something more definite on this subject than has yet seen the light. We have here taken only a step in that direction. Later we may find time to dovetail together in systematic order the curious revelations and other documents that we have had sent to us, and which deal particularly with flagellation in all its Protean shapes and forms. The study is needed and already numbers many amateurs. In fact the rage for whipping is in England very great, since even the humble author of these lines has been menaced — if we are to believe a certain public journal — with a "horse-whipping" by an irrationally irascible father smarting under an imaginary wrong. [1]

We are glad to assure our alarmed readers that, as this feverish gentleman has not yet appeared on the horizon, there may be still some chance of our bringing out a new work before his advent.

[1] He pretended that a circular had been sent to his address in a closed envelope and opened, in his absence, by his daughter "[illegible]"! But what are we to think, even if the story be true, of a young female of this tender age who opens her father's letters while he is out. Suppose the letter had been from his "lady-friend"? Would he have horse-whipped *her*?

CHARLES CARRINGTON.

PARIS, November, 1897.

TABLE OF CONTENTS

[illegible]

[illegible]

[illegible]

[illegible]

[illegible]

[illegible]

[illegible]

TABLE OF CONTENTS

THE ARTICLE

ON

"FLAGELLATION IN FRANCE"

IS GIVEN AWAY WITH THIS BOOK AND, BEING OF UNIFORM TYPE AND SIZE, BOTH VOLUMES MAY BE BOUND UP TOGETHER.

THE PHYSICIAN

OF

LOUIS XI.

I ever
Have studied physic, through which secret art,
By turning o'er authorities I have,
Together with my practice, made familiar,
To me and to my aid the blest infusions
That dwell in vegetives, in metals, stones;
And I can speak of the disturbances
That nature works, and of her cures; which doth give me
A more content in course of true delight
Than to be thirsty after tottering honour,
Or tie my treasure up in silken bags
To please the fool and death.

Pericles, Act. III, Sc. 1.

THE PHYSICIAN OF LOUIS XI.

If led by idleness or curiosity, you had a few years ago turned your steps to the Rue Saint-André-des-Arts, a few paces from the Cour du Commerce, so rich in historical associations connected with the Revolution, you would have noticed an edifice of modest architecture, purposely simple in style, the construction of which was being actively pursued. On enquiry, you would have been informed that the building then being constructed on this spot, was destined to be a college for girls, to be named, after the "Swan of Cambrai:" the *Lycée Fénelon*. If you pushed your researches further you would evoke an entire epoch of long-forgotten history.

* * *

Let us for a moment carry our thoughts four centuries back, and endeavour, with the patience of an archæologist, to reconstitute this corner of ancient Paris, now menaced by the pickaxe of the demolisher. In this quarter, called in the XVth century the Faubourg-Saint-Germain; let us draw an irregular square, bounded by the Rue des Fossés-Saint-Germain, the Rue de l'École de Médecine, the Rue du Paon, the Rue de l'Eperon and the Rue Saint-André-des Arts. A long, narrow street, called the "Cour de Rouen," cut this irregular square diagonally into two nearly equal parts. In that part of the square nearest to the Rue du Paon, was situated the "Palace of the Archbishop of Rouen," in the other part touching the Rue Saint-André-des-Arts, as far as the eye could reach, stretched out gardens, marshy fields and tumble-down hovels. This entire quarter was called the "Séjour de Navarre."

After having been for many years an appanage of the crown, the Séjour de Navarre passed into the hands of Louis XII, then only Duke of Orleans. On the eve of setting out on his expedition to Brittany, the young Duke, who wanted to turn all he could into money, sold the mansion of his sires. The purchasers are now known to have been: Guillaume Ruzé, a counsellor to the Parliament; and Nicolas Violle, lord of the manor of Noizeau a corrector of the Chamber of Accounts. Jean Hurot, an advocate of the Parliament, bought the third lot, which he very soon hastened to dispose of, on the 27th January 1489 to Jacques Coitier, late first physician to Louis XI and his intimate adviser.

* * *

Coitier, whose name is variously spelled, by different historians *Coictier*, *Coittier*, *Cottier*, and lastly *Coitier*, retired there, quite at the end of the town, near to the ramparts, after having made his fortune. It was not, as the legend for a long time had it, in order to flee from the fury of the monarch, that he had thought of retiring. The anger of Louis XI was no longer to be feared, he having already been six years in his grave, when Coitier purchased the grounds, situated opposite the Buci postern, nearly touching the rampart of Philippe-Auguste.

Scarcely had the new owner taken possession, than the workmen were busily employed. In a few months, arose the two wings of a mansion, with crenellated front, behind which was a closed gallery, resting on pillars such as may be often seen in lordly mansions of the Middle Ages. At the angle formed by the meeting of the two wings was a court, with a winding-staircase ; a medley of incongruous buildings, forming a small mansion.

A second court contained a well, which deserves to draw our attention for a moment. This well, which could still be seen a few years ago, was more exactly a cistern with a low coping, on the middle of which there stood a dolphin's head.

Let us not forget to mention two gardens, a pleasure-garden and a fruit-garden, and lastly a Gothic chapel. Over the principal entrance Coitier caused an elephant with a tower on its back to be sculptured.

Upon a turret over one of the doors, a shield had been sculptured, in the field of which were represented a tree bearing fruit, an orange-tree and an apricot-tree, * and images

* We adopt the version of the *abricotier* (Apricot-tree) in order not to give denial to the legend which says that Coitier wished to play upon words, by a sort of sign or rebus.

In this case *A l'abri Coitier* would mean that the doctor deemed himself fortunate to have retired, like the sage, to a safe shelter from all importunate annoyances. But it is equally probable that it is an orange tree, the arms of the arch-physician bearing " An orange tree or."

of the Virgin, Saint James and Saint Nicholas, with the following inscription in letters running into each other, as are usually observed in the writing of that time:

JACOBVS COICTIER
MILES ET CONSVLARIVS
AC VICE PRAESES CAMERAE COMPTORVM
PARISIENSIS
AREAM EMIT ET IN EA OEDIFICAVIT
ANNO M.C.C.C.C.X.C. *

* * *

Coitier's mansion, known by the name of the "House of the Elephant," was not demolished until 1739. It stood on the site of Nos. 47, 49, 51 and 53 of the Rue Saint-André-des-Arts †. In 1740, the place where the mansion of the King's doctor had stood was occupied by buildings devoid of character, and this act of vandalism was perpetrated notwithstanding the protests of the journalists of the period.

Coitier lived for nearly fifteen years in his House of the Elephant, overwhelmed with honours and dignities, enjoying peaceably the riches he had amassed. He was not satisfied with having a mansion in town, he must also have a country-house. At the distance of a few gun-shots

* The translation of this inscription is as follows:
"Jacques Coitier, knight, counsellor to the King, vice-president of the Chamber of Accounts, has bought this plot of land and has thereon built this edifice in the year 1490."

† By a curious coincidence, it was in the house bearing the number 53 Rue Saint-André-des-Arts that the eminent toxicologist Orfila died, on the 4th March 1853.

from the forest of Bondy, near to the celebrated abbey of Livry, there existed an ancient castleward, the lordship of Aulnay; he bought it for 3,000 gold crowns. This lordship included: a castle with drawbridge, a dwelling-house situated in the court-yard of the castle, two ponds, two water-mills, a warren, etc., to say nothing of the broad acres, the woods and meadows, which made of this property one of the finest domains in the neighbourhood of Paris.

Coitier could, if he had a fancy to do so, have played the lord of the manor on his lands. In fact the castleward was endowed with incontestable rights and prerogatives: right of high justiciary, dues on sale of wood, rights of high, mean and common jurisdiction. History fails to tell us whether he ever exercised these rights. Had Louis XI been still alive, there is but little doubt that the peasants would have had to endure the lot of the serfs of days gone by, and the feudal practices would have been seen to flourish on this spot of land. But Coitier was no longer in favour at Court, and neither Louis XII, nor Charles VIII, felt inclined to feed his ambition. At the death of Louis XI, the Burgundian doctor had lost his appointment as chief physician to the Court, also that of President of the Chamber of Accounts, and had managed only, thanks to high influences, to retain the secondary post of Vice-President of the same Chamber.

At all events the King thought fit, to take into consideration the "great and agreeable services that the said counsellor, master Jacques de Coitier hath rendered unto our lord and father, during his illness", as it said in the charter of Charles VIII, afterwards confirmed by Louis XII: "by reason of the great esteem and perfect confidence" that he had in his "well-beloved and trusty" Jacques de Coitier.

Assuredly this was no disgrace, but seems something very much akin, to those who are acquainted with the extraordinary career of this unscrupulous physician during the preceding reign, whom a pusillanimous King had overwhelmed with liberalities, in order to drive away the death he so greatly dreaded.

* * *

Coitier must indeed have exercised a great ascendency over this suspicious monarch, dreaded by all who approached him, and who yet gave way so easily to all his physician's demands, however haughty and imperious they might be!

How was it that a mere village doctor, or nearly so, could have risen to become the medical adviser of the most distrustful of all monarchs? How did he succeed in gaining his confidence? All these enigmas remain yet to be solved.

Not only is the date of the birth of Coitier unknown, but nothing whatever is known either concerning his boyhood or his youth. All that is known is that he was born at Poligny, in the Franche-Comté, and that he was of an honourable family in pretty comfortable circumstances.

No traces of his career as a medical student are to be found in the registers of the Faculties of Paris or of Montpellier. Perhaps, but this is merely a conjecture, he took his degrees at the University of Dôle, where he was remarked by Philip, Duke of Savoy, who made him his physician.

If we are to credit Louis Guyon, it was the Duke of Savoy who presented him to Louis XI, and caused him to be accepted by the King about 1470. He soon managed to persuade that monarch that until then he had been badly treated, that his ordinary physicians understood nothing about his malady: that he had carefully studied his case, and that he alone could succeed in combating it. In order to convince him, he did not fear to speak to him in a brutal tone, to which the King was hitherto little accustomed. He was so rough with him, says Comynes, "that no one would use towards a valet such contumelious words." And when the King seemed to kick against it, he would boldly answer him: "I know well that you could send me where you have sent so many others, but by . . . (here a tremendous oath) you would not be alive eight days afterwards." And from fear of death, the King granted him all he asked for, —and heaven knows what an itching palm he had!

* * *

First of all Coitier demanded the post of "Clerk in ordinary" to the Chamber of Accounts, which brought him about 9 francs a day, without counting allowances for robes, cloaks, gloves, mufflers, hats, caps, harness, housings, horses, door-fees, pen-knives, stationery, etc." At the end of three years, at the death of the titular possessor of that place, he was appointed Vice-President of the above Chamber.

At the end of another three years, and "in consideration of his good, agreeable and continual services," the King granted to his physician the revenues of the castle of Civray.

A little later, by letters patent dated from Lyons, Coitier was granted the castle and lordship of Rouvres, with all its dependencies.

After that came the castleward of Poissy bestowed upon him besides a dwelling-house situated within the precincts of the castle of Plessis-du-Parc, the favourite residence of Louis XI.

His ambition had henceforth no limit. What he cannot obtain by ruse, he will get by violence acting as informer and laying accusations, anything that answered his purpose.

A certain personage, Jean de Ladriesche, had the title of bailiff or door-keeper of the King's palace and that of President of the Court of Accounts: Coitier had no rest until he obtained his dismissal. This post of bailiff, besides a yearly salary of 1200 livres (36,000 francs), gave many other important advantages. The bailiff exercised high and ordinary justice, he alone had the right to assign their places to the mercers or to withdraw them; without taking into account a host of other privileges not less lucrative. Of course Coitier was privileged to pocket the profits and emoluments of his functions without ever fulfilling the duties. The condition of his august patient required his constant attendance, and the sovereign himself exempted him from the discharge of his official duties.

As if he dreaded to see the King die before he had realized the dreams of his ambition, he hastened to get him to sign deeds which gave him possession of the domains of Poligny and of Grimont, in his native country; the lordships of Brazey and of Saint-Jean-de-Losne; of a house at Dijon, paid for by Louis XI out of his privy purse, besides other presents of lesser value.

It is but just to add that if he did not forget his own interests, he also thought of those of his family. One of his nephews, Pierre de Vercey, canon of Bayeux, was, thanks to him, appointed Bishop of Amiens, without the least effort on his own behalf.

* * *

At this time the King had fallen into such a state of intellectual depression and physical weakness, that he could no longer refuse anything to the insatiable ambition of his doctor.

In 1481, a fit of apoplexy, which seized him as he rose from table, almost deprived the King of his power of speech. From that moment, he passed alternately from slight amelioration to successive relapses; he thought himself surrounded by imaginary dangers, and caused his castle of Plessis to be walled in with a perfect cuirass of iron.

One day he took it into his head that his body exhaled a pestilential odour, and had himself deluged from head to foot with perfumes.

Another time, he thought that music would relieve him, and immediately musicians were called into requisition to enliven him.

Debarred from hunting, his favourite pastime, he took pleasure in having rats and mice hunted by dogs in his apartments.

He consulted quacks and soothsayers, tried all sorts of remedies, natural and supernatural, had the holy ampulla brought to him from Reims, and went so far as to get relics sent to him by the Sultan.

"Two ships were fitted out to fetch something for the health of the King". Something! Some exotic drug apparently, from which marvellous results were anticipated

A surgeon of the name of Sixtus was sent for from Germany. A noted physician of Reims, Gérard Cochet, was also called in, as well as a matron or *chirurgienne*, Guillemette Dubuys. But all was of no avail, and did not prevent the King, as Comynes says, from "passing where others have passed."

* *

Despite all the surgeons and apothecaries, Louis XI breathed his last on the 30th of August 1483.

His physician survived him for twenty-three years, and did not die until the 29th October 1506.

* * *

As Coitier, during his life, had sinned not a little, on approaching the portals of eternity, his sole thought was to redeem his former errors. Two churches and sixteen congregations had a share in his posthumous liberality: all his godchildren, and they were numerous, poor orphans and servants, received their share in his inheritance, and to crown his good works, the repentant sinner requested to be buried in the chapel of Saint-Nicholas in the church of Saint-André-des-Arts, which thenceforward was known as the Chapel of the Coitiers.

Finally, by his will, Coitier bequeathed his library to the Chapter of Poligny, and founded in the church of the same place, a mass to be daily said in perpetuity for the repose of his soul.

Could he more worthily have ended his career of scheming and unrest. *

* For the biography, properly speaking, of Coitier we have closely followed the excellent, though rather compendious study, of Dr. Chereau, which appeared in the *Union médicale* of 1861. We have however considerably condensed it, retaining only the essential points.

THE PEREGRINATIONS OF CARDINAL DE RICHELIEU'S BODY.

I saw a Potter at his Work to-day,
With rudest Hand he shaped his yielding Clay,
"Oh gently, Brother, do not treat me thus,
I too, was once a Man," I heard it say.

We all are Puppets of the Sky, we run
As wills the Player till the Game is done,
And when the Player wearies of the Sport,
He throws us into Darkness One by One.

Whatever is, by Fate was erst designed,
The Maker now his Labor has resigned,
And all our Striving can avail us Naught,
For all our Acts were long ago defined.

OMAR KHAYYAM.

THE PEREGRINATIONS OF THE MORTAL REMAINS OF RICHELIEU.

It is always profitable to ransack a collection of old Reviews; from them it is more than often possible to exhume interesting documents which gain from being once more brought into full light.

It was thus that in shaking the dust form some old papers we chanced upon a number of a provincial archæological journal, called the *Revue du Bas Poitou*.

At the first glance, this title did not seem attractive, but urged by the demon of curiosity, we decided to cut the leaves, and, as the following will show, without having cause to regret so doing. We there discovered a gem worthy to be set in our collection of curious documents: nothing less than a notice on the necropsy of Richelieu, according to the minute, perhaps official, account of the opening of the body of the great cardinal.

Not to submit the curiosity of our readers to a longer ordeal, we will at once place before them *in extenso* the most diverting passage—all the worse if the words loudly protest at being so coupled together—of this necropsy.

* *

"illustrious men" — let us bear in mind that this document is signed by two advocates of the Parliament — "illustrious men almost always have some singularities in the composition of their temperament. We have a recent example in the person of the great Cardinal de Richelieu, first minister of State.

"We learned from his surgeon in ordinary, that after the Cardinal's death, he had orders to embalm the body, which he did in the presence of several persons of distinction and of the highest quality. He found in the interior parts of the body a very fine conformation, corresponding to that of the members and of the external figure. When he opened the head to extract the brain, he noticed the most extraordinary singularities.

"He first remarked that the two plates of the skull were thin and porous, and that at the thickest parts there was but little of that spongy bony substance called diploe (*sic*), so that a blow with the fist might easily have fractured this part of this skull, extremely hard and thick in other persons, so as to be able to resist exterior impressions when not too violent."

All this is but quite superficial observation, but what more could be expected in the XVIIth century?

But what follows quits the scientific domain to approach the limits of the grotesque:

. . . "Having opened the brain" — it is always the person who performed the autopsy who is speaking — "I found it all greyish, and of a firmer consistence than usual. *It had a soft and agreeable odour*, instead of being as usual whitish in colour, soft, aqueous, and of a rather fetid odour."

This brain that emits an agreeable perfume, is it not a genial discovery, an act of posthumous adulation, worthy to be admired?

But a far more astounding fact, is "that in this brain, there was double the usual number of ventricles, each one having another above it, forming two stages, both in front and behind, and particularly in the middle, *in which are formed the purest spirits of the discursive power, serving the operations of the intellect, the front ventricles furnishing the imagination and those at the back furnishing movement, sentiment and memory.*"

It would be rather risky to pretend, that in these few lines Broca's theory of cerebral localisation had been foreseen. It may perhaps, if one chooses, be considered as an incalculary forecast of the theories which are current at present, and which in fact may still be judged too far-fetched.

*

But what strange peregrinations this great Cardinal had to be subjected to after his death: he who had been so dreaded during his lifetime, and whose head had thenceforth to roam so long about the earth like a spectre escaped from the realm of shadows; for by an inconceivable fatality, the man before whom the mightiest had trembled, was doomed to have no repose from the day that he had entered into eternal peace.

On the very morrow of his death his tomb* nearly suffered a first profanation. The Minister had accumulated around him, during his lifetime, such an amount of hatred, that the common people talked of nothing less than of casting his remains into the common sewer: a threat which they would undoubtedly have executed if the doctors of

* The tomb, placed in the centre of the choir of the church, had been originally placed on the spot previously occupied by the prior of the Collège de Cluny.

the Sorbonne had not deemed it prudent to cause his coffin to be concealed for a time.

The tomb of Richelieu was respected until the Revolution. But on the 19th Frimaire of the year II (19th December 1793), an order was given to search the tombs in the Sorbonne, on the declaration of a certain Leblanc, a member of the Convention, that "a supposed treasure was suspected of having been deposited there in the former church". The tombs were then opened and officially searched on the 19th, 20th, 21st, 22nd and 23rd of the same month.

While the search was being carried on, an individual, "whose name," said one of the commissaries in his report, "he did not remember, but who was provided with an order from the department", caused the tomb of Richelieu to be opened, descended into it and came up again "without taking anything away", and then caused the tomb to be closed again. But what is also mentioned in the report, is that an hour was given every day to the workmen "for their dinner", and that during that time there was no supervision. Was it at this moment that the robbery, of which we are about to relate the circumstances, took place, or was it during the visit of the "individual" mentioned above? This appears rather difficult to determine.

But at all events the head of the cardinal was stolen* and probably by a man named Cheval, known to be one

* This was not the only robbery committed. In the Bibliothèque Mazarine by the side of the bronze bust of Richelieu in a crystal rocket is a little finger of the great Cardinal, which finger had been stolen by one of the workmen employed in the researches, and who had cut it off in order to more easily remove the rings which encircled it. This human digit became afterwards the property of Mr. Petit-Radel, brother of the librarian of that name, who gave it to the Bibliothèque Mazarine.

of the most ardent patriots of the section of the Thermes.

* *

Cheval was a hosier in the Rue de la Harpe, or in the Rue Saint-Jacques, at a stone's-throw from the Sorbonne. One day, that an honourable ecclesiastic, the Abbé Arnéz had gone to this man's shop to make some purchase, the tradesman led his client into a back-room, and there confided to him that he possessed the head of Richelieu! On saying this he exhibited to the astounded gaze of his visitor the features of the Cardinal, still enveloped in a stained piece of strong cloth, an authentic fragment of the shroud in which he had been wrapped.

At the request of the Abbé Arnéz, Cheval several times consented to show the relic he possessed.

After the 9th Thermidor, fearing to be looked after on account of his advanced opinions, and also that the robbery might one day be discovered, Cheval begged and prayed the Abbé Arnéz to disencumber him of a possession he deemed to be compromising.

Later on, the Abbé made a present of the precious relic to his brother.

On the return of the Bourbons, Mr. Arnéz wrote to the Duke of Richelieu, then Minister of Foreign Affairs. Did this letter go astray, or was it that the noble duke cared but little to possess this family souvenir? At all events Mr. Arnéz received no reply.

The relic now came by right of inheritance into the possession of the son of Mr. Arnéz. This gentleman, who afterwards became a member of the French legislative assembly, took all sorts of steps to be enabled to restore the relic that had been confided to his care.

In June 1846, at a meeting of the Historical Committee of Arts and Monuments, Mr. François Grille informed the President, the Count of Montalembert, of the intentions of Mr. Armez: but notwithstanding the efforts of the Society, the head still remained sorrowing for its body.

In 1840 the head of Richelieu served as a model to a historical painter, Mr. Bonhommé, who was thus enabled to make from nature, the portrait of the cardinal destined for one of the rooms of the Council of State.

It was not until 1866, that Mr. Armez, writing to the Prefect of the Côtes-du-Nord, charged him to cause the skull of the eminent prelate, to be placed in the hands of Mr. Duruy, then minister of Public Instruction.

On the 5th December of the same year 1866, the Minister presented in grand pomp, at the Sorbonne, to the Archbishop of Paris, Monseigneur Darboy, "what remained of the great Statesman."

After the usual speeches and prayers, the casket containing the precious remains was lowered into the tomb excavated beneath the mausoleum, which had been erected there in 1694 by the heirs of the cardinal.

* * *

As might be expected, the authenticity of the treasure of Mr. Armez was contested: one collector of curiosities went so far as to maintain that he alone possessed the head of the great Minister.*

* When the celebrated publisher Dentu, died in 1884, there was found in his collection of "rare and precious objects", a head, or rather a fragment of a head, which seems to have been the posterior part of the skull of Richelieu: duly authenticated documents attest that this well-known amateur obtained this lugubrious relic from Mr. Armez.

Richelieu must therefore have been bicephalous! But historians would no doubt have drawn attention to this peculiarity.

Did Mr. Armèz then possess only a spurious skull? The solution of the enigma was soon discovered: the collector possessed the back part of the skull,* but Mr. Armèz possessed the face of the dreaded cardinal.

* It is this posterior portion of the skull that Mr. Quatrefages deplored having been unable to examine.

The anthropologists of course could not let such an occasion escape them to determine the phrenological characteristics of the material covering of that mighty brain, whose vast conceptions had astounded the world.

At the meeting of 20th December 1866, of the Paris Anthropological Society, Mr. Duhousset, placing before the Society the model of the face of Richelieu, read the following note:

"The oval is long and regular. As for the outlines in general, the proportions of the different parts which constitute the features approach by their regularity to the type of handsome.

The forehead surpasses in height the length of the nose, and it widens considerably above. The glabella (space between the eyebrows) is flat, and joins the eyebrows without forming a prominence.

"What nevertheless rather disturbs the general harmony of the features is a slight asymmetry in the frontal region: the left side projects more than the right; further, besides these general signs of superior intellect, the forehead presents in the upper part a slight inclination towards the summit, which characterises the long dolicocephalous cranium of the Celt, were it not that the width at the upper part is the same.

"The sub-nasal length exceeds that of the nose; this peculiarity added to the median thickness of the lower lip, of which it is easy to trace the outline, though dried up, indicates disdain; the chin shows fineness, cunning and strength. The teeth are complete on the right side; the four which are wanting on the left side of the lower maxillary, were probably detached during the occurrences which followed the violation of the tomb, and which hindered this illustrious head from being restored to its resting-place until 1866."

The face of the cardinal, was besides, in an admirable state of preservation.* The skin was dried up and grumous, the eyes seemed hidden in the deeply excavated orbits,

To this Mr. Quatrefages added: "It is to be remarked that the posterior part of the skull is wanting. I have had the skull in my hands. The temples presented a sensible depression, the forehead was considerably larger at its upper part.

"The same features are to be seen on the statue by Girardon. But in the statue the skull appears to be brachycephalous, the left frontal protuberance is largely developed; to the right the forehead is perfectly smooth."

Since then, Colonel Duhousset has published in the *Revue Scientifique*, 1895, the results of the anthropological study he had been able to make of the skull of Richelieu, in the study of the Minister, Mr. Duruy, two days before it was again deposited in the tomb at the Sorbonne.

* In the midst of the Terror, a man who on many occasions risked his life to save from destruction the most precious monuments of art, the art guardian Lenoir, was present in the church of the Sorbonne at the moment when it was invaded by a band of barbarians bent upon knocking to pieces the tomb of Richelieu.

In the scuffle, Lenoir received a bayonet-wound, but the marble remained intact.

These vandals satisfied themselves with dragging the body from the grave and shamefully trampling upon it on the pavement of the sanctuary.

"The Cardinal, whom I saw taken out of his coffin, presented to view the aspect of a dried up mummy in good preservation. Dissolution had not altered his features. The skin was everywhere of a livid hue. His cheek-bones were prominent, the lips were thin, the beard reddish and the hair of the head whitened by age.

"One of the myrmidons of the Government of 1793, believing in his fury that he was avenging the victims of this cruel Minister, cut off the head of Richelieu and showed it to the spectators who were present in the church."

Was the body placed back in the coffin? Did it suffer the profanation of the sewer, like so many others? This is still an open question.

With regard to the head, we have just seen what a strange destiny it had.

but the eyelids still preserved their lashes. The cartilaginous portion of the nose had given way, probably under the weight of the shroud. The mouth was still garnished with nearly all its teeth. It was easy to recognize some vestiges of the moustachios and of the pointed chin-beard which in his lifetime gave him that characteristic appearance which is so well known from his portraits. The face itself was of a brownish colour, due to some particular varnish: Mr. Armez, having one day perceived that insects were attacking it, had confided it to a Mr. Hamon, a pharmaceutical chemist at Rennes, who employed this coloured varnish to prevent further destruction.

* *

The characteristics noted by anthropologists on the face, were verified on the statue by Girardon, representing the Cardinal, which was at the chateau de Meilleraye.

A detail but little known, is, that the head of this same statue, mutilated during the Terror by some of the desperadoes of that period, became who would believe it? . . .* the counterpoise of the turnspit of a Limousin patriot!

* In order to write this chapter we have retouched two articles previously written; one published, in the *Journal de médecine de Paris* (nº. 16, of 1892); the other, in the *Gazette des Hôpitaux* (nº. 20, of 1894).

THE TEETH OF LOUIS XIV

Within the hollow crown
That rounds the mortal temples of a king
Keeps Death his court, and there the antic sits,
Scoffing his state, and grinning at his pomp,
Allowing him a breath, a little scene,
To monarchize, be feared, and kill with looks;
Infusing him with self and vain conceit,
As if this flesh which walls about our life
Were brass impregnable, -and, humoured thus,
Comes at the last and with a little pin
Bores through his castle wall, and -farewell king!

Richard II, III, 2.

THE TEETH OF LOUIS XIV.

It was proclaimed a miracle when Anne of Austria, after twenty years of sterility, gave birth to a splendid dauphin.

If miracle there was, it was rather that the infant already possessed two teeth when he came into the world! *

This anomaly, it is true, is not very common. There are undoubtedly several historical personages who have presented this peculiarity: Curius Dentatus, Robert the Devil, Richard III of England, Mazarin, Mirabeau, and, in our days, Doctor Broca: but the list closes there, which sufficiently proves the rarity of this freak of nature. †

* Mercier, *Tableau de Paris*, t. IX, p. 162.

† According to our colleague Dr. Witkowski, the ancients predicted the highest destinies to male children born with teeth and the illustrious names we have cited seem to give some credence to this prejudice. But on the contrary the same anomaly is considered an evil presage for the female sex. For instance Valeria, the daughter of Diocletian, and wife of the emperor Valerius Maximinus, being born with teeth, the augurs announced that she would cause the ruin of the town into which she would remove, and this prediction, says Pliny, was accomplished. But history has neglected to inform us what town

We will not go so far as to say, with our ancestor Dionis, that this may tend to explain the *great* appetite of the *great* monarch, a rather bold induction; but what we may venture to affirm, on the authority of a serious document, is that it was several times necessary to change nurses because the royal infant used to bite their nipples.*

The first nurse of Louis XIV was Elisabeth Ancel, the wife of Jean Longuet, lord of the manor of la Giraudière, King's procurator at the Finance Office of Orleans. Elisabeth Ancel suckled the young prince during three months only; notwithstanding which, she was entitled, by decree of the 4th of May 1639 to continue in the enjoyment of the pension granted to the nurses of the infants of France (*Vieilles archives de la guerre*, vol. 56, p. 107).

Perrette, or Pierrette, Dufour took the place of Elisabeth. It was this Pierrette Dufour who had most to suffer from the teeth of the lion-cub. After repeated bitings, she suffered from certain "indurations of the breasts" which obliged her to cease suckling during several days. We are to suppose that it was to this wise precaution that the nurse owed the cure of her breasts for the "indurations disappeared rapidly enough †.

had this mishap. However the tragical end of this Empress, who was beheaded at Thessalonica by order of her own son, partly verifies the sad prognostic of the augurs.

* Don Carlos, the son of Philip II. came into the world with teeth, which he used to so bad effect as to lacerate the breasts of his nurse, even until the age of three years. (Gachard, *Don Carlos et Philippe II*; Brussels, 2 vols. in 8vo).

† The Queen, very superstitious naturally, attributed this cure to supernatural intervention, as is attested by the following curious document, reproduced by Jal in his excellent *Dictionnaire critique*:

"Her Majesty (the queen-mother of Louis XIV) in order to testify

After or before Perrette Dufour, there was another nurse who seems to have played but a very humble part, Marie de Segneville Thierry, whose name appears in the royal accounts.

An account of 1667 mentions also Jeanne Potteri, Anne Perrier, Marguerite Garnier, and Marie Mesnil, with the title of *King's nurses*; but they were more strictly speaking cradle-rockers, for they did not receive more than 30 livres salary. *

* * *

According to an old tradition, children who come into the world with teeth are like those *born with a caul*, certain of happiness and fortune for life.

As for Louis XIV, who can venture to assert that the prophecy was realized?

"The Louis XIV of the doctors," wrote one of our pre-

the credulous veneration that she entertained for the holy relic sent to her by Your Eminence (the grand-master of the Knights of Malta), has related to me how by a miracle the nurse of Monseigneur the Dauphin (Louis, born the 5th September 1638, at Saint-Germain-en-Laye), named Pierrette, the wife of a carter at Poissy, having had some hardness of the breasts which were ulcerated by the teeth of H. R. H., she had prayed for cure to St. Anne (patron Saint of the Queen) and scarcely had the injured parts been touched by the relic, than by a miracle (so said the Queen) the pains ceased, the hardness disappeared and the intemperate heat caused by the pain on and around the nipple, and the nurse continued to give suck to H. R. H." (Cited by Jal as an extract from the *Relation of the Embassy, Journey and sojourn at Court, of M. le Bailly de Fourbin, Ambassador extraordinary of His Eminence and of the Order of Saint John of Jerusalem, charged with the mission of congratulating the King and the Queen on the happy birth of Mgr. the Dauphin.* (Bib. Nat. Mss. Suppl. fr., n°. 1755.)

* Jal. *Dict. de Biog. crit.*, loc. cit.

cursors in the line we are following, "is not at all the brilliant hero that has been pictured to us, but rather a sickly young man often subject to very serious illnesses; then, later, a man always suffering, bound to observe a strict diet, obliged to submit to grave operations; and lastly, a gouty old man, continually tormented with gravel and whose existence ends finally with gangrene." *

Such is indeed, the exact portrait of Louis XIV, as he is depicted in the *Journal of the King's health*.

This journal, as we shall have occasion to repeat, besides furnishing us an idea of the medical manners of the XVIIth century, the oddities of the physicians of the period, so happily ridiculed by Molière in his immortal plays, this journal, we observe, is a unique collection of documents, indispensable to any one who wishes to study the thousand and one complaints with which Louis XIV was afflicted.

We have perused it in order to derive our information respecting the disease with which the young sovereign was affected after certain youthful excesses; † we will now again consult it with regard to the different dental annoyances which plagued the King during his long existence.

*

One of the medical historiographers of the health of Louis XIV, D'Aquin, has let us into the secret, that during all his life his royal client was afflicted with a deplorable dental system; but it was not however until he attained the age of 38 years, in 1676, that he began seriously to complain.

* *Journal de la Santé de Louis XIV*. Introduction, p. IX.

† *A youthful indiscretion of Louis XIV*, in *The Secret Cabinet of History*, first series.

It was at the moment of the campaign in Flanders. During the campaign the health of the King had been pretty good, although "the fatigues of the war had not been slight, so that his rest was often interrupted, even to passing several nights without sleeping." This however had no ill effect upon the King's health, except some "very obstinate toothaches." *

As he had *naturally very bad teeth*, he was subject to toothache, which however could generally be calmed by a simple application of essence of cloves or essence of thyme. But as it was not advisable to use essences, which have the inconvenience of *burning the mouth and of causing nausea* they were only had recourse to "in the extremity of pain." †

Two years later, in September 1678, the King who went out hunting in all kinds of weather, caught cold and a dental abscess showed itself. The right cheek, and the gum were swollen and "the abscess having suppurated internally by the use of a poultice made of bread and milk, it was opened with a lancet, and there issued matter from it and the pain ceased with the tumour." * This was evidently a *suppurating periostitis*.

* *

In 1685, the year of his marriage with Madame de Maintenon, the King showed every appearance of being in excellent health, although he was attacked by caries of the maxillary and perforation of the sinus.

It became necessary to extract all the teeth on the left side of the upper jaw, so bad were they, and after that

† *Journal de la Santé de Louis* XIV. p. 135—136.
* Idem. ibidem, p. 140.

operation there remained such a hole in the jaw that when the King drank, or gargled his throat, the water would go from the mouth into the nose, "from whence it would flow as from a fountain."

This hole had been caused by "the splitting of the jaw-bone, a portion being carried away with the teeth; it had now become carious and there sometimes flowed from it sanies emitting a bad odour, the more so that this hole could only be stopped by the augmentation of the gum, which could not reproduce itself except upon a healthy soil, that is to say by first curing the caries of the jaw-bone however deeply situated it might be."

By the advice of D'Aquin, seconded by Felix Tassy, first surgeon to the King, and Dubois, dentist attached to His Majesty's service, it was judged that "fire only could combat the action of this disease."

The patient consenting, "cauteries were made large and long enough to fill and burn all the sides as deeply as the caries required."

On the 10th of January, actual cautery was applied fourteen times, Mr. Dubois, who held the instrument "appeared to be more tired than the King who endured it."

After the application of the cautery, the doctors recommended the King to pass three or four times a day, from the mouth through the nose, a liquid or gargle "composed of one quarter spirits of wine, the same of distilled vulnerary water, and one half of orange flower water, to combat the putrefaction, facilitate the falling of the eschars, and advance the renewa of the gum."

Caustic had to be applied three times; and finally the fistula closed. The King never left his apartments during the whole course of his illness.

A morbid effect followed almost immediately upon the malady from which the King had just recovered: after the closing of the fistula, there remained for some time an unpleasant smell in the nostrils, caused by the stagnation of pus in the maxillary sinus, of which the inflammation continued for some time longer. *

It is not unworthy of remark that certain historians have attributed to that serious buccal affection the particular state of mind in which Louis XIV must have been when he decided to sign the fatal revocation of the edict of Nantes (November 1685).

*

It was not until eleven years later (1696) that the King again had another dental abscess.

On Saturday 12th May, the King having walked a great deal, felt "worn-out, his face burning, hot flying pains in the limbs; he had no appetite for dinner; his pulse was irregular and he had a little fever until the evening."

He perspired copiously, and appeared to be relieved.

He thought himself well again, when "a fluxion showed itself on the right cheek and it became much swollen near the maxillary glands."

After dinner, the King having worked with M. de Pontchartrain, and again in the evening after his walk, had vapours, lassitude and fever; the cheek was red, and much swollen. The King having had no sleep during the night, remained in bed on the Wednesday morning,

* *Journal de la Santé de Louis XIV*, p. 152--161.

and slept well from noon until half past two in the afternoon. He woke up without fever, but the tumour increased in the evening and his rest was disturbed.

The following night he was better because the abscess broke, which "diminished the pain and the fluxion." But the King having insisted on going out on Friday, "to go to Mass," the tumefaction reappeared, first of all hard, but progressively softening, until it disappeared altogether on the following Monday. *

The patient was not completely relieved until "three pallet-fuls of blood had been drawn from him." The blood-letting was followed by a purgation, because the King had had an attack of gout; but a week later he was well enough "to touch seventeen hundred sick persons, on Saturday the eve of the Pentecost."

* * *

As the monarch advanced in age, his illnesses became more serious. Gout, which had hitherto only given him reminders at long intervals, tortured him more and more every day. The system of diet he adopted was besides, not of a nature to favour his return to health. Great banquets, variety of dishes, and particularly his ravenous appetite and the want of teeth, which prevented him masticating his food, increased more and more his tendency to dyspepsia and to congestion.

It was only during Lent, "by reason of the moderation of his meals, which to him meant abstinence," that he had some respite.

His teeth would nevertheless not have made him suffer

* *Journal de la Santé de Louis XIV*, p. 228.

too much, if he had not had the unlucky idea to torment "the stump of a lower tooth, the point of which incommoded him, by endeavouring to draw it out." (1707).

The same evening he felt pain and hardness and tumefaction, which involved the whole of the lower jaw accompanied by considerable induration.

The pains extended to the nape of the neck, to the left shoulder, the right arm, the joint of the shoulder, at the same time that a slight sore throat became manifest.

"A copious stool, mingled with incessant humours," and a profuse perspiration caused these unfavourable symptoms to disappear; the tumour subsided, and the pains ceased.

On the following Wednesday, 16th of the month, the King had the stump drawn, which came out almost without pain, and all the accidents were at an end.*

* *

During the following eight years until the death of Louis XIV, his health did nothing but decline, but his extraordinary appetite never failed for an instant. It was only during the last week of his life that he ceased to eat as much as usual.

But his condition was getting worse every day. Notwithstanding the optimism of his physician Fagon, the chief surgeon, Marechal, more frank of speech, did not dissimulate his anxiety.

On Friday, the 9th August 1715, the King, although much fatigued, hunted the stag at Marly, as usual.

On the 11th he complained of violent pains in the legs, symptomatic of a phlebitis on the point of declaring itself.

* *Journal de la Santé de Louis XIV*, pp. 201–203.

On the 13th, Madame de Maintenon, giving news of the King to the Archbishop of Rouen, did not however seem to be very anxious.*

* * *

But the next day, the left leg of the patient was much swollen, the pain in the thigh and hip persisted and the

* The unpublished letter, that we print below, and which we owe to the kindness of one of the most enlightened Parisian amateurs, Mr. Paul Dablin, informs us fully as to the health of the King at that date, that is to say twenty days before the death of the sovereign. It is addressed by Madame de Maintenon to the archbishop of Rouen.

Saint-Cyr, the 13th August 1715.

"Since we have returned from Marly the King has complained of a slight pain in the left leg which he feels only in walking or moving. It is a sort of gouty cramp, he looked depressed and out of sorts, the pulse is very good and the appetite has come back he will remain in bed to-day to see if the heat will diminish the pain; he passed these last days in my room amusing himself as usual and he looked very well, he is vexed and with good reason about this affair of the Church. Messrs. of the Parliament refuse this declaration, Mr. Joli-Fleury will not speak, the King wishes to go there himself and there is no obstacle. the party is astonishingly insolent, threats are made against the Cardinal de Rohan it is said that he and the other Cardinal de Bissi (?) are killing the King whilst the Cardinal de Noailles makes him unhappy. It is said that the latter has diminished his household and has now only two servants this is a thing to be verified before it is spoken of I am not surprised, Monsieur at the contradiction and persecutions you are suffering for they reach even to the King anxious about my condition in the midst of so many misfortunes that I have drawn down in wishing the Archbishop of Paris where he is, pray for us I do not doubt but that you will do so.

The bishop of Chartres is to be here towards the 19th or 20th of the month for a procession. (The want of punctuation has been scrupulously preserved in this letter [*Transl.*]).

King was obliged to remain in his room and not move.

On the 26th, the pain and swelling were considerable and symptoms of gangrene were evident.

In spite of empirical remedies,* the gangrene progressed, from the foot it gained the knee, then invaded the thigh, the muscles of the abdomen, and ascended even "to the throat"; and death at last supervened on coma, on Sunday the 1st September 1715, at a quarter past eight in the morning.

The *Roi-Soleil* had succumbed without an effort, like a candle that dies out. †

* V. Corlieu, *La mort des Rois de France.* 1873, p. 113.

† *Journal de Dangeau*, 1st September 1715, Vol. XVI. p. 130.

THE
CLANDESTINE ACCOUCHEMENTS
OF
MADEMOISELLE DE LA VALLIÈRE.

"'Tis better to be lowly born,
And range with humble livers in content,
Than to be perked up in a glistering grief,
And wear a golden sorrow."

Henry VIII. ii, 3.

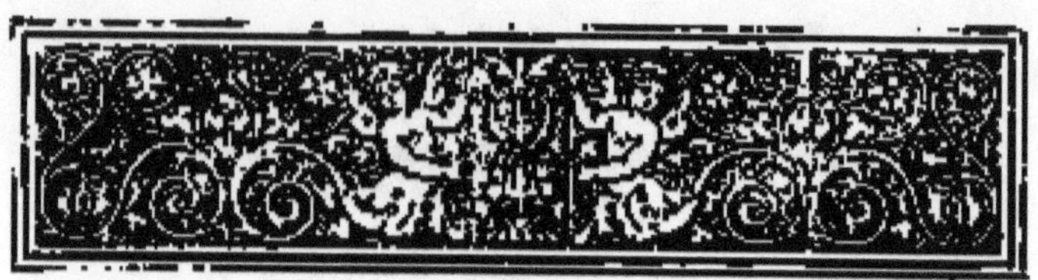

THE CLANDESTINE ACCOUCHEMENTS OF MDLLE. DE LA VALLIÈRE.

The amours of the great Monarch with Mdlle. de La Vallière led to the birth of four children.

History has preserved only the names of the two who survived: Mdlle. de Blois, born 2nd October 1666; and the Count of Vermandois, who saw the light, the same day, one year later. She is almost dumb with regard to the two first born, who died shortly after their birth.

It was in 1663 that the royal favourite was first observed to be pregnant.

At Court no one ignored the relations existing between the young sovereign and the maid of honour of Madame (a), but the secret was so well kept that nothing had transpired outside. Louis had confided his secret to one man only: "absolutely trustworthy, a man, of sure confidence, a worthy servitor whose only thought was to serve him," *

(a) Princess Henrietta of England, the wife of the King's brother, Gaston Duke of Orleans (Transl.)

* Mémoires de Choisy, t. I: p. 110.

Jean-Baptiste Colbert, who, on this occasion played a part which does not seem to have offended his dignity.*

Being at war with the Duke of Lorraine, the King had been obliged to leave suddenly for Marsal, the 25th August, leaving his mistress in a situation that was causing him some uneasiness. It was then that he spoke to Colbert of the service he expected from him.

* *

It so happened that Madame Colbert, a respectable bourgeoise, was to a certain extent a fellow-country woman

* An apologist of Colbert, Mr. P. Clement, admits, notwithstanding the great admiration he professes for his hero, that the latter had been obliged, in order to strengthen his position, the attainment of which was to himself a source of astonishment, to receive the most intimate confidences of the King, and to assist, and favour his amours.

It was Colbert who intervened, as we shall show, between the King and the favourite, when the latter had for the first time retired to the Convent of Chaillot, and who managed to bring her back.

Later on, it was Colbert who had the mission of making Mme. de Montespan listen to reason, when she had threatened to "speak to his wife."

Mr. Clément, in order to incline us to indulgence, pretends that these royal freaks should not be judged according to XIXth century notions: "and one ought not be astonished", says this mild censor, "at the compliance of this most austere Minister with the failings of the King, at a moment when Louis XIV exhibited himself publicly in the same coach with Marie-Thérèse, La Vallière, and Montespan, while the people as they passed said under their breath: '*There go the three queens*': when he had all his bastards made legitimate by the Parliament, etc.... it must be considered that, to some extent, the King had the tacit support of the ideas and manners of his time."

Without being more hypercritical than necessary, we cannot but deplore the sorry part played under certain circumstances by the greatest Minister of the grandest of our Kings. Fortunately the "domestic services" occupy but little space in the life of J. B. Colbert.

of Mdlle. de La Vallière: she was in fact from the Blésois country, where she had known the families of La Vallière and of Saint-Remi. But the principal reason why she was chosen by the King, was that she was "expert in nourishing children," having brought up seven of her own.* She was besides esteemed and respected, for Mazarin himself had recommended his nieces to avail themselves of her good offices.

It was understood that Colbert should act as intermediary, we dare not employ a more brutal term, between the King and the favourite; during the two months that the expedition lasted, Colbert was charged to receive and transmit the letters between the lovers.

On his return to Paris, the King took means to provide for his mistress all that her condition required. It was again to Colbert that he had recourse in this delicate conjuncture; it was he who was entrusted with the mission of finding some discreet and quiet retreat wherein to shelter his liaison, and the fruit that was likely to result from it.

A gentleman of the name of Brion, more troubled with want of money than with scruples, had built in the garden of the Palais-Royal, at the side abutting on the Rue de Richelieu, near to the former rue des Bouchers, one of those pleasure retreats called *Folies*.†

In order more effectually to conceal this accouchement the King made a present of the Brion mansion to Mdlle. de la Vallière and by this means "withdrew her from the apartment of the ladies of honour of Madame, among whom she was."§

* Lair, *Louise de la Vallière et la jeunesse de Louis* XIV. p. 122.
† Lair, *loc. cit.*
§ The passages between inverted commas are taken from a manu-

It was necessary at once to find "a young girl, in whom confidence could be placed, to act as lady's-maid." Colbert fixed his choice on a Mdlle. du Plessis. "All the linen and all the other things required on the occasion" were got ready, probably by Madame Colbert, and introduced into the Brion mansion, under pretext of being "the wearing apparel" of Mdlle. du Plessis.

For suckling the infant, Colbert had arranged with a certain Beauchamp and his wife, formerly valet and maid-servant in his family, who resided in the Rue aux Ours, to whom, says the person who serves us as guide in this narration, "I declared in confidence that one of my brothers, having got a young lady of quality with child, was obliged, in order to save her honour to take care of the child and to confide it for suckling to their care, which they accepted with joy."

* *

Meanwhile, the King wrote several notes about the affair, "nearly all of which," says Colbert, "I have burned; but among others I have preserved two, one, in which His Majesty apprizes me of an accident that has occurred to the said *demoiselle* (it is always La Vallière who is in question), and another ordering me to see that Master Boucher[*] holds himself in readiness."

* *

script in the handwriting of Colbert, entitled: *Diary Kept for each week of what has happened likely to be useful to the history of the King, from the 14th of April 1663 to the 7th of January 1665*, republished by the *Revue rétrospective*, vol. IV, p. 251 et sequitur.

[*] We have found no other bibliographical notice of Boucher, than

Master Boucher was the accoucheur, perhaps designated by Colbert, but certainly accepted by the King. The word *Master*, which we purposely underline, leaves no doubt as to the sex of Boucher, and that is why we can hardly explain how an erudite and most estimable man should have ventured to say "that it was a midwife of

the following extract from the book of Dr. Witkowski: *Accoucheurs et sages-femmes célèbres*; and we cannot even then venture to assert that it relates to the same Boucher mentioned in the following lines:

"François Boucher or Bourbel, son-in-law of La Cuisse, had also some reputation. He remained in a chamber adjoining that in which Marie-Thérèse of Austria was being confined, to give his assistance if necessary, and," says Dionys, "when Monseigneur was born, he examined the infant, without the Queen being cognizant of it."

In his *Mémoires sur les grands jours d'Auvergne*, Fléchier has devoted a few lines to this *accoucheur* which are not wanting in a certain amount of irony.

Boucher had been called in by the President (Judge) de Nevion to give his services at the confinement of his daughter, Mme. de Ribeyre:

"All the ladies, on this occasion, paid court to the president and to the lady who had been confined, and Mr. Boucher was the object of extraordinary honours. He was visited by all the town and received many presents, such as are bestowed on persons of great distinction or whose position causes them to be highly considered, in the provinces. Everybody regarded him as a person to be revered and the poor little faculty of medicine and of surgery of Clermont tendered him most humble homage. He was called in, *honoris causa*, to several consultations, and M. de Nevion never failed to treat him with all the civility due to a man of science who had come all the way from Paris to render him service abandoning for that purpose a practice that could not but be important. His expenses were paid and he received 1800 francs; he was also gratified with many presents, but all that did not prevent him from rather complaining of the results of his journey. Mme. de Fleury, who was brought to bed a month previously, was not sorry to have employed only a good midwife, who had the reputation of being skilful in her profession and who was very moderate in her demands."

the name of Marguerite Boucher who delivered Mdlle. de La Vallière." *

This error having been imputed to Mdlle. de Montpensier, we cannot do better than quote the fragment of her *Memoirs* alluded to, and which to us bears a different interpretation.

"I have often heard it related," writes Mdlle. de Montpensier, "that when La Vallière was about to be confined, Madame passed through her chamber on her way to hear mass at the Sainte Chapelle; Boucher who was delivering her had to be hidden. She said to Madame "I have the colic fit to kill me!" As soon as Madame had passed, she said to Boucher: "Make haste, I want to be delivered before she comes back again."

It was on a Saturday; there was card-play in her room until midnight. She partook the same as the others of the "medianoche" (*a*), her head was uncovered, just as if she had not been delivered that morning." †

This passage seems to us sufficiently explicit; but we can bring another authority to support it, rather untrustworthy it *is* true, but which, in this question of identity deserves to be quoted.

The version of Mr. d'Ormesson is somewhat romantic in its details, but, in the historical basis, it agrees so exactly with the actual facts, as Colbert himself has revealed them to us in his official journal, that there is no reason to suspect its veracity.

As the grave counsellor d'Ormesson says: "I will here

* Le Roi. *Union médicale*, 1861, no. 97.

(*a*) Spanish for midnight supper (*Transl.*)

† Quoted by Witkowski, *Les Accouchements à la Cour*, p. 188. Mdlle. de Montpensier here alludes to the third confinement of the Duchess: we shall revert to this subject later on.

write a history that is reported everywhere and which may be of importance.

"On Tuesday, 18th December 1663, the Marquise de Villeroy, being about to be confined, begged of Boucher not to accept any other engagements, or at least to leave word where he might be found in case of need. It is said that on Wednesday morning, having come to the Marquise de Villeroy, after having been sought after all night long, he related, that being at home the previous night, he was called for; a carriage was in waiting, on entering which he was blindfolded: the coach proceeded rapidly, and in about half a quarter of an hour, he was ushered into a house, where, after mounting a staircase, he was introduced into a chamber in which, the bandage being removed from his eyes, he saw a lady in bed, her face covered with a mask, with ten or a dozen people round her, unmasked, the bed and the tapestries covered with cloths, and that having happily delivered the lady, he was again blindfolded and replaced in the carriage, which conveyed him home, after receiving a proper remuneration." *

There is nothing of all this in the journal of Colbert, who was not a man to employ useless phraseology, and simply relates that "on Wednesday, 19th December 1663, at half past three in the morning, Mdlle. de La Vallière gave birth to a boy, three days after the full moon of the same month of December which "had been on the fourteenth."

"A few minutes after the accouchement," continues Colbert, "Boucher let me know, by a note that it was a boy giving the hour of its birth. The same day, at six in the morning, the said Boucher carried the child across the garden of the Palais-Royal, and committed it by my

* *Journal d'Ormesson*. t. II, p. 69 and sequitur.

order into the hands of the said Beauchamp and his wife who were waiting for me at the *carrefour* opposite the Hôtel de Bouillon."

During that time, the King had gone away hunting, but not without having left instructions with Boucher to give him news through Colbert.

That same evening Colbert received the following message from *the accoucheur*: "We have a fine strong boy. Mother and child are doing well, thank God. I await your orders." *

We have seen what these orders were: to remove the child from the mother as quickly as possible, and to conduct it to a safe place.

The same day, 19 December, the new-born infant was taken to Saint-Leu and baptized under the name of Charles, "the son of Mr. de Lincour and of damoiselle Elisabeth de Beux."

The register is signed by "Guy Focard, named Beauchamp, to whom the said child is confided," Clémence Pré, his wife and D. Lecomteulx.

* * *

On the 7th January 1665, at noon, "the last quarter of the moon having been on the sixth" Mademoiselle de La Vallière was delivered of a second son, at noon precisely.

"The same rules were observed as for the preceding one; for the King wished the matter to be kept secret. The *sieur* (master) Boucher, who had served him in the first accouchement, served him again in this; for that purpose, he entered the Palais-Royal by the back-gate of the garden." †

That same evening, at nine o'clock, Colbert waited to

* Colbert's MS., *loc. cit.*

† Lair, p. 179—180.

receive the infant. The child was carried by a valet; from his hands it passed into those of Boucher and of Colbert, successively, and was by them carried to the Hôtel Bouillon.

There it was confided to a certain Bernard, the husband of demoiselle Ducoudray, both of whom had been in the service of Colbert.

On the following day, 8th January, the child was taken to the baptismal font of the church of Saint Eustace, and the baptismal register was drawn up in the following terms:

"*On Thursday, the 8th January 1665, was here baptized Philip, son of François Dersy le Bourgeois and of Marie Bernard his wife residing in the Rue Montorgueil. God-father, Claude Tessier, a poor man; God-mother, Marguerite Biet, daughter of Louis Biet, burgher. Signed L. Biet.*"

Neither Philip nor Charles, the first-born, lived more than a year. The last died suddenly from the fright caused by a clap of thunder, as Mademoiselle de Montpensier says in her *Memoirs*, adding maliciously enough, that "such a fright was unworthy the son of a King." On his side, Mr. d'Ormesson says that Mdlle. de La Vallière, had already lost a son and a *daughter*. In a pamphlet published before 1666, mention is also made of a daughter of Mdlle. de La Vallière.

But the testimony of Mdlle. de Montpensier, and particularly that of Colbert, contradict these assertions, and these latter have in our eyes a far greater value than the gossip of Mr. d'Ormesson and that of a hired pamphleteer.

* * *

Three months had scarcely elapsed after the death of her second son, when Mdlle. de La Vallière was again taken with the pains of labour. She was at that moment at Vincennes, where the Court had taken up its quarters from the 19th of August 1666. The King's mistress occupied a chamber which served as a sort of passage to the grand apartments. "It was therein that she was obliged to take to her bed, to call in the doctor and to dissimulate her pains so that her shame should not be publicly known." *

While in the midst of the throes of labour, Madame Henriette, her former rival, passed, and cast upon her a glance of contempt, without pity for her sufferings.

The child, well delivered, was a girl, known afterwards as Mdlle. de Blois; she was of course immediately taken away from the mother.

The latter, wishing to hide from the Queen the offence she was guilty of towards her in her own palace, ordered her room to be filled with odoriferous plants and flowers, without considering how injurious such emanations might be to a woman in her condition; she dressed, received visits, and gave dinners. This second torture, worse than the first, lasted twelve hours.

Meanwhile, the King had gone to Versailles, and visited on his way, a manufacture of French point-lace! in the Rue Quincampoix.

* * *

The unfortunate Duchess seems to have been doomed always to bear children in pain and in mystery.

In 1667, on Friday, 2nd October, while at Saint-Germain, she was taken prematurely with the pains of labour, and as formerly, was obliged to smother her cries. The next

* Lair, *Louise de La Vallière.*

day she was delivered of a boy who was immediately borne away before she had time to give it a caress.* Every one suspected that she had been confined; it was known, though she wished no one to know it." *

This love-child was not acknowledged by the King until two years later, the 20th February 1669, and legitimated under the name of *Louis, Count of Vermandois.*

The only details we possess of the birth of this fourth adulterine child are those given, according to *La France Galante*, by the verbose Touchard-Lafosse in his amusing *Chroniques de l'Œil de Bœuf*. We cannot undertake to guarantee the veracity of his narration.

"We have at Court," writes Touchard, "new fruit, but forbidden fruit, that of which the arch-fiend made the first woman eat.

"Three days ago, the King, more dressed out than usual, was with Mademoiselle de La Vallière; His Majesty was preparing to take his pleasure in that way to which women, resigned and submissive mortals, lend themselves too readily.

"All at once, the effect of an event which had happened nine months previously, announced itself in such fashion as to oblige the Prince to put off his gallant enterprise. Matters proceeded so rapidly that, in a few moments, Louis XIV found himself in the most embarrassing situation possible. He was obliged to open a window and call for help, giving orders to fetch immediately Madame de Montausier, Madame de Choisi, any one no matter whom, as long as it was a woman.

At the same time a midwife was being sent for, the

* *Mémoires de Mdlle. de Montpensier*, Maestricht edition, t. V, p. 288.

King not wishing his mistress to have the assistance of a professional man, fearing no doubt that the shrine at which he had sacrificed his royal love might be desecrated by profane regards.

"A crowd of willing dames hurried up, but too late to prevent a vest, embroidered with pearls and precious stones, from being deluged with marks of the event. The ladies found His Majesty bathed in perspiration, supporting, as well as he could, La Vallière who, clinging to her lover's neck, was tearing to pieces in her clutches a lace collar worth a thousand crowns. Soon the young mother, had a violent pain followed by a prolonged fainting fit; they thought she was dead— . 'In God's name,' said the King, bursting into tears, 'give her back to me, and take all I possess.'

"This tender monarch knelt at the foot of the bed, pale, unmanned, motionless and uttering from time to time such lamentable cries as to draw tears from the ladies present, and from His Majesty's doctors who had been summoned as a desperate resource.

"At last, the final result of this prolonged labour appeared upon the scene: it was a little boy who entered as a bastard into the noble family of Henri IV."

* * *

We do not know whether the doctors had been called in as *a desperate resource*, as Touchard-Lafosse so boldly asserts, but, refering only to the facts as they are given us by the *Grande mademoiselle*, (a) we find that Boucher

(a) Mademoiselle de Montpensier, a Princess celebrated for her eccentricities and for her masculine proclivities. (*Transl.*)

was present at this accouchement as he had been at the three others.

What is less contestable is, that from that moment the King ceased to be enamoured of the Duchess. The real explanation of this change may perhaps be traced to a malicious report recorded by the Princess Palatine: the King had been led to suspect that the child (the Count of Vermandois) *was not his, but Lauzun's.*

The delay taken by the King before he acknowledged him, and the slight regret he expressed at his death, would give credence enough to this opinion, but as the Princess Palatine says with her usual bluntness: "It would have been well if all the King's bastards had been as undoubtedly his own as that one. Madame de La Vallière was not a giddy inconstant mistress.... She was a person altogether agreeable, good, gentle, and tender. She did not love the King to gratify her ambition, but she entertained a sincere passion for him, and during all her life she never loved any other man but him."

* * *

Mademoiselle de La Vallière had retired from the world and had already taken the veil some years before, when the news was suddenly brought her of the illness, and immediately afterwards of the death, of her last born. She managed, under these trying circumstances, to master her emotion: to a friend who said that tears would relieve her, she simply replied: "Everything must be sacrificed, it is for myself I must weep." *

Others attribute to her the following reply, which

* P. Clément, *Réflexions sur la miséricorde de Dieu*, of Mdlle. de La Vallière, t. II, p. 176.

however affected it may appear, is not wanting in a certain grandeur: "When I shall have wept enough for having given birth to him, I may then mourn his death." *

The birth of the Count of Vermandois had been fatal to his mother. From that moment, each day brought nearer to the favourite the final separation from her lover.

After her last confinement, her plumpness disappeared, the brilliancy of her eyes was dimmed, her face lost its freshness; she had no more charms to retain a lover who was no longer enamoured. Already lame from her youth, by reason no doubt of a coxalgia at birth, she became, and remained, almost paralyzed on the whole of one side of her body.

This physical falling-off marked the beginning of her disgrace. A haughtier beauty had captivated the senses and the heart of the Monarch.

And as in France all finishes and begins with songs, the following railing couplet circulated:

On dit que La Vallière
S'en va sur son déclin;
Ce n'est que par manière
Que le Roi suit son train.
Montespan prend sa place,
Il faut que tout y passe
Ainsi, de main en main. †

* This reply has been variously interpreted, according to the authors who have quoted it: Voltaire, Mme. de Caylus, the *Journal de Verdun*, etc.

† La Vallière's star is on the wane
She has lost the King's protection
And if he visits her now and again
It is more from use than affection.
One's rise is another one's disgrace
Montespan now takes her place
As King Louis' last selection.

THE FIRST ACCOUCHEUR
AT THE COURT OF LOUIS XIV.

Shorten my days thou canst with sullen sorrow,
And pluck nights from me, but not lend a morrow;
Thou canst help time to furrow me with age,
But stop no wrinkle in his pilgrimage;
Thy word is current with him for my death,
But dead, thy kingdom cannot buy my breath.

Richard II. i. 3.

THE FIRST ACCOUCHEUR AT THE COURT OF FRANCE. THE CONFINEMENTS AND THE DEATH OF MADAME DE MONTESPAN.

PREVIOUS to the end of the XVIIth century, matrons (midwives) were alone entrusted with the accouchement of the queens of France and of princesses of blood royal.

The Court physicians and surgeons remained in an adjoining chamber, but there is no case mentioned in which their services were required.

Julien *Clément* was the first accoucheur who officially assisted the princesses of the Court of France in their confinements. Until the delivery of the Dauphine, Anna-Maria-Victorine of Bavaria, the queens and other princesses had always been assisted by midwives.

Marie de Medecis, wife of Henri IV, had employed as midwife the celebrated Louise Bourgeois. Anne of Austria, wife of Louis XIII, had been delivered by Mme. Peronne, and lastly Maria Theresa of Austria, wife of Louis XIV, is said to have employed Marguerite Boucher *.

* This at all events is what is pretended by Mr. Le Roi. But has he not rather confounded Marguerite Boucher, the midwife, with the *accoucheur* of that name, François Boucher?

The Dauphine, Victorine of Bavaria, being particularly delicate, the greatest precautions had to be taken while she was *enceinte*. The King, who ardently wished for a grandson, must have been specially anxious about the exact time when the confinement would take place. It is probable that Louis XIV consulted his physicians on that important matter, and among these, the man whom he honoured with his utmost confidence, the illustrious Dr. Fagon. This physician, the medical attendant of Mme. de Montespan, recommended to the King the accoucheur Clément, of whose talents he spoke highly, so much so that Louis XIV would hear of none other to deliver the Dauphine.

Julien Clément may then be considered as the first officially appointed accoucheur of the princesses of the House of Bourbon.* Not only did he usher into the world all the children of the Dauphine, daughter-in-law of Louis XIV, but he was also the *accoucheur* of the Duchess of Burgundy, of her sister the Queen of Spain,

* It does not appear quite certain that Clément was official *accoucheur by title* to the Princesses of the blood royal, and we must be satisfied with what Dr. Chéreau says on the subject.

"All that I can state," says our colleague, "is that I have among my papers the lists of the persons officially attached to all the royal family under Louis XIV, and therein no mention is ever made of the appointment of an *official accoucheur*, a post pertaining to the *commensaux* and to the domestic officers of the royal household. We find a chief physician, a physician in ordinary, eight physicians (attached), a number of other physicians unattached, a "spagyrist" physician, a chief surgeon, eight surgeons (attached), four apothecaries, four assistant apothecaries, an apothecary-distiller, three bone setters, one operating oculist, two operators for the stone, one dentist and nine barbers. But there is no record of any *accoucheur* having *free table and livery at Court*, according to the expression of that time." (*Union médicale*, 1861, t. IX, p. 80.

whom he delivered of three successive Princes, and of all the great ladies of the period. From Clément's time onward none but accoucheurs were employed at Court, instead of midwives.

Under Louis XV it was Levret who delivered the Dauphine.

Under Louis XVI, the accoucheur Vermond delivered Marie-Antoinette.

Under the First Empire, as soon as Marie-Louise became *enceinte*, Baudelocque was appointed to assist her, and as he died shortly after his nomination, Antoine Dubois took his place.

Under Louis-Philippe it was Moreau who assisted the Duchess of Orleans.

Lastly under Napoleon III, as soon as the Empress Eugénie showed the first symptoms of pregnancy, Paul Dubois was appointed accoucheur to the Court.

Of these several personages, some held the appointment without the title, such were, Clément, Levret, Antoine Dubois, Moreau; whereas during the Regency, under the Republic and the Consulate, under Louis XVIII, Charles X and during the first years of the reign of Louis-Philippe, any *accoucheur* that might have been appointed would have had the title without any duties to perform. Paul Dubois was perhaps the only one who had both.

This digression has taken us away from Clément, an obscure personage, but who, by the sole fact of having been the first accoucheur appointed at Court, deserves that his name be not buried in oblivion. Clément was besides, the *accoucheur* most in vogue in the XVIIth century, and that in itself is worth recording. Among other notable clients, he had Madame de Montespan, which is not his least title to glory. It has been said that he had also delivered the Duchess of La Vallière of the children she had by Louis XIV; but this is manifestly an error.

At the time of the first accouchement of Mdlle. de La Vallière, in 1663, Clément had not yet attained his fifteenth year (having been born at Arles in 1649); that alone refutes the idea of his having assisted the favourite. What is particularly droll, as we shall show further on, is that there appears to have been a confusion with Mme. de Montespan, for all the details given by the historian Astruc, and after him by Suë, * the ancestor of the novelist, on the part played in this circumstance by Clément, apply perfectly to the daughter of the Mortemarts (*a*).

* * *

Julien Clément already had a great reputation when Fagon pointed him out to the notice of Louis XIV. After having studied the humanities in his native town and gone through his apprenticeship as surgeon, he went to Paris where he entered, as sub-assistant surgeon, into the

* In his *Essais historiques sur l'art des accouchements*, Suë the younger says that Clément delivered the Duchess of La Vallière of the children she bore Louis XIV. "At her first confinement," he writes, "as she desired the utmost secrecy, Clément was taken to a house in which he found Madame de la Valliere (sic) her face hidden beneath a hood, and it is asserted that the King was hiding within the curtains of her bed." This is but an idle tale, as we believe we have proved.

(*a*) Mme. de Montespan.

house of Jacques Lefevre, one of the most famous *accoucheurs* of his day. His zeal and skill soon gained him the favour of his master, who shortly afterwards bestowed on him the hand of his daughter.

It was at Bariges, where Fagon had accompanied the Duke of Maine,* that the King's chief physician had occasion to appreciate the qualities of the young master in surgery. Clement had, thanks to his efforts, obtained this degree, which his talents deserved.

The Dauphine being close upon the critical moment, Fagon remembered his *protégé*, and spoke favourably of him to the King. "So formal a recommendation, coming from Fagon, had such weight on the mind of the monarch that all the efforts of rival surgeons of good repute to supplant him were fruitless, the King, adhering absolutely to the recommendation of Fagon."

From that moment, his fortune was made. The dames of highest quality, the most distinguished *bourgeoises* "generally inclined to ape the ladies of highest rang,

* The Duke of Maine came into the world with a club-foot. The chief physician judged it necessary to send him to the waters of Bariges. A person of confidence was sought for to take charge of the child. Louvois went secretly to Paris and proposed this mission to Scarron's widow, who accepted it.

The letters addressed by her to the King under these circumstances, pleased him so much that they were the commencement of the connexion, perhaps the intimacy, between them.

Some years previously, the widow Scarron had urgently solicited Louis XIV to allow the pension of 1500 livres paid to her late husband to revert to her. The King had persistently refused, and it was not until later, at the instance of Madame de Montespan, that he granted her a pension, not of 1500 livres, but of 2000 (*Vide*, on that subject the *Mélanges historiques, satiriques, anecdotiques*, of Mr. de B... Jourdain, t. II.

would no more, as far as they could help, have any other accoucheur than the one in favour at Court."

A few years later Clément was summoned three consecutive times by the Queen of Spain, sister of the Duchess of Burgundy. He thus ushered into the world successively three princes, to the great satisfaction of their august parents.

"In the year 1711, Louis XIV, wishing to worthily recognize the services rendered by this skilful man to the royal family, besides the liberalities he had already received from His Majesty, and among others, the dignity of first gentleman of the bed-chamber to the Duchess of Burgundy, which had been conferred upon him, was graciously pleased to grant him letters patent of nobility, charging him at the same time, not on that account to abandon his profession, so that the princesses of blood royal, whose happy fecundity had given so many princes and princesses to his royal family, should not be deprived of a help so efficacious to augment its number, and that other noble and distinguished dames, as well as those of different condition, might also be enabled to have the advantages of his services." *

* *

Clément continued to practice as *accoucheur* for some time longer, giving his help with equal readiness to rich and poor, until the fatigue of his professional duties obliged him to retire.

* The passages between inverted commas are borrowed from a biography of Clément published in the *Index funereus*, and which reappeared for the first time in the *Union Médicale*, 1861, t. XI, p. 87 et sequitur.

He died on the 17th October 1728, aged 80 years, and was buried in the church of Saint-André-des-Arts, as attested by the certificate of his death.

"This Saturday, ninth of October 1728, was interred here Mr. Jul. Ant. Clément, first gentleman of the Chamber of Madame la Dauphine, deceased the preceding day in his house, rue Christian, at the age of about 80 years. Were present: Master Alexandre Julien, Counsellor to the King in his Court of Parliament, the lord of the manor of Feuillette, his son; master Claude-François, De la Ville du Portault, King's counsellor at the Court of Taxes, undersigned:

De la Ville du Portault.

Clément de Feillet. Clément.

Clément had no children by his first marriage.

By his second marriage, he had two sons: the eldest, King's counsellor at the Court of Parliament of Paris, the other invested with the dignity of counsellor before the grand Council.

It was to the good offices of Clément that Louis XIV had recourse, when Madame de Montespan was found to be pregnant by him.

* * *

Mme. de Montespan had not less than seven, some say eight offspring of royal lineage.

The first-born died at the age of three years, without having been acknowledged.

The next four were: The Duke of Maine, the Count of Vexin, Mlle. de Nantes, Mlle. de Tours.

Then came the Count of Toulouse and Mdlle. de Blois, who must not be mistaken for the Princess of Conti, daughter of Louis XIV and the Duchess of La Vallière.

The first pregnancies of Mme. de Montespan were most carefully hidden from observation. When she could not do otherwise than appear in public, Mme. de Montespan donned a dress so ample, and the folds of which were so ingeniously disposed, that every one was immediately aware of what was sought to be hidden. As the Duchess of Orleans says, with her habitual malignity: "When she puts on a dress of that kind, it is as if she has written on her forehead that she was enceinte; at Court, everybody said: Mme. de Montespan has put on a wide gown, Mme. de Montespan is therefore enceinte." By antiphrasis, these gowns were called *innocent robes*.

> Une robe de chambre, étalée amplement
> Qui n'a point de ceinture et va nonchalamment,
> Pour certain air d'enfant qu'elle donne au visage
> Est nommée *innocente*, et c'est du bel usage.

So says Boursault in his *Mots à la mode* (*a*).

* * *

Who can better inform us concerning the pregnancy of Mme. de Montespan, than that malicious gossip Bussy-Rabutin, whose stories must be received with a certain amount of caution, but who was so much addicted to listening at half-opened doors, that he must sometimes have been well informed?

(*a*) A morning gown of ample space
And without a girdle;—a careless array;
From the childish look that it gives to the face
Is "an innocent", called, and the fashion to-day.

It is in this fashion that Bussy * relates the birth of the Duke of Maine (31 March 1670); although not obliged to believe implicitly all his statements, one cannot but recognize a certain piquant relish in his chronicles.

Let us now hear what he says:

"Some time after Monsieur de Montespan had been exiled to his estates by order of the King, for having boxed the ears of Mme. de Montespan who, having found a relish in the caresses of the King, could no longer suffer those of her husband and refused to henceforth grant him anything whatever, Madame his wife became enceinte; and although she was perfectly aware that everybody knew what was going on between her and the King, that did not prevent her being in some confusion when she was perceived to be in that condition. That was the reason which made her invent a new fashion very advantageous to women who wish to dissimulate their pregnancy, which is to dress like men, excepting a very wide skirt, over which at the waist the shift was made to puff out as much as possible so as to hide the belly.

"However the time for the lying-in of the lady approaching, the King withdrew to Paris, where he seldom went, hoping that she might be there confined more secretly than if he remained at Saint-Germain, where he usually resided.

"When the time arrived, a lady's-maid of Mme. de Montespan, in whom the King had particular confidence, got into a coach, and presently went to the rue Saint-Antoine, to the house of Clément, the celebrated *accoucheur*, whom she asked if he would come with her to deliver a woman who was in labour. She at the same time told

* In the *France Galante*, published *à la suite*, of *L'Histoire amoureuse des Gaules*, of Bussy-Rabutin.

him that his eyes would be bandaged, because it was not desirable that he should know where he was going. Clément, who was accustomed to this sort of thing, seeing that the maid who came to fetch him looked respectable, and that this adventure could not be otherwise than to his profit, accepted, and told the woman that he was ready to accompany her, and having allowed his eyes to be bandaged, he mounted into the coach with her, and after having been taken by a roundabout way, was finally led to a superb apartment where the handkerchief over his eyes was dropped.

He was not however, given much time to examine the place; in fact the candles were put out, after which the King, who was hiding behind the bed-curtains said to him that he might be without fear. Clément replied that he feared nothing, and coming nearer, he examined the patient. Seeing, however, that the delivery would not be immediate, he asked of the King, who was next to him, if the place in which they were was the house of God, or if it was not permitted to eat and drink therein, that, as far as he was concerned, he was very hungry, and would be glad to have a bite of no matter what.

"The King, without waiting for any of the chamberwomen to do that service, made haste to serve him, and finding in one of the cupboards a pot of jam, he went to find some bread elsewhere, saying that it could not be wanting in the house. After that Clément had eaten, he asked if it was not possible to have something to drink. The King went himself to fetch a bottle of wine from a cupboard, and poured him out one after another several glassfuls. Clément having drank first, asked of the King if he would not also take a glass, and His Majesty having refused, Clément added that the lady might not be delivered so well, and that if he wished her to be promptly delivered, he would do well to drink to her health.

"The King did not think proper to make any reply; and Mme. de Montespan being just then taken with pain, this interrupted the conversation. Meanwhile she clutched the hand of the King who exhorted her to take courage, and he repeatedly asked Clément if the affair would not soon be over. The delivery was laborious, although it did not last long; and Mme. de Montespan having given birth to a son, the King testified much joy; but he objected to its being immediately made known to her lest the emotion might injure her health.

"Clément having done all that pertained to his trade, the King poured him out some more wine, after which he again retired behind the bed-curtains, it being necessary to light a candle, so that Clément might see that all was right before leaving. Clément having assured himself that his lady patient had nothing more to fear, the young woman who had fetched him, handed him a purse containing one hundred louis d'or, and then blindfolded him once more; then having made him again get into the coach, she escorted him with the same ceremony to his house; that is to say, after the coach had taken a roundabout route as before."

* * *

Hardly had the babe seen the light than the widow Scarron (a), whose acquaintance Mme. de Montespan had made at the house of the Maréchale d'Albret was sent for. The obliging widow took away the child, hidden beneath

(a) Later, Mme. de Maintenon.

her scarf, and with her own features concealed beneath a mask; she returned to Paris with her precious burden. Mme. de Caylus, who gives us the details of these minute precautions, adds: "and what fears did she not feel that the infant might begin to cry!"

The widow Scarron already aspired to play a first part, and her intrigues so far succeeded that she managed later on to supplant her friend, the favourite of the day, and to become queen in her turn, and not a queen of the left hand, but queen in fact—the legally married wife of the King.

On June the 20th 1672, the third illegitimate child of Mme. de Montespan by Louis XIV was born.

On this occasion it was Lauzun, a man ready for all jobs, the most agreeable as well as the most repugnant, who took the future Comte du Vexin in his cloak and deposited him in the coach of the serviceable widow Scarron, who had been boldly introduced into the very chamber of the confined lady.

Clement had been fetched with the same precautions as on the previous occasion, only this time he received a fee of two hundred louis instead of one hundred as before. "The same conditions were observed each time that his services were required and he received as much as four hundred louis for delivering Mme de Montespan of her fourth child. But, whether this seemed excessive to the lady, who was naturally inclined to economy, or for other reasons, the Great Alcander (Louis XIV) having again got her in the family way some time afterwards, she sent to treat with Clément, that he might send one of his assistants to Maintenon, where she had resolved to be confined. There she passed as one of the good friends of the Marquise de Maintenon, so that the assistant who delivered her was not aware that he had delivered the mistress of the great Alcander." *

In reality, Mme. de Maintenon had but little love for Mme. de Montespan, of whom she was jealous, and was eager to supplant her; and if she was prodigal of caresses to the children of her rival, it was less her friend whom she sought to please than Louis XIV.

* * *

In 1675, the widow Scarron had gained ground in the esteem of the monarch and at that moment she began to hope to become favourite, the King either because he was beginning to get old, or because he was moved by religious scruples, having separated from Mme. de Montespan.

This separation did not last long and ended in a reconciliation, Mme. de Montespan came back to Paris, and took the sacrament at Easter, to the great edification of everybody, and distinguished herself by most pious conduct.

The reconciliation took place in the apartments of Mme. de Montespan. It was understood that the saloon in which the two interesting lovers should meet, was to be embellished by the presence of the "most respectable and grave Dames at Court."

At the appointed hour, the King appeared. A moment afterwards he took the favourite with him into a window corner, where they conferred quietly, shed a few tears, simulated or sincere, then courteously saluting these venerable dames, they went into an adjoining chamber; whence resulted, says Mme. de Caylus, *Mme. the Duchess of Orleans, and afterwards, the Count of Toulouse.*"

* Bussy-Rabutin, *loc. cit.*

The birth of the Count of Toulouse, was for Mme. de Montespan what had been for La Vallière the birth of the Count of Vermandois, it tolled the funeral knell of the King's love, and was the signal of the disgrace of the Montespan.

* * *

Mme. de Maintenon, who now comes forward on the scene, took care to throw the last shovelfuls of earth upon the defunct amours, and it was not without some secret joy that she wrote the following rather cruel lines:

"Mme. de Montespan neglected nothing to regain her influence over Louis, and he tried what he could to free himself; she feared that the birth of the Count of Toulouse would leave her some malady which might disgust the King. She was imprudent enough to ask if this was the case, and the King was cruel enough to admit it. He had just come from the hunt, bathed in perspiration. Mme de. Montespan, more irritated at the coldness by which she felt more insulted than by the insult itself, answered angrily, that she might indeed support his faults, he having so long put up with her own, and reproaching him at the same time, said, that ambitious love may perchance tolerate that which sensual love can never pardon. This last stroke was too much for the King. He could never forgive it. In vain Mme. de Montespan, on her knees, embraced his foot; he lifted her up again, without showing either anger, love or pity." *

There was an other reason for this coldness of the

* *Mémoires de Madame de Maintenon*, passage quoted by Dr Witkowski in his *Accouchements à la Cour*.

King: Mme. de Montespan was getting old, approaching sixty, and the only lien attaching her to the King consisted in her children.

She thenceforward dragged on a few years of an abandoned existence, until death as saith the Scripture, came to deliver her from her remorse and from her pains. *

* * *

The funeral of Mme. de Montespan was scandalous. "The body," says St. Simon, "remained a long time at the door of the house, while the canons of the chapter of the Sainte Chapelle de Bourbon and the priests of the parish were disputing their respective prerogatives, with much indecency."

The church was almost deserted. Mass being over, the body was deposited in a common tomb; it was not until some time later, that the Duke of Antin, † the only legitimate heir, had it placed in the family tomb at Poitiers.

* Madame de Montespan died at Bourbon l'Archambault, an inland watering-place already in repute owing to the visits of Gaston d'Orléans, the brother of Louis XIII, of Boileau, of the Maréchal de Meilleraye, etc. Madame de Montespan came there several times to recover from the fatigues of her semi-royal confinements.

† The Duc d'Antin, having been informed of the hopeless condition of his mother, went post-haste to Bourbon, and without leaving his coach or even asking news of the dying lady, required that the casket of Madame de Montespan be delivered into his hands. He was answered that she always carried the key about her person. He at once went into the apartment of the dying Duchess, searched in her breast, took possession of the key, emptied the casket, and started away again with the letters and jewels he found therein, without expressing a word of grief, sorrow, or regret. A few moments later, Madame de Montespan expired. (Allier and Dufour, *L'Ancien Bourbonnais*).

But even the body did not arrive intact at its final destination.

"This body formerly so perfect," (it is still St. Simon who is speaking), "became the prey of some sort of apprentice surgeon from heaven knows where, who being then at Bourbon wanted to open it, without knowing how to set about it."

According to a tradition, the Duchess, before dying, had bequeathed her heart to the convent of La Flèche, her body to the Abbey of Saint-Germain and her entrails to the Abbey of Saint-Menoux.

La Flèche and Saint-Germain duly received their melancholy legacy; but a peasant having been commissioned to convey the entrails to the Benedictine convent at Saint-Menoux, and perceiving on the way that they were beginning to putrefy, threw them into a ditch, where some dogs and a lot of pigs tore them to pieces. *

* * *

Had Louis XIV any sorrow for this lamentable end?

The King, after attending a stag-hunt, walked about the gardens until evening †; and, having heard the news, he calmly replied, that from the moment he had dismissed her, he had hoped never to see her again, and had thenceforward considered her dead to him. ‡

That was all the funeral oration vouchsafed to her by the man to whom she had borne eight children.

* *L'Ancien Bourbonnais, loc. cit.*

† Dangeau, *Mémoires.*

‡ Saint-Simon, *Mémoires.*

ILLUSTRIOUS REMAINS

AND

ANATOMICAL RELICS.

Mme. DE MAINTENON'S SKELETON AND Mme. DE SÉVIGNÉ'S SKULL.

O amiable lovely death!
Thou odoriferous stench! sound rottenness!
Arise forth from the couch of lasting night,
Thou hate and terror to prosperity,
And I will kiss thy detestable bones;
And put my eye-balls in thy vaulty brows;
And ring these fingers with thy household worms;
And stop this gap of breath with fulsome dust,
And be a carrion monster like thyself:
Come, grin on me, and I will think thou smilest,
And buss thee as thy wife. Misery's love,
Oh! come to me!

K. John, III, 4.

ILLUSTRIOUS REMAINS AND ANATOMICAL RELICS.—THE SKELETON OF MADAME DE MAINTENON AND THE SKULL OF MADAME DE SÉVIGNÉ.

It is a foible of the human mind, or rather an endemic mania, for it seems to have prevailed in all times, to venerate human remains because they are vestiges, most often of doubtful authenticity, of individuals who living, were the object, for some reason or another, of public attention. Superstition plays so considerable a part in this connection that it borders upon insanity.

Feuillet de Conches, the special historian of curious matters has left us some astounding revelations on this subject.

Artemisia, he says, from pure love, drank down the ashes of her defunct husband, mixed with water and pounded pearls.

In our days a lover is said to have found a solace in drinking from the delicate porcelain cup that he had caused to be kneaded with the ashes of the hair of his dead mistress.

In 1751, the lovely marquises between their gallant adventures and their delicate suppers, played with human skulls. The virtous Maria Leczinska had one, which she called her *darling*, and which she pretended was that of the lovely Ninon de Lenclos.

The case of Artemisia drinking the ashes of her dead husband, is not a solitary one. We remember also a tale once published by Mr. Jules Claretie, in his lively and picturesque chronicles in the *Temps*, and re-edited by Philippe Gille, at the head of his Reminiscences of his grand-father Louis-François Gille, reminiscences known under the title of: *Mémoires d'un conscrit de 1808*.

Mr. Gille, the father, had at one time in his possession the bones of Madame de Maintenon! He had seen them, had handled them. Returning from Caprera and from the British pontoons, the grandfather of our eminent colleague of the *Figaro* had become steward's clerk at the royal School of Saint-Cyr (*a*) about 1814. The school was then under the direction of General d'Albignac; the head steward was a Mr. Guillaumot. In the lodging given to Gille was a cupboard, in which was a mysterious box bearing on the lid the following half-effaced inscription: *Bones of Madame de Maintenon*.

In 1793, the tomb of the widow Scarron had been desecrated like many others, the lead covering of her coffin had been stolen, and her bones had been dragged, through the streets of Saint-Cyr by the wild fanatics of the village. After having been carried about on a hurdle,

(*a*) School founded by Mme. de Maintenon for the education of the daughters of needy King's officers. They were required to prove at least four quarters of nobility. (*Transl.*)

they were thrown down near to the Polygon (a). It was there that a worthy abbé bound them up and brought them back during the night to the School. This fact was certified to Gille by the author of *L'Histoire des Français des divers Etats*, the erudite Alexis Monteil, then professor at the School of St. Cyr, and by the surgeon attached to the School. This latter personage, an ardent Jacobin, added even the following detail: that the worthy priest had taken one bone too many, and that this bone was the tibia of a cow!

General d'Albignac was several times most anxious to give a proper sepulture to the remains of the mistress of the *Grand Monarque*. He wrote to the Minister, he spoke about it to the Duchess of Angoulême. He addressed himself to the Duke and Duchess of Berry. But he met with the cold shoulder everywhere. The Bourbons, it was said at the time, finding so many pretenders to the title of Louis XVII, were afraid of meeting with some new impostor, who might claim to be a lineal descendant of Louis XIV by Madame de Maintenon.

The bones of the foundress of the School of Saint-Cyr remained therefore in the hands of Mr. Gille. But, one evening, after a dinner to which he had been invited by some of his Caprera comrades, one of the guests, by name Palnel, afterwards secretary to Baron Athalin under the government of Louis Philippe, wished, by bravado to just take a taste of a bit of the broken skull. It made him ill.... from fright no doubt, but he consoled himself by boasting everywhere: "All the same I have eaten a bit of La Maintenon!"

It was not until the government of Louis-Philippe had

(a) The butt for artillery practice. (*Transl.*)

come into power that these bones were replaced in the tomb still existing in the chapel of the school.

* * *

While some time ago seeking information regarding the death of Madame de Sévigné, we became acquainted with the wanderings of her skull: we will confine ourselves now to what strictly concerns this lugubrious odyssey.

When the violation of the tomb of Madame de Sévigné happened, the municipal authorities were present, the local administration, followed by a number of citizens, had gone to the church of Saint-Sauveur for the purpose of finding a considerable quantity of lead in the family tomb of the Counts of Grignan, in which the body of Madame de Sévigné had been deposited.* A mason of the place, twenty years old, who was employed to raise the slab over the tomb, wanted to have some part of the remains of the celebrated Marquise.

He cut off a lock of her hair, of which he gave a part to the naturalist Faujas de Saint-Fond; the rest he wrapped up in paper and hid it in a hole in a coach-house.

Later on, this last relic was divided by the eldest daughter of the mason between Mr. Charles de Payan-Dumoulin, lieutenant in the navy, and Mr. Devès, clerk to the Justice of Peace of Grignan.

This latter gentleman preserves preciously, in a box, the portion of the lock of hair that came to him, and which it is said, is quite white and stained with lime. The

* Three or four of the workmen present descended into the vault and broke open six or seven coffins that were there, in order to steal the lead, which was sent by the municipality to the district of Montelimar.

mason also took possession of a morsel of the brocaded frock that enveloped the remains, and which was almost intact.

The Justice of the Peace of Grignan, at the time of which we speak, Mr. Pialla-Champier, * was also present at the exhumation. He had *the skull of the celebrated Marquise sawn in two*, and forwarded the upper part to a school in Paris that it might be the subject of an anthropological examination.

Mr. Saint-Surin, one of the editors of the correspondence of Madame de Sévigné, asserts that he heard that this anatomical specimen was submitted to the examination of Dr. Gall. We shall see later on what was its fate.

We may add that another eye-witness of the exhumation, Mr. Veyrene, notary at Grignan, got possession of a fragment of a bone of the Marquise (a piece of one of the ribs $0_m.04$ in length), that he had enclosed in a glass frame, over which he wrote the following verses:

De sa beauté voilà les tristes restes,
Le trait fatal ne les respecte pas.
Mais si tout passe et s'enfuit ici bas,
L'esprit survit aux temps les plus funestes. (*a*)

The medallion in which this bony fragment is enshrined belongs now to Mr. Louis Faye. †

* *

(*a*) Her beauty now lies shrivelled and wrecked.
The fatal dart showed here no respect.
But though here below all dies and decays,
Wit still will survive the mournful days. (*Transl.*)

* Mr Pialla also had one of the teeth of Mme. de Sévigné handed to him; this tooth, set in a gold ring, was given to Mme. de Cordoue de Tain; whose daughter was, afterwards, educated along with Mme. Pialla-Champi.

† Le Mire, *A propos of the second centenary of the death of Mme. de Sévigné*.

We shall now assist at the last act of this drama which, in some of its aspects, so closely approaches to farce.

In April, 1870, the old stone pavement of the sanctuary and choir of the church of Grignan was being taken up and replaced by the fine pavement of compressed cement which can be seen there to-day. Besides a large quantity of bones, mixed with lime, spread about in disorder in the soil, there appeared a skull, very regularly sawn in two, and the exterior of which, relatively clean, showed that it had been formerly handled. Mr. Leopold Faure took the impression of the contour of the section made by the saw on a piece of paper which he preserves as a voucher for comparison, in case the upper part—sent to Paris—should happen to be found again. The half of the skull just discovered was then put back again, in the presence of witnesses, in the place where it had been found, and the sepulchre was immediately closed with a sealed stone slab.

It appears therefore evident that the tomb at Grignan contains but one half of the skull of Mme. de Sévigné. Where the other half may be is a question we have been unable to determine.

At one time we rather hoped to find it in the collection of celebrated skulls at the museum, called the *Collection of Gall and Dumoutier*; but Mr. Manouvrier, the professor of anthropology, whose authority is universally recognized, and who has made a profound study of this collection, assured us that the skull of Mme. de Sévigné did not figure therein.

Directing our investigations in another direction, we searched in a bundle of papers collected some time back for a work on *Illustrious anatomical remains*, to see if it might contain something concerning the skull of Mme. de

Sévigné, and chanced upon the following slip, no doubt cut out of some daily Parisian newspaper:

"We read in the Nancy papers:

"Many people are not aware that our town possesses the skull of the celebrated letter writer of the XVIIth century, known in her day as the all gracious Marquise de Sévigné, née Marie de Rabutin de Chantal, grand-daughter of Saint Jeanne de Chantal, who founded the Order of the Visitation.

"This relic is preserved at Nancy, in the library of the Dominican Fathers; the lower maxillary of this skull is wanting, having become detached during its removal from Provence to Lorraine.

"The skull of Mme. de Sévigné was given to the monastery founded at Nancy by Lacordaire, by a collateral descendant of the Marquise. Further, all the proofs of authenticity and the historical documents are contained in a compartment forming a double bottom to the casket in which the skull is preserved."

Possessing these indications, we at once wrote to the Prior of the Dominicans at Nancy, the Very Reverend Father Tripier, who honoured us with the following reply:

"Nancy, 15th June 1896.

"To Doctor Cabanès,

"Sir,

"We possess a skull, which *tradition asserts* is that of the illustrious letter writer of the XVIIth century.

"M. de Saint-Beaussant resided at Nancy when Father Lacordaire came there to preach a mission in the cathedral. He became a monk, and gave Father Lacordaire a little house which, with a few modifications, forms now the actual nucleus of our convent.

'M. de Saint Beaussant was an artist, and a distinguished collector of curios: it is he who gave us the skull *so-called that of Mme. de Sévigné.*

'The monks, his contemporaries, have disappeared, leaving, to my knowledge, no document to establish the authenticity of the skull.

'The skull is in a circular box of card-board, six or seven inches in height: it appears to be of a respectable age.

'On the cover is fixed a card, with the following inscription in old handwriting:

Tête de Madame de Sévigné	pour Monsieur Gamelin.

Chez Monsieur de Rochefort
Rue Caumartin. No. 13.

'I have endeavoured faithfully to reproduce the dimensions of the card and the writing.

'The skull is large, widening out somewhat behind, a little narrower in front. The frontal bone is very regular in form and rather largely developed.

'The length of the skull is fifteen and a half centimetres.

'The width of the frontal bone above the eyes is 11½ centimetres (4⅝ inches).

'The width of the skull at the back is fourteen centimetres.

'The competence and caution of M. de Saint Beaussant, the inscription of which I have given you a fac-simile, and the tradition preserved in the convent at Nancy, are the sole evidence we possess.

"The authority of Mr. de Saint Beaussant, a good connoisseur and artist, is the only source of the tradition.

"At the convent of our Fathers in the rue du Faubourg Saint-Honoré, the Very Reverend Father Faucillon, formerly Prior at Nancy, might perhaps be able to furnish you with more precise information as to how and whence the skull came into the possession of M. de Saint Beaussant, and which we should be glad to know was that of Mme. de Sévigné.

"Please accept, Sir, my respectful salutations

"P. Tricia, *prior.*"

* * *

In order to complete our research, we paid a visit to the V. Rev. Father Faucillon, who received us with a courtesy that we are happy to acknowledge. He, however, could but simply confirm the information so obligingly supplied to us by his colleague at Nancy.

"Mr. de Saint Beaussant," said he to us, "was a man of the world who entered our convent at Nancy, the first founded in France, after having attended the preachings of Father Lacordaire. From whom he obtained the object in question, I do not know. At any rate, he was no relation of the Rabutin family. He belonged to an ancient Lorraine family, and had never inhabited Provence. All I can tell you, is that he was an amateur of enlightened taste, and that, if he thought to make us a present of the skull of Mme. de Sévigné, he did so in perfect good faith. He may himself have been mystified; the thing is possible, and I will admit to you that if we never presented that anatomical relic to any museum or to a medical collection, it was because we had in hand no document to vouch for its absolute authenticity. Nevertheless, it appeared certainly to be the skull of a woman, and the grain, the polish, the ivory hue of the bone testified to its antiquity. The box also in which it was contained had an ancient look. On this box a card had been affixed, looking much like a playing-card with the back turned upwards, and which was fixed there with sealing-wax all dried up and crumbling away. In any case, it would be to-day impossible to determine precisely who had been the original possessor of the skull now in the custody of the convent at Nancy.

"Mr. de Saint Beaussant, who alone could have enlightened you usefully, died at Oullins, in one of our convents, and he has left no family. Under these circumstances . . ."

It would seem therefore as if there were two skulls of Mme. de Sévigné about in the world: the true one, or rather a portion of it, and an imitation? *

* *

Some time back — and this is a tale of yesterday — a small leaden box was offered to one of the great Paris museums, containing some bones, with the following inscription engraved upon it:

Remains of Gaspard de Coligny, Admiral of France, killed on St. Bartholomew's day, the 24th August 1572, etc.

This same box had been already presented thirty years

* Our article on the *death of Mme. de Sévigné* from which the fragment here reproduced is taken, appeared in the *Revue hebdomadaire*, of the 11th July 1896.

previously to the Archæological Society of Orleans, but the Society had refused it.

It is very certain that in this manner the danger of being the victim of a gross fraud was avoided.

In 1851, the remains of the illustrious Admiral had been replaced in a case which was sealed up into one of the walls of the ruins of the castle of Chatillon-sur-Loing, where they probably still repose, unless the fragments of bone contained in the case have been abstracted by some fanatic or . . . speculator!

* * *

Towards 1830, Mgr. de Quélen, the Archbishop of Paris had the relics of St. Vincent de Paul transferred to the chapel of the Lazarist Fathers in the Rue de Sèvres, although the skeleton had been burned in one of the great auto-das-fé of the Revolution.* It is true, it had been asserted that a notary had preserved it in his house during all that stormy period. But who has ever furnished the proof?

* * *

I know of no one, wrote Mr. Aimé Giron, speaking of Duguesclin, whose mortal remains have been more disputed and pulled to pieces, the tombs more mutilated and displaced, and the ashes more maltreated than those of the Constable of France.

Duguesclin had expressed a wish that his body should be transported to Dinan, to the funeral chapel of his ancestors. The journey to Brittany was commenced.

The first halt was at Le Puy. There, in the convent

* De Fonvielle, *La Physique des Miracles*, p. 66.

of the Jacobin friars, a service was to be celebrated, the body exposed during one day, then embalmed, notwithstanding the rule in such cases to incinerate it and put the bones in a sack. Accordingly on the 23rd July there was "great pomp and every abundance of mortuary triumphs" with fifty wax candles, a cloth of gold emblazoned and with black embroidery—further, a funeral oration by the theologian of the convent.

Now it chanced that the Viscounts of Polignac had their sepulture in the church of these friars. Considering themselves to be in some degree at home there, and being under obligation to the Constable, who once had come to their assistance, they suddenly declared their formal intention to keep his entrails, which were thereupon well and truly "entombed in a fine monument . . ."

For about two centuries the eternal repose of the great Breton captain was not disturbed. But in 1567, the unfrocked knight of Malta, Blacon, lieutenant of the Baron des Adrets, at the head of 8000 Huguenots, camped in the convent and did not quit until the church had been ravaged and the monument mutilated.

The tomb remained in this state until the year VIII of the Republic when a certain prefect had a fancy to see, and did see, "the said entrails."

In 1833 the coffin was restored and removed to a chapel. . . . In the sarcophagus was found a double round leaden box. On the smaller, which was quite modern, was inscribed: "Here repose the ashes of the heart and viscera of Constable Duguesclin entombed in the church of St. Laurent and exhumed the 5th complementary of the year VIII of the French Republic under the prefecture of Citizen Lamothe."

This little box contained merely a few pinches of ancient ashes. The only spectators were some priests, curious, respectful, and silent, as they stooped to regard the relic, scarce daring to breathe, for the least puff of air would have sufficed to scatter what remained of the entrails of the great Constable.

Let us now return to the year 1380, when the body left Le Puy in its coffin. The escort had already reached Le Mans, when the orders of a third party—Charles V—reached them and were bound to be obeyed. The King commanded that the body of Duguesclin should be interred at Saint-Denis "in a high tomb, with great solemnity, in the chapel that he had caused to be constructed for himself," says Froissard.

The body was therefore conveyed to Saint-Denis, "Where the King had his obsequies performed as if it had been for his own son." A white marble statue of him was carved and set upon a tomb of black marble, before which night and day there burned a lamp.

Duguesclin's lamp continued burning until 1709, when some repairs displaced and extinguished it. Eighty-four years later, the Revolution came and violated at the same time all the tombs in the basilic of Saint-Denis.

Of the Constable there remained but a few bones, but the head was entire, from which some of the hair was plucked.* From these remains, thrown pell-mell into the same pit with the ashes of Kings—the skull was piously abstracted.†

* De Goncourt. *Histoire de la Société française pendant le Directoire* p. 287.

† *Le Figaro*, October 1895.

"I have been assured," adds Mr. Giron, "that it is in Paris, in the possession of the rector of the church of Saint-Thomas d'Aquin, the abbé Rigat. But I have not been there to see."

With regard to the heart of Duguesclin, it found a refuge in the Cathedral church of Saint-Sauveur. A white marble cenotaph was erected for it, and, on a shield, in bright golden Gothic letters, is the following inscription: *Here lies the heart of Sir Bertrand du Glesquin, in his lifetime Connestable of France who quitted this life the XIIIth day of July of the year one thousand IIIc IIIIxx of whom the body rests with those of the Kings at Saint-Denys in France.*

* * *

The body of Turenne was long preserved in the Museum of Natural History.

Beaumarchais, in a letter printed in the journal *La clef du cabinet des Souverains*, published by the widow Panckouke, asked the minister François de Neufchateau to put an end to such a scandal. Beaumarchais wrote in 1798; two years later Bonaparte had the body of Turenne transferred to the *Invalides*.

The heart of Turenne was so small in volume that when the army surgeons charged with the embalming examined it, they could not overcome their astonishment. The hero furnished them another subject of surprise: he possessed but one kidney.[1]

* * *

The vicissitudes of anatomical remains! what chapters

[1] Vigneul-Marville, *Mélanges d'histoire et de littérature.*

pregnant with revelations for the lovers of the curious in history do they not present!

We remember, in this connection, to have rendered ourselves guilty of an indiscretion which raised, at the time, a fine hubbub. In running through the pages of a volume of medical anecdotes, we discovered the following unexpected statement: that the medical men who had made the autopsy of the great Emperor had been obliged to interrupt their work at nightfall; and next morning the heart of Napoleon was no longer to be found... because it had been eaten by the rats!

My erudite colleague, Dr. Bremond, had picked up this fact in the *Memoirs of Dr. Antomarchi*, one of those who were present at the last moments of the exile of Saint Helena.

So that the curious thousands who had filed before the tomb in the *Invalides* had knelt before the heart... of a sheep! for it was the viscera of this peaceable animal which had been substituted for that of the conqueror of the world! *

The same misadventure had occurred to the heart of Arnaud, the hermit of Port-Royal, and also to the heart of the Regent. A splendid Danish dog, without the least respect for these dead muscles, had simply gobbled them up without any ceremony. †

* * *

A simple reflection to conclude with. Is there any

* See *Intermédiaire des chercheurs et des curieux*, 1864, p. 46; 1865, p. 42; 1879, pp. 98, 151; 1887, pp. 580, 658.

† See for *Hearts devoured*, the *Intermédiaire*, 1881, pp. 58, 216.

It was asserted that the heart of Louis XIV had undergone the same fate. The following is what we found in an old journal of which uninterest in preserving in our museums the skull of Richelieu or the brain of Talleyrand, *unless indeed they*

fortunately we cannot now remember either the title or the date. We give the extract simply as a matter of curiosity:

"About ten years ago, at No 101 of the Rue du Faubourg Poissonnière, there existed a house where was installed a Catholic professional school for young girls, under the direction of lady patronesses. Messrs. Cochon, Son, & Co. the proprietors, have had the house demolished and have built over the garden planted with trees attached to it. The site is now occupied by three modern houses.

"An extremely curious souvenir is attached to this ancient mansion. Before the Revolution, it was the residence of a wealthy Englishman, Doctor Buckland, whose name has become legendary, by reason of a fact which has perhaps no precedent in history.

"One day, Labouchère relates, the authentic heart of Louis XIV was brought to the Doctor to have his opinion on this singular relic. It was somewhat dried up and shrivelled having much the appearance of a bit of leather. The learned doctor examined it closely with the greatest attention, smelt it for a long time, so long that at last he swallowed it!!!

"Did he do so on purpose or inadvertently? It was never known exactly. The adventure created a terrible sensation; but as restitution was out of the question, the matter ended there. We may add that the remains of Dr. Buckland repose at Westminster, but the heart of Louis XIV had been digested long before the doctor died.

"Unfortunately a recent discovery altogether contradicts this story.

"The Musée Carnavalet, came into possession, about two years ago, of a letter from the Count de Maurepas, minister of Louis XV, dated at Versailles, 10th March 1730. Mr. de Maurepas informs the Duke of Artois, that in obedience to an order from the King, the heart of Louis XIV will be deposited on the next following day, 21st March, in the church of the Jesuit Fathers in the Rue Saint-Antoine. He begs him to arrange with Mr. Robert de Cotte, architect of the King's buildings, and with the comptroller of the household, Jules de Cotte, in order to place the heart "in the mausoleum constructed to receive it."

To this letter is joined the official record of the ceremony, which, in fact, took place in the morning of the 21st of March.

present some peculiarity from an anthropological point of view?

And again, ought the hair of Maximilien Robespierre and the pretended head of Charlotte Corday to find a place next to our most remarkable masterpieces of ancient and modern art? particularly as we are always exposed to the most grotesque mystifications.

Among others of this sort, one which caused some laughter at the time was the following: the maxillary of the author of *Tartuffe* had been found again. Mr. Durel who had received it for the Musée de Cluny from the heirs of Dr. Cloquet, had offered it to the administrator of the Théâtre Français, the only sepulchre worthy of such a relic. *

* See with regard to Molière's jawbone the *Intermédiaire*, I, 100, 245; VIII, 452, 598; X, 561. And the pamphlet entitled *Reliques de Molière*, by Mr. Ulrich Richard Desaix. In this latter publication mention is made of a reliquary belonging to Vivant-Denon and containing, besides a bone-fragment of *Molière*, a lock of hair of *Agnès Sorel*, another of *Inez de Castro*, part of the moustache of *Henry IV*, a bit of the shroud of *Turenne*, some of the hair of *General Desaix*, one of *Voltaire's* teeth, fragments of bone of *Héloïse* and of *Abélard*, of the *Cid* and of *Chimène*, of *La Fontaine*, and lastly a lock of the hair of *Napoleon I*.

On the fate of the body of *La Bruyère* see *Intermédiaire*, 1887, p. 678.

On that of *Voltaire*, fragments of which were disseminated about almost everywhere: *Petite Revue*, 1866, t. II, p. 182; *Intermédiaire* I, 62, III, 8; XVIII, 340, 452, 536; XXI, 12; *Revue des autographes*, 15th August 1880; *Revue de la Révolution* (unpublished documents) t. VII, p. 100.

On the skull of *Mirabeau*, the *Intermédiaire*, XX, 452.

On the anatomical remains of *Dante*, the *Amateur d'autographes*, t. IV, pp. 175, 192.

But unfortunately, its authenticity had been much contested. One irreverent humourist went so far as to insinuate that this jaw-bone of Molière was at the most that of Regnard!....*

It would be well if, these frauds could only cure our aberration. Shall we at last some day come to understand that the memory of a great man, and above all the example of his deeds, are of higher value than this abdication of our reason before matter, fatally condemned to destruction?

On the head of *Stofflet* (*a*), the *Intermédiaire*, 1892, II, pp. 15, 308.

On the corpse of *Descartes*, *Journal de Médecine de Paris*, 1890, pp. 662—663.

On the head of *Coligny*, the *Intermédiaire*, XV, 395, 430, 498, 593, 655.

(*a*) One of the most heroic, and certainly the most energetic and active of the commanders of the Vendéan royalist insurrection against the first Republic. After performing wonders, to the admiration even of his enemies, he was at last taken prisoner by the Republican troops, and shot on the 23rd February 1796. (*Transl.*)

* Regnard, a comic poet, dramatist and novelist of considerable talent, of the 17th century. In comedy, he is said to be second only to Molière. He has left a great number of works, many of which are highly esteemed. (Transl.)

THE PHYSICIAN

OF

MADAME DE POMPADOUR.

Have more than thou showest,
Speak less than thou knowest,
Lend less than thou owest,
Ride more than thou goest,
Learn more than thou trowest,
Set less than thou throwest;
Leave thy drink and thy whore,
And keep in-a-door,
And thou shalt have more
Than two tens to a score.

K. Lear, I, 4.

THE PHYSICIAN OF MADAME DE POMPADOUR.

THE eighteenth century, so much ransacked, and still so fertile in surprises, is it to be considered only as the epoch of delicate suppers, of charming women, of vapours and of patches? Is it not presented to us somewhat as a perpetual fairy scene in which only libertines and idlers play the principal parts?

The writers of scandalous stories deceived us then when they caused to pass before our fascinated gaze the spectacle of that mad saraband in which *marquises* and courtly *abbés*, beaus and noble duchesses, all rode the legendary broomstick that carried them straight to the witches' sabbath?

When the reign of Louis XV was spoken of, it was with a meaning look, and on the lips a smile full of indulgence or of hauteur. Ah! what a time of secret scandals, of quiet abductions, of arbitrary rule and of licence without check!

One of the most singular characteristics of this epoch, so full of singularities, is the contrast between a life of easy pleasures and one of hard work. The old world is tumbling down, the ancient regime is falling to pieces, the citadel of superstition is cracking, and no one pays attention; the fiddles are ordered, the ball is at its height, the growling of the storm can be heard, but the clouds are yet far off, we are still in shelter. *Après nous, le déluge!*

The Encyclopædists have generally been credited with having been the pioneers of the Revolution; of having prepared by their writings the way by which advanced the bold Titans who made of it a huge but superb reality. It is forgotten, that in this labour, they were aided by others, of more modest aspect, who accomplished their task without noise or ostentation.

At that time there were assembled a handful of factious individuals who conspired without intending it, and that in the very apartment of Madame de Pompadour,—that upstart *bourgeoise*, but yesterday only Mme. d'Etioles, to-day the real Queen of France—of the left hand.

Whilst, in an adjoining chamber, the courtesan endeavours to revive the faded senses of her royal lover, at the same time that with exquisite hand she signs disgraces or distributes favours, that she crushes beneath her heel a Choiseul, a Bernis or a Machault, all ready devotedly to kiss her hand, certain independent spirits express the broadest and most subversive opinions, without heeding who might be listening at the doors.

There were times even when their discussions made the walls tremble, for these conversations were often animated.

Sometimes the favourite condescended to take a seat at that table where the most ingenious paradoxes, the boldest theories circulated.

Here we might recognize most of those who later on would wield the pen to stigmatize abuses, ignoring the past and preparing the future. Here were to be seen dining together, d'Alembert, of cynical face; Duclos, so well described by Jean Jacques Rousseau as a straightforward clever man; Diderot, who is ruminating in his vast intelligence the Encyclopædia; Marmontel, the unfrocked priest, author of certain *moral* tales, so-called by euphemism. Buffon, careful of his ruffles, which did not prevent him from being a great genius in natural history; all these enjoy the hospitality of the host, who seldom utters more than a few words, but each equivalent to a sentence,—the celebrated Doctor Quesnay.

* * *

Louis XV had given Quesnay a lodging in the apartment of his mistress, close to the boudoir of the favourite. The doctor was rather cramped for room in his apartment, but, he consoled himself with the philosophical reflection that he was lucky to have before his eyes an unbounded field of observation.

But the amiable doctor had another whim which served to dissipate his ennui, if he ever had time to feel any.

He might be seen wandering about the palace of Versailles, close shaven, with smiling countenance and laughing eye. You saw him obsequious and polite, fulfilling conscientiously his duties as court physician. Undeceive yourself, Dr. Quesnay was reflecting * beneath the mask of

* Louis XV had surnamed him *The Thinker*. When he ennobled him, he asked him to choose for himself his coat of arms. He chose three pansies (*pensées*) on a field argent, with fesse azure, and the device: *Propter cogitationem mentis*, "a sort of riddle, if you like," says d'Alembert, "like many other escutcheons, but an honourable rebus, because it is true."

polite idleness, on the most arduous problems of social economy.

Whilst in the Boudoir of Madame de Pompadour the question of peace or war was being decided, and the choice of generals, the maintenance or revocation of ministers, was being deliberated upon; our doctor, as indifferent to what was going on at Court as if he were a hundred leagues away, was quietly writing down his axioms of rustic economy. *

He resided at Court, ignoring the language of the place, not seeking to acquire it, nor to have any intimacy with the inhabitants. †

The only persons with whom he loved to converse were the men of letters or the philosophers who came to see him.

First of all there were the writers of the *Encyclopedia*, to which he himself was one of the most assiduous contributors. §

There was Duclos, the royal historian, for whom he professed an evident sympathy, based on community of ideas and of temperament. Next came Buffon, and Turgot, then quite young, who later on, when in power, put the ideas of the Master into practice.

* * *

In this society, Quesnay maintained his freedom of speech.

A large collection might be made of the witticisms

* Marmontel, *Mémoires*.

† *Mercure de France*, Nov. 1778, loc. cit.

§ For that dictionary he wrote the articles *Farmers and grain*, and also *Evidence*, which shared the fate of most articles of the kind that of being but little read, less understood, and strongly criticised.

that escaped him in the heat of discussion. Nothing ever hindered him from bluntly saying what he thought was the truth.

At the time of the conflicts between the clergy and the Parliament, he heard in the saloon of Madame de Pompadour, a courtier propose to the King to use violent measures, saying: "It is with a halberd that a kingdom is led."

"And who, Sir," answered Quesnay, "wields the halberd?"

And seeing that the further explanation of his thought was expected, he continued,

"It is public opinion; and it is public opinion that must be considered."

On another occasion, the Dauphin, the father of Louis XVI, Louis XVIII, and Charles X, was complaining of the troubles of royalty.

"Now what would you do if you were King?" said he, turning to Quesnay?

"Your Highness, I should do nothing."

"Then who would govern?"

"The laws!"

* * *

It may now be asked what was Quesnay's attitude towards Louis XV.

It was more than respect, it was affection that the Doctor entertained for the monarch. He proved it many times, but more particularly on the following occasion.

In the middle of the night, Madame de Pompadour woke up her maid of the bed-chamber, worthy Mme. du

Hausset, who has preserved for us the details of the incident.

"Come quickly," she said, "the King is dying." The maid hastily put on a petticoat, and much alarmed, came to the King.

What was to be done? They sprinkled water on him, which revived him; and made him swallow some drops of Hoffmann's liquor.

"Let us make no noise," said the King as soon as he could speak. "Only go to Quesnay and say that your mistress is taken ill, and tell his servants to say nothing."

Quesnay came at once, and was much surprised to find the King so ill. He felt his pulse and then said: "The crisis is past, but had the King been sixty years old, it might have been serious."

He returned to his apartment to fetch some drug, probably the drops of General Lamotte, and afterwards deluged the King with scented water.

A cup of tea was then given to the patient, who returned to his apartment, leaning on Quesnay's arm.

* * *

The next day the King handed secretly to Quesnay a note for his mistress, in which he said: "My dear friend must have been much alarmed, but let her be tranquilized, I am now well, as the doctor will inform you."

Quesnay received a pension of one thousand crowns for his care and discretion, and the promise of a situation for his son.

The doctor was reassured for the time, but he often had

fears as to what would happen if the King were to die suddenly.

Mirabeau once said to him: "I think the King looks very ill, he is getting old."

"So much the worse, a thousand times the worse!" said Quesnay; "it would be the greatest loss to France, should he happen to die."

And he detailed all the consequences of that event, which might have, according to him, such deplorable results.

* *

We have already said that Quesnay respected the King. This respect was not unmingled with a certain terror.

One day that the King had been conversing with him in the saloon of Madame de Pompadour, the doctor seemed to be very uncomfortable. When the King had left, the favourite said to him: "You seem to be embarrassed before the King and yet he is so good!"

"Madam," he answered, "I was forty years old when I quitted my village, and I have but little experience of the world, to which I accustom myself with difficulty. When I am alone with the King, I say to myself; there is a man who can have my head cut off, and the thought troubles me."

"But ought you not to feel reassured by the justice and goodness of the King?"

"That is very good as a reasoning," said he; "but sentiment is quicker, and inspires me with fear before I have had time to say to myself that which should dispel it." *

* Madame du Hausset, *Mémoires.*

He had at the same time an unmitigated admiration for Louis XV, either when expressing approval of those who spoke highly of him, such as Turgot and Duclos, or when expressing his own judgment.

"Louis XIV," said he, "loved poetry, and protected poets; that may have been well in his time, because one must begin somewhere; but this century will be far greater; and it must be admitted that Louis XV sending astronomers to Mexico and to Peru to measure the earth, presents something more imposing than the arranging of operas. He has opened the gates to philosophy, notwithstanding the outcries of bigots, and the Encyclopedia will honour his reign."

* * *

Of a positive nature, strongly inclined to exact science, Quesnay had but little taste for the beauties of poetry, and expressed marked contempt for the protection granted to poetry by the "Grand Roi."

Being one day asked if he did not admire the great poets:

"As I do the great players at cup and ball," answered he, in that tone which rendered every thing jocose that he said. "But I have myself made verses and I will recite them to you. It is an epigram on a Mr. Rodot, an intendant of the navy, who took pleasure in speaking ill of physicians and of physic. I made these verses to avenge Æsculapius and Hippocrates:

"Antoine se médecina,
En décriant la médecine
Et de ses propres mains mina
Les fondements de sa machine;

Très rarement il opina
Sans humeur bizarre ou chagrine,
Et l'esprit qui le domina,
Était affiché sur sa mine.

* * *

Quesnay, the grave Quesnay, was not above trying to be a wit, happily it was but seldom that he indulged himself in this luxury. His conversation was usually of a more serious turn.

The first physician to the King being one day in the salon of Madame de Pompadour, the conversation suddenly turned upon madness and mad people. The King who was much interested in everything connected with medical science, was listening with attention.

"I will undertake to recognize the symptoms of madness six months beforehand," said Quesnay.

The King at once asked, if there were any persons at Court liable to become mad?

And Quesnay promptly answered: "I know one who will be an imbecile before three months are over."

Being pressed to mention the party, he for some time refused, but at last allowed the name to escape him: "It is Mr. de Séchelles, comptroller general. At his age he wants still to do the gallant, and I have noticed that he loses the connection of his ideas."

The King began to laugh; but three months later, he came to Madame and said to her: "Séchelles has been talking nonsense in full Council, it will be necessary to find him a successor."

A little later, Quesnay foretold to the Keeper of the privy Seal, Berrier, that he would have a fit of apoplexy, which occurred four days later.

* * *

Quesnay as may be seen, diagnosed extremely well. He could judge men at first sight, reading their very souls, laying them bare, so to speak, without their knowledge. And then, with great happiness of expression with a single word he would describe their character.

One day mention was made of "the curled and scented" Minister Mr. de Choiseul.

"He is but a dandy," said the Doctor, "and if he were but better looking, would do well for a minion of Henri III."

Another time, the Count de Saint-Germain, who boasted that he could transform little diamonds into big ones, came to the Court to make some experiments.

"It is possible," said Quesnay, "that M. de Saint-Germain may be able to fatten pearls, (a) but he is none the less a charlatan since he professes to make the elixir of life, and gives out that he is several centuries old!"

He never failed also to expose charlatans whenever there was an opportunity.

A certain physician, named Renard, and he well justified his name, had prescribed for Madame de Pompadour, who suffered from violent palpitation of the heart, to walk about her room, to lift weights and to walk fast. "If the movement increases the palpitation," he said to her, "it will prove that they proceed from the organ, otherwise they proceed from the nerves." This singular treatment having been brought to the knowledge of Quesnay:

"That is the conduct of a wise man," he simply answered.

On one occasion the Queen, had recourse to the services

(a) *Grossir des perles*, to fatten pearls, is equivalent to drawing the long bow, or telling a lie. (Transl.)

of the King's physician, for "heart trouble," caused as follows.

It was a year or fifteen months before she fell into disfavour. Whilst at Fontainebleau, the Queen sat down at a little desk, to write; above it was suspended a portrait of the King. When she had finished her writing, she closed the desk, the portrait fell down, and struck her violently on the head. Quesnay was sent for, and having had the accident explained to him he prescribed bleeding and sedatives.

* * *

The relations between the Doctor and the lady of the chamber of Mme. de Pompadour seem to have been close; but nothing goes to prove that there was anything between them other than a sincere friendship, at the utmost a Platonic attachment.

Madame du Hausset does not deny that the Doctor inspired her with sympathy. She assisted at his suppers and used often to converse with him here and there. In several places in her book she declares that "he had wit," that "he was very merry," and that she used to consult him "as an oracle," but we cannot see anywhere the shadow of anything compromising.

She also says that he "was a great genius;" but she added, "all the world says so."

He liked to converse with her about the country, and having been brought up there, he used to get her to talk to him about the pastures of Normandy, of Poitou, about the rich apple-orchards, and the best means of cultivation.

She admits again that at Court "he was far less occupied

with what was going on there, than with the best manner of cultivating the land." Her confidences however end here.

Quesnay was too much absorbed by his passion for study to allow himself to be diverted from it by trifles.

* * *

Work was necessary to a man of his active disposition.

During the month which preceded his death, he wrote three pamphlets on subjects of political economy, which caused a man of high position to say that he had a head of thirty years on a body of eighty.

At the age of 70, he betook himself with ardour to the study of mathematics, and, notwithstanding the supplications of his friends, published his pretended discovery of the squaring of the circle.

He wrote also on theology. But at any rate he had the good sense to consult on the subject with Father Desmarets, the King's confessor, who gave him useful indications.

His *Tableau économique* gives a better measure of his talent. It was published at Versailles, by express order of the King, together with his *Extract of the royal economies of Sully*; and His Majesty insisted on striking off a few copies himself. But they were so carefully concealed, that even during his lifetime, and shortly after their publication, as Mirabeau has stated, it was impossible to discover a single copy.

* *

After an existence so well employed, he was 80 years of age when he came to the end of his long and well-employed existence. Quesnay was in no way alarmed at the approach of death.

Overcome by age and infirmities,* he quitted this life, according to the words of an ancient poet, as though he quitted a banquet, without disgust, but without regret, with all the tranquility of a sage.

As his servant was shedding bitter tears:

"Console yourself," said he gently to him, "I was not born to live for ever. Look at this portrait before me; read below it the year of my birth, and judge whether I have not lived long enough..."

He did not guess, at this supreme moment, this too modest great man, that his last journey would lead him to the portals of immortality.*

* From the age of 20, he was gouty, which induced him to give up surgery and take to medicine.

* The statue of Quesnay was inaugurated at Méré, near Montfort-l'Amaury, in 1896.

THE INFIRMITIES

OF

SOPHIE ARNOULD

Beauty is but a vain and doubtful good,
A shining gloss that fadeth suddenly;
A flower that dies when first it 'gins to bud;
A brittle glass, that's broken presently;
A doubtful good, a gloss, a glass, a flower,
Lost, faded, broken, dead within an hour.
And as goods lost are seld or never found,
As faded gloss no rubbing will refresh,
As flowers dead lie withered on the ground,
As broken glass no cement can redress,
So beauty blemished once, for ever's lost,
In spite of physic, painting, pain and cost.

THE PASSIONATE PILGRIM.

Duke. Women are as roses, whose fair flower
Being once displayed, doth fall that very hour.
Vio. And so they are: alas, that they are so;—
To die, even when they to perfection grow!

TWELFTH NIGHT, II, 4.

THE INFIRMITIES OF SOPHIE ARNOULD.

WHAT amusing gleanings may be picked up with the aid of chance, or Providence, in the catalogues of autographs!

Such catalogues are indeed sometimes an historical epitome, and of true history, because the personages come before us in undress and without the slightest disguise.

No doubt such documents are often dry, on account of their intentional brevity, but those who know how to read between the lines, can give them life, and they may then become the source of most unexpected consequences.

Thus it was, that a few days since, we chanced upon one of the said catalogues. In which, in two lines, there was advertised for sale a letter from Sophie Arnould, the divine songstress, to Belanger the architect, whom she used in the freedom of intimacy, to call her "*Bel-ange.*"

Belanger had quite succeeded in gaining the good graces of Sophie. He was indeed much more and better than her lover, he was at all times her faithful body-guard.

Belanger was however something more than an architect, he was a man of wit, and in such matter, to be able to cope with Sophie Arnould, required wit indeed, and that of the best.

But poor Sophie, alas! was not always in a joking humour, and, notwithstanding her mad thoughtlessness, she had often cause to shed bitter tears. Disease, in fact, paid her frequent visits, confining her to her bed, and in such doleful moments, her thoughts reverted to her friend, the confidant of her sorrows, and she summoned him to her bed-side. "How on earth is it possible, '*mon bel ange*', the best and oldest of my friends, that I should be ill, as I have been so seriously and dangerously, for over four months, without having any news of you, without receiving from you the slightest token of sympathy, of friendship! I could never have believed it, were it not for my sad experience."

Her eldest son had brought to see her a practitioner from Paris, but she preferred her village doctor, a genuine Sganarelle, always singing '*Bottle, my darling,*' from which he seldom parted ...." But that mattered little, for he managed to set her on her legs again.

He was a great "*botanist*" and employed only simples for her cure.

* * *

It was alas! but a reprieve.

A little later on, Sophie will write again to her habitual correspondent. Yes, indeed, she has been *very bad* during fifty-three days .... "but particulary for *thirty-five*, during which she was at the last gasp .... however, *petit bonhomme vit encore*."

Now begins the chastening of this charming but sinful

woman, who will have to undergo a thousand agonies before inevitable Fate shall sever the thread of her existence.

"From the age of thirty-three to that of forty she was obliged to have recourse but only moderately, to the mineral waters of Barèges and of Bagnères, which it was necessary to bring from the distant Pyrenees. Except the waters of Barèges, these baths served only to relax the fibres and to swell the vessels of a *certain part*, which should not be tormented by any excess. The regimen imposed on her was to avoid spiced dishes and things of that nature and, to walk a great deal. Never to be bled except by leeches! and then only when indispensable."

In spite of this severe regimen, which she herself recommended, but was careful not to observe, Sophie is a continual martyr to pain. As she so nicely says, her health is always so *dolorous*. "The learned Esculapians Pelletan of the Hôtel-Dieu and Boyer of the Charité" have visited her and are not at all devoid of uneasiness.

The fact is that Sophie has a scirrhous tumour of the rectum the result of a fall, since which the symptoms have daily become more serious.

One day, there was a medical consultation, and each doctor in his turn had to view the secret seat of the evil. It was then that the talented actress is said to have sorrowfully murmured: "I am now obliged to pay for showing that which formerly..."

* * *

Formerly indeed, she cared so little to show *it*, that she found nothing better (to combat certain injurious suspicions of a lover who accused her of having contaminated him), than to get from the surgeon Morand the following most explicitly indiscreet certificate: "I certify that I have very scrupulously examined Mdlle Arnould, and that I have found upon her no mark or symptom whatever of venereal disease. Paris, this 10th December, one thousand seven hundred and sixty two. Morand."

She has now something else to do than to reply to calumny.

Now, her health begins to be her dominant care: it is so terribly shattered that she can but seldom find time to laugh at her sorry fate.

But let things but brighten up a little, and that her "scirrhus disgorge some of its humour," she becomes again the joyous Sophie whose witty jests are the joy of all Paris. After all, was not perhaps *incontinence* the root of her evil?

* * *

But soon the smile freezes upon her lips, and her torments begin again. She however still looks forward to better days. "That worthy Æsculapius, Boyer, who has visited the place with eye and finger, is pretty well satisfied, as is likewise Doctor Michel." When she says to the latter that she still has some rather sharp pains, he replies "that it must be so..." Therefore *bene sit*... However there is a temporary improvement. "The tumour is sensibly diminishing; although it is far from being ready to disappear."

It was indeed so considerable that "the satisfactory operation produced by the remedies" seems to her almost a miracle. She was then taking 72 grains of extract of hemlock, without counting "lotions, fumigations and injections, three or four times a day," according as the pains may render them necessary.

Add to that "the purgative required to be taken as brooms to sweep away the filth from inside the body."

How sad must be the look she casts into the past, when her thoughts revert to the time when she was made much of, idolized by all Paris, when the greatest wits as well as the most learned men were all disputing for her favours.

If her lap-dog fell sick, it was quite an event.

And she took good care not to confide poor doggie's health to Lionnois, the veterinary surgeon in vogue, but to the illustrious magnetizer Mesmer, who in three or four passes sent doggie off *ad patres.*

This at once gave rise to the following verses which went the round of the capital :

Le magnétisme est aux abois
La Faculté, l'Académie
L'ont condamné tout d'une voix,
Et même couvert d'infamie.
Après ce jugement bien sage et bien légal,
Si quelque esprit original
Persiste encore dans son délire,
Il sera permis de lui dire :
Crois au magnétisme... animal ! (a)

* * *

(a) The following is an attempted translation of the above, unfortunately the joke in the last line cannot be rendered into English.

Notwithstanding her acquaintance with the charlatan Mesmer, Sophie was none the less on the best terms with the Faculty, and even with the Royal Academy of Surgery.

She was disputed and contended for, as de Goncourt says in his very curious monograph.* And at the dinner, known by the name of the *Dominical*, where every Sunday around the table of the celebrated surgeon Louis, were gathered the members of the *Caveau*; (a) into this temple of wit and song, amongst Vadé, of Crebillon *fils*, of Barré, of Coqueley de Chaussepierre, only one woman was admitted, Sophie Arnould.

* * *

But now evil days have come upon her, the invalid is condemned to remain a great part of the day sitting motionless on a chair, when it is not indeed a close-stool!

Magnetism has gone to decay,
Since all the Academy big-wigs swore,
In a quite unanimous solemn way,
That it was a swindle and nothing more.
After this judgment—sage, or blind,
If some man of original mind
Still persists in his foolish creed,
He may divert the dilemma indeed
By asserting it's only the "animal" kind.

* E. & J. de Goncourt, *Sophie Arnould*, p. 51.

(a) An assemblage of the choicest and merriest spirits who used to meet to "eat, drink and be merry." After dinner original witty songs were sung, often severely criticising and castigating the political abuses of the day. (*Transl.*)

"There one must remain sitting on one's rump like an old monkey." Or move about "with the elegance and quickness of a tortoise; so that one is reduced to gaze at the people passing by and get weary of doing nothing... What is to be done? Suffer and then die? A fine conclusion!..."

If she is "too old for love," is she not still "too young to die?" If she could only escape to the country!

But the doctors have ordered it otherwise. They say that she is not yet in a condition to support without great inconvenience the jolting of a coach, particularly of a public conveyance.

And again her son Constant "Our hussar," has announced that he will soon arrive in Paris; and she is obliged to give him a good welcome. But where is she to lodge him? She does not know where to put him to sleep. He is no longer little enough to share her bed, "not that anything good or bad would come of it, *but the world, dear Agnes, is so strange!*"

* * *

The evil, in spite of all, continues its havoc. Sophie again suffers fiendish torment, although the doctors are charmed with the results of the treatment. "But they are singing victory, whilst she is crying for woe!"

The unfortunate woman is dying and has now but two months to live. She is dying deprived of the comfort which her poverty prevents her from procuring.

. . . She is dying because she cannot procure the proper remedies to alleviate her sufferings! *

Ad. Lance, *Dictionnaire des Architectes français*, Article on *Denayer*.

On the 22nd October 1802, talent, charm, wit and seduction, all had passed away.

In a few dry sentences the papers of the day recorded the death of this Magdalen, whom the representative of God here below* had pardoned, because she had loved too well.

* Sophie Arnould was buried in the Montmartre cemetery. The curé of Saint-Germain-l'Auxerrois received her last breath. The only biography in English of this famous Frenchwoman is that by Mr. Robert B. Douglas, who has published a fascinating account of her career, under the title: "Sophie Arnould, Actress and Wit."

This work contains seven charming *copper-plates* etched by Adolphe Lalauze, (*Carrington Paris*) 1898.

There is no occasion for us to quote the sallies of Sophie Arnould. It is well known how caustic or simply mischievous she could be at times. We will merely recall, because it enters into the order of this study, the cruel joke she made at the expense of La Harpe, who was afflicted with a shameful leprosy? (syphilis or eczema), "that is all he has of the ancients" was the rather wicked remark of Sophie.

The critic hardly forgave the insult.

WAS GUILLOTIN THE INVENTOR

OR

THE GODFATHER OF THE GUILLOTINE?

Ven, muerte, tan escondida,
Que no te sienta venir;
Porque el placer del morir
No me vuelva á dar la vida.

Escriva.

"Come Death, but gently come and still; —
All sound of thine approach restrain,
Lest joy of thee my heart should fill
And turn it back to life again."

WAS GUILLOTIN THE INVENTOR OR THE GODFATHER OF THE GUILLOTINE?

ALL has not yet ever been said on a subject which, at first sight, and to superficial minds, would seem to have been exhausted. But on pushing our enquiries further, we made fresh discoveries which amply rewarded us for our trouble.

We at first despaired of being able to write an article, after so many other authors, on *Guillotin and the Guillotine*.

On Guillotin? But all the biographical dictionaries and publications which pretend to be well informed give whole columns of closely printed text on the subject. How resist the temptation of playing the easy and humble part of a plagiarist? How many of these second-hand pundits are there not to encourage us to conform to their example?

Well, whatever may be the result, we will not follow their perfidious advice, but boldly endeavour to compose a new variation on an old tune.

* * *

Was it a calumny on Guillotin to attribute an invention to him which others might more justly claim? Did he take but slight part in it, as some have insinuated?

Without repeating here the history of the guillotine,* let us recall briefly the real part played by Guillotin.

Until 1789, capital punishment was effected in various ways. The stake, drowning, the gibbet, different modes of torture, mutilation, were inflicted on unfortunate beings, guilty in most cases of insignificant offences. It was from an essentially humane principle that Guillotin proposed to substitute for such barbarous methods one more prompt and less cruel.

On the 10th October 1789, Guillotin proposed that "offences of the same nature shall be punished by the same kind of penalty, no matter the rank and condition of the culprit."

On the 1st December he mounted the tribune in the assembly, and drawing a moving and vivid picture of the fearful punishments that were then in force, and which dishonoured humanity; the gibbet, the wheel, the stake, etc., he concluded "that in every case where the law should pronounce the pain of death against a criminal, the punishment shall be the same, no matter the nature of the crime he may have committed." He added, "the criminal shall be decapitated, and that by means *of a simple mechanism.*"

He went so far as to give a description of the machine before his colleagues.

Forgetting for an instant that he was a legislator,† in

* Vide, *Curiosités littéraires de Marie*, pp. 13 & 282; *Curiosités des Traditions*, p. 301 and sequitur; the works of Chéreau, of L. Du Bois and of Dubois d'Amiens on the guillotine; *Le Vieux-neuf* of Ed. Fournier, t. I, p. 318, note, etc.

† *Journal des États-généraux*, t. IV, p. 235; 1789 in 8vo.

the heat of his oratory he permitted the following phrase to escape him, the terms of which went beyond his thought: "the mechanism falls like lightning, the head flies, the man is no more."

The assembly, while approving in principle the motion of Guillotin, adjourned the question of deciding upon the mode of execution to be inflicted on criminals condemned to death: Guillotin succeeded only in obtaining that nobles or peasants, etc., should be punished in the same manner.

It was not until the 3rd of June 1791, that is to say twenty months after Guillotin's first speech, that Lepelletier de Saint-Fargeau got the assembly to vote that "every culprit condemned to death should be decapitated."

* * *

There remained but to have a machine made, sufficiently expeditious to spare the criminals who would first have to try it all unnecessary suffering.

The National Assembly, taken by surprise, thought to get out of the difficulty by applying to the perpetual secretary of the Academy of Surgery, Antoine Louis, already known for his highly valuable scientific labours. Louis hastened to draw up "a report upon beheading." This report, adopted without discussion, was published in the *Moniteur* of 20th March 1792. *

The only thing now to be done was to have the machine constructed. An active correspondence on the subject was carried on between Louis, Roederer, the procurator-syndic

* In part only. Vide, *Union médicale*, 1870, t. X, pp. 132 and 134 and *Revue des documents historiques*, 3rd year, pp. 47 and 48.

of the Department of Paris, and Clavière, the Minister of public taxes. Guillotin was consulted merely for the sake of form.* In reality it was Louis who directed everything.

He first of all requested the State carpenters to send in a specification † of the cost of constructing the new apparatus; but in view of the exaggerated demands of "master carpenter Guédon," who asked not less than 5,660 livres for the "first machine," § on account, as he alleged, principally of "the difficulty of finding workmen to execute a work which shocks their principles," Clavière and Roederer decided to dispense with his services.

Louis then addressed himself to "*another artist*," of German origin, a *manufacturer of pianos* named Tobias Schmidt, whom he recommended to the Directoire.**

On the 17th April 1792, at ten o'clock in the morning, the first trials of the machine now finally constructed, were made in the amphitheatre or rather in a small adjoining court of the hospital of Bicêtre, in presence of the chief officials of the establishment, of Doctors Philippe Pinel and Cabanis, the friend of Mirabeau; of Doctors Louis, Cullerier and Guillotin; of the Procurator-Syndic of the commune; of a crowd of notabilities of the national assembly, the members of the committee on hospitals, etc. ††

* *Union médicale, loc. cit.*, p. 214.

† *Ibid.*, 215, 216.

§ *Ibid.*, 217.

** *Revue des Doc. hist., loc. cit.*, 48 and 49.

†† On this subject here is a letter written by Doctor Louis to Dr. Michel Cullerier, at that time surgeon to the General Hospital:

"Dear Sir, The mechanic employed to construct the machine for decapitating, will not be ready to experiment with it until Tuesday. I have written to the Procurator General Syndic, requesting him to give orders to the person who will have to operate in public, to be

The executioner Sanson and his assistants laid down a dead body between the two supports of the machine, the face downwards. At a signal given by one of his workmen, Sanson pressed upon the button which held the cord. The knife, heavily weighted, slid swiftly down between the grooves and severed the head from the body, as Cabanis himself said, "with the rapidity of a glance." The bones were cleanly severed. Two other similar trials, which followed succeeded equally well.*

at the place chosen for the experiment at two o'clock next Tuesday. I have informed the Director of the zeal you have shown in aiding in the accomplishment of the general wish in this sad matter. Therefore until Tuesday.

"In order to ensure the efficacy of the fall of the blade or axe, the machine must be fourteen feet in height. From that you will be able to judge whether the experiment can be made in the amphitheatre or in the little adjoining court.

"I remain, etc., ... "Louis."

(A. Husson, *Étude sur les Hôpitaux.*)

* Paul Bru, *Histoire de Bicêtre*, p. 87.

We think it worth while to relate the following anecdote, of which, however, we cannot guarantee the authenticity.

While the spectators were congratulating the two doctors whose invention would make capital punishment more expeditious and less painful, old Sanson (the executioner), alone, his gaze rivetted on the corpse from which the head had been so swiftly separated, without further effort on his part than pressing a knob, muttered sadly: "A fine invention indeed! provided that no abuse is made of the facility!" . . . The spectators quitted the place and hastened to give an account of the new invention, some of them to the National Assembly, others throughout the city. As for the prisoners at Bicêtre, they eyed each other as they got down from the window-ledges where they had climbed to behold the sight.

"That," said one, "is the famous plan for equality. All the world to die the same death.

On the 25th April 1792, a murderer and robber named Pelletier, was beheaded by the new axe. *

* * *

The question has been often mooted, who was the godfather of the guillotine, and Guillotin has always been named.

The following may have given some credence to this opinion.

The *Journal de Perlet*, of 20th March 1792, says expressly: "The legislative committee has caused a decree to be adopted regulating the mode of decapitation of criminals condemned to death. It was adopted without being read or discussed. This decree is nothing but a proposal of M. Louis, perpetual secretary of the Academy of Surgery, who suggests, for the execution of this article of the penal code, a machine similar to that *which the inventor had christened the guillotine.*"

On the other hand, one can read in the journal Les *Actes des Apôtres:* †

"There was a considerable difficulty in finding a name for this instrument. Is the language to be enriched by the name of its inventor? Those who are of that opinion found no difficulty in giving it the gentle and smoothly flowing name of *guillotine.*"

Other appellations had been proposed for this instrument

"Yes," said one of the wits of the prison, "it's a levelling measure!"

(*Histoire anecdotique des prisons de l'Europe* by Alboize and A. Maquet.)

* *Chronique de Paris*, no. 118, 26 April 1192.

† No. X.

of execution: the *mirabelle*, the *Louison* or *Louisette* (a), but the word guillotine was finally chosen.*

*

According to one version, it was while assisting, several years before the Revolution, at the performance of a pantomime of the *Quatre fils Aymon*, at a theatre on the Boulevards, that the first idea of the instrument presented itself to Dr. Guillotin. It is more probable that he found the model in certain authors of the XVIth century, who have given a detailed description of it.†

There is not the least doubt that Guillotin had precursors. But another point which is equally beyond dispute is that he was the first to *propose* and to *obtain the adoption* of the principle of a decapitating machine.

Whether he himself gave the name or bequeathed it to the instrument, he certainly could not, were he to return to this world, disclaim its paternity.

(a) In allusion no doubt to Dr. Louis. (*Tr.*)

* Saint-Edme, *Biographie de la Police*, 1829, in 8vo, p. 253.

† *Union médicale* loc. cit. pp. 869–872; *Bulletin de l'Alliance des Arts*, 25 Fev. 1846, 261; Ibid. 10 Dec. 1846, 202; *Musée universel*, 1872–73, t. I, p. 179; 1873, t. II, p. 118; etc., etc.

THE REAL

CHARLOTTE CORDAY.

HER PERSONAL APPEARANCE.

Ah, since the Future's Riddles none can guess,
Come fill the Cup, the Cup that drowns Distress.
Ah, Love, yon Moon will often rise again,
Will rise and miss us in Her loneliness.

Before us twain were many Nights and Days,
The Stars have long pursued their Heavenly ways.
But tread with Lightest Foot upon this Dust,
I was once an Eye that beamed with Loving Rays.

Omar Khayyam

THE REAL CHARLOTTE CORDAY.

PROLOGUE.

I. *Her personal appearance.*

Painters and poets are always to be consulted with a certain amount of distrust: they often sacrifice to art too much historical truth. What individual has ever so greatly tempted the brush of the painter and the pen of the historian as Charlotte Corday? Who has transmitted her features to us without idealising or deforming them? Even after the lapse of a century new controversies spring up: it is as difficult to agree about her personal appearance as it is about the motive and the moral of the act she committed. Was it crime or sublime folly? On this point again the case is far from being finally judged. *

The following is the appreciation formed of her by Mr. A. Casimir-Perier, whose well-poised judgment is known, in a remarkable article on Charlotte Corday, published in the *Revue des Deux Mondes* (1862):

'Her name will pass down to future ages with the remembrance of an act for which the crimes of the victim afford no excuse. Never can any cause however just, however innocent of all complicity it may

At any rate the world is agreed that the appearance of Charlotte Corday was rather charming than otherwise, and that her features were most prepossessing.

There can be no doubt on that score if we are to credit only those who were her contemporaries, who had opportunities to see her often. They concur in portraying to us "her oval countenance, her eye so blue and penetrating; a well formed nose, a lovely mouth with pearly teeth, auburn hair; hands and arms worthy to serve as models." Others go further, and tell us that "her complexion had the transparency of milk, the carnation of the rose and the downy softness of the peach. The tissue of her skin was of rare delicacy; one seemed to see the blood circulating beneath the petal of a lily. She blushed with extreme facility and was then indeed most bewitching. Her eyes, slightly veiled, were well formed and very handsome; her chin, just a little prominent, did not mar a charming ensemble full of grace. The expression of this lovely face was of indefinable sweetness, as was also the sound of her voice."

Her voice had a particularly agreeable tone.* "Never was there heard a more harmonious and enchanting voice; never was there seen a glance more angelic and pure, a more winning smile. Her light auburn hair was admirably suited to her features; she was indeed, a superb woman."

Quite different does she appear to us in a passage from

be, see its defenders take to the poniard without a great prejudice to those inflexible principles of public morality which it is the prime duty and supreme interest of honest men of all parties to respect and defend."

* "Her voice, like a child's," writes Mr de Ségur (Les Femmes, I. 111), "was always in harmony with the simplicity of her appearance and the imperturbable serenity of her features."

a demagogic paper of the period, in which she is described as follows: "This woman, often said to be pretty, was not so in reality; she was a *virago* more fleshy than fresh, without grace, and dirty, as female philosophers and wits almost always are. Her face was hard, insolent, *erysipelatous* and ruddy . . ."

However much our sympathy may be enrolled on her side, this last detail is not without importance, coupled with the testimony of an octogenarian who had known Charlotte, found in a pencil note among the papers of Mr. George Mancel, formerly librarian at Caen:*

* A woman of the name of Berlant, condemned to death in 1812 for participation in the Montaigu riots and pardoned, whilst giving details of this event to Mr. George Mancel, librarian of the city of Caen, was led to speak of Charlotte Corday.

Her words were taken down textually by Mr. Mancel and recorded in his note-book, on the 10th May 1859.

This woman was then 76 years old. She related as follows:

"Charlotte or Mademoiselle de Corday, *ouvrière* (sic) at the Abbaye aux Dames, was the first to teach me how to handle the bobbins for making lace, when I was six years old; she was marked with the small pox; rather tall than otherwise, and not handsome, but she had a gentle air, so gentle that one already loved her before she spoke; she was one of God's angels." (*Unpublished papers of Vatel.*)

To this testimony may be added the following extract from a much esteemed work:

"An aged nun (of the Abbey of the Holy Trinity at Caen), who is still living (1840), who knew Charlotte Corday, relates that she at first attached herself with great fervour to religion; but she already gave evidence of a certain amount of pride and of obstinacy which caused her to be reprimanded.

"She learned in the convent to read, to do embroidery, to draw, in which last accomplishment she attained much skill; and later, Charlotte could draw very well." (Lairtullier, *Les femmes célèbres de la Révolution*, I. 158.)

"Mlle. de Corday was *pitted with the small-pox*, rather tall than short and *not handsome*, but she had a gentle manner: so gentle that before she opened her mouth, one already loved her: she was one of God's angels!" *

* * *

These contradictions would not fail to be somewhat disconcerting to our judgment had we not more convincing documents to go upon. If we are to believe one of the most truthful biographers of Charlotte Corday, who published his book at a time when there were many people still living who had known the young girl, it appears beyond doubt that she was irresistibly charming.

"All the historians of Charlotte Corday," writes Mr. de Monteyremar, "are agreed as to the beauty of the young girl, on the hue of her blue and penetrating eyes, on the perfect form of her nose and mouth, on the regularity of her features, gentle but serious, on her graceful appearance, but they differ about her height, which according to some was short, while others say that she was tall.

* "The name of Corday was much venerated in the country, I noticed in my numerous excursions round about the castle.

"Mme. Jules de Corday informed me that it amounted to a sort of superstition in the district.

"Mme. de Corday was a Mauvers.

"Her mother was herself a Chézot, and the Chézots descended from the Baillculs, descendants of the Scottish King.

"Now, it is a well known popular prejudice that Kings had the privilege of curing by touch the King's evil: therefore sick persons used to come to get touched by Mme. de Mauvers and her sister. Children afflicted with mesenteric atrophy were also brought to be touched." (Extract from an unpublished letter of Ch. Vatel.)

According to Mr. Hauër, Charlotte Corday was tall, and rather robust looking.

With regard to the colour of her hair, there can no longer be any doubt whatever * she was *fair.*"

*

Concerning the height, † of Charlotte Corday, her pass-

* The proof that doubts were possible, is that even some of the contemporaries of Charlotte who had themselves seen her could not agree on this point.

"I remember one day," writes Mr. Ratisbonne in the *Débats*, "arriving at the editorial office of the paper in the midst of a stormy debate, the vivacity of which rather astonished me, but which I was careful not to interrupt. It was as to whether *she* had been blonde, or chestnut. The two disputants were Mr. Barrière and the venerable Mr. Delécluze. *She* was Charlotte Corday, *whom both remembered to have seen in Paris, in their infancy.*"

See also the *Figaro* of 24th August 1868.

† The Marquise de Saint-Léonard, *née* de F., aged 87 years, wrote to Vatel on the 11th October 1862, as follows:

"Mdlle. de Corday was tall, without however surpassing middle height: she was plump without excess; she was dark and resembled the medallion which is here. She held herself badly, with her head bent down, which made her seem to look from underneath her eyebrows. My father was constantly saying to her, 'Cousin, your chin will stick to your breast! Do show us your eyes, they are handsome enough for that.'"

Found among the papers of Vatel was another letter, from which we detach the following post-scriptum, which confirms what we have said about Ch. Corday being rather tall than otherwise.

"P.S.- Charlotte Corday was a very fine woman of about 5 feet 2 inches, old measurement, in height: *(a)* she was rather pale in the face.

"There are a great many portraits of her; but Mdlle. Augustine de Corday, owner of the Chateau de Glatigny, a relation of Charlotte, who knew the original, has never seen an exact portrait of our heroine."

(a) 5 feet 6 inches modern English measure. (*Transl.*)

port will at once authentically enlighten us. It is as follows:

"*Let pass freely the citizeness Marie* * *Corday, born at Mesnil-Imbert, residing at Caen, district of Caen, département of Calvados, aged twenty-four years, height five feet and one inch (5 ft., 6 in. English), hair and eyebrows auburn, eyes grey, forehead high, nose long, mouth medium size, chin round, double pointed, face oval; etc.*"

This official document, notwithstanding its laconicism, is absolutely exact. There is no possibility of there being any mistake as to height; it is a measurement obtained with mathematical exactness.

With regard to the *colour* of her hair, we must again rely upon this official document, although in this respect it is necessary to give some explanations.

* * *

We must here again have recourse to Mr. de Monteyremar. "It was at the tribunal that Hauër sketched the portrait of Charlotte Corday. It was during the trial and not in the prison that the accused maiden, during a momentary interruption of the trial, cut off a lock of her hair and offered it to the painter, who was far more troubled and affected than she was herself, saying: 'I know not, Sir, how to thank you for the deep sympathy you seem to feel for me and for the care you have taken in tracing my portrait. This is all that I can offer you, please take and preserve it as a souvenir.'"

* Her real baptismal name was *Marie*.

In Hauër's portrait Charlotte Corday is represented with fair hair. *

We may further notice the following detail: The painter Hauër had given a clergyman of his acquaintance, the Abbé Dinomé, then vicar of the cathedral of Blois, a portion of the lock of hair which had been given to him by Charlotte. It is stated that the Abbé Dinomé had assured Mr. de Monteyremar, who relates the incident, that the hair, unfortunately lost through the ignorance of a servant, was auburn, of a real and beautiful blond, that is to say neither red nor ash-coloured. †

Mr. Lenotre, who has worked so patiently to reconstitute Paris during Revolutionary times, considers that these details are open to suspicion or else insufficient.

Mr. Lenotre managed to make the acquaintance of Mme. Hauër, the daughter-in-law of the painter of the portrait

* Hauër, then an officer of the section of the Théâtre Français, was called to the tribunal by reason of his functions as garde national. It was while gazing at the maiden that the idea came to him to make a rough sketch of this beautiful model. (De Monteyremar, *Ch. de Corday*, pp. 115–116.) It was not until much later, that Hauër, with the help of this sketch and of his souvenirs, composed the picture which is to be seen in the picture gallery of Versailles.

This portrait was purchased in 1839, ten years after the painter's death, by the Director of Museums, for 600 francs (£24), from the heirs of Mme. Hauër (*De Monteyremar*, loc. cit., p. 117.)

† George Duval, in his *Souvenirs de la Terreur*, published in 1840, asserts that he knew Hauër, and that he saw at his house not only the portrait, but also the lock of hair of Charlotte Corday. "This portrait," says he, "that I have seen, and which has been recently purchased by the Civil List for the Museum at Versailles, does not in the least resemble the other portraits of Charlotte, which represent her with dark hair, whereas here it is of a light blonde. The lock of her hair, still in the possession of his family is a proof of the same." (T. III, c. XXVIII, p. 357.)

of Charlotte Corday: and according to this respectable lady, it was not at the trial, but in the prison itself, a few minutes before leaving for the place of execution, that Charlotte gave this noted lock of hair to the painter who had been authorized to visit her in her prison.

This lock of hair remained a long time in the possession of the artist, until it was one day lost in the trouble accompanying a change of lodging. "I never heard," added Mme. Hauër, "that a portion of the lock of hair had ever been given to any one, * my husband would have known it; and as this loss was a source of positive regret to him, he would certainly have demanded the return of it to him from the person to whom it had been given. The colour of the hair of Charlotte Corday was *light auburn*. My husband had many opportunities of seeing it."

Hauër was not the only one who had seen that her hair was light auburn: we need seek no other proof for the moment than the following two *testimonies* taken from the *Papiers inédits de Vatel.* †

Chéron de Villiers (p. 55 of his work on Ch. Corday), asserts however that he saw a lock of the hair of Charlotte in the possession of a Madame Forget. This lady had it from the painter "who made the last portrait of Marie de Corday."

† We thought we had exhausted all the sources of investigation when the idea struck us of going to the Versailles library, where, we had been told, were preserved the *papers of Vatel*. For the information of those who may not know, be it known that Vatel is the accredited historian of Charlotte Corday, her *cavaliere servente*, and has been aptly called her posthumous lover. During his lifetime this amiable scholar had collected with fervour all the relics that could remind him of the virgin martyr, of the saint to whom he had plighted his troth.

First, that of a Mme. Bignon, residing at Rouen, aged 81 years (letter dated 11th September 1862, addressed to Vatel):

" ....Her skin was white and rosy, and her hair *light auburn.* When the known portraits of Charlotte Corday were shown to us, my mother exclaimed: 'It is quite astonishing, I do not in the least recognize the features of Mademoiselle de Corday. She is here made to look like a big, dark, frigid woman; but it is altogether incomprehensible. She was not at all like that. She was *fair*, with a fresh complexion, and handsome.' "

The second testimony comes from a Mme. Françoise *Proud*, widow Cauchois, born at Lacombe in March 1774. We transcribe it here without changing anything:

" .... She (Ch. Corday) very much resembled her father, she was of a *nice height*, well made and upright, her face rather long and pale, *she was fair*, of the same colour as myself. She often wore a round cap with a ribbon encircling it. She wore her hair plain or plaited falling behind on her shoulders, she used *powder*, but moderately, because she was *very fair.*"

Thanks to the great kindness of Mr. Taphanel, the guardian of these treasures, we were allowed to visit the *Charlotte Corday Saloon*, where a quantity of souvenirs of the heroine are preserved: the bed in which she reposed as a young girl, the celebrated portrait by Hauer, and a number of miniatures, engravings, etc., which in the silent meditation in which we were wrapped enabled us to evoke that noble countenance.

Our pilgrimage terminated, we asked to see the *Vatel papers*: and from distant recesses were brought to us some thirty portfolios crammed with manuscripts, the fruit of nearly thirty years laborious research!

It was necessary to make a selection: this task was greatly facilitated by the aid given to us by Mr. Taphanel and also by that of Mr. Viret whose cooperation on this occasion was particularly valuable.

But we now come to a rather different opinion, emanating from a contemporary of Charlotte, *Marie Anne Gilette*, born the 5th November 1771, at Saint-Jean-de-Caen, aged 88 years; she was sixteen years old in 1790.

This good dame states that Charlotte Corday's hair was: chestnut.

"....I have seen Mme. de Corday more than a hundred times. She was neither fair, nor was she dark, but something betwixt the two, she was chestnut; her face was rather large; she had fine eyes and a pleasing look. Her nose was not aquiline, she had a superb complexion, with a very fresh colour; altogether she was a pretty person, but she did not seem to be aware of it; she never gave herself airs; her manner was simple and her dress quite unpretending."

Lastly, we take from a letter addressed to Mr. Vatel by Mr. Cosnard-Desclosets, the following passage:

"....She (Ch. Corday) was tall and strongly built, which did not prevent her being graceful: her features were irregular, but her complexion was admirable I purposely retain the word *her hair was light* chestnut. Her eyes were blue and very expressive; her hands large."

* * *

All these contradictory opinions are rather disconcerting.

One point seems settled, that the colour of Charlotte Corday's hair was auburn, but inclining to blonde, contrary to the generally received opinion, and to the popular lithographs which generally represent her with quite dark hair.

Mr. Vatel remarks that, in the portrait by Hauër, "*the death of Marat*," Charlotte Corday *is powdered*. In the painting by the same artist, Charlotte Corday before the Revolutionary Tribunal, she is also represented with her *hair powdered*.

This in itself is the only detail of any value in the discussion: Charlotte, in fact, was in the habit, according to the custom of the day, to slightly powder her hair.

We may here quote incidentally a witness whose evidence may have some value. It is the hair-dresser who gave his professional services to Charlotte Corday, on the very day when she was about to accomplish the act which was destined to immortalize her name.

A certain hair-dresser named "Charles-Alexandre Person, hair-dresser and barber to the Ecole Polytechnique and to the Collège Henri IV, residing in Paris, at the Barrière d'Italie,"* used to relate as follows:

* The two following letters, taken from the Vatel papers show what care this conscientious scholar took to obtain information, even the least important, of a nature to shed a light upon the biography of his heroine.

The first of these letters is signed by a well-known name, that of Mr. Dauban, the author of a work on Madame Roland which is considered trustworthy.

Sir,

The hair-dresser whom I mentioned to you was named Person. He resided in the Rue Descartes, 42. He has now retired to the Barrière Fontainebleau, near to the fortifications. I could not obtain his number, but I am assured that he is very well known in the quarter and it will be very easy for you to find him out. This information has been given to me by the hair-dresser who succeeded him, and I give it you as I had it.

Yours very truly

20th August 1861. Dauban.

(Mr. Person, as it is said in a note, "is an old man, but very well preserved, not appearing more than sixty years old.") We will now allow him to speak for himself:

"I was born in 1787.

"In 1805 I was apprenticed to a hair-dresser named Férioux, in the Rue des Vieux Augustins; he had a little shop looking on the street; in the morning he used to wait upon outside customers; in the evening he was employed at a gambling-house in the Palais-Royal, n° 129.

"This is what I heard him relate:

"In the morning of the day of Marat's assassination, he was summoned to a neighbouring hotel in the same street, between the Rue Pagevin and the Rue Montmartre, on the right-hand side. He went there and found a young lady alone in her room; *he dressed her hair and powdered it*; while he was proceeding with his business, he noticed on a commode a knife in its sheath.

"In the evening news was brought of the death of

The other letter, written by a less known person, Mr. Felix Jubé, is not less interesting:

Paris, 30th Sept. 1867.

Sir,

I have to regret not having been able to reply earlier to the letter with which you honoured me. It was only yesterday that I ascertained with certainty the existence of Mr. Person *in the full possession of all his faculties*. He still resides at the *Maison-Blanche*, opposite to the omnibus station of the line Pointe St. Eustache to the Maison-Blanche.

I should have wished to have been able to inform you that I had seen him, and have been glad to confirm my remembrances concerning a fact which appears to interest you.

Please accept, etc.

Felix Jubé,
Rue des Feuillantines, 47.

Marat, and the next day, the officers of justice having visited the hotel, he found that the young woman whose hair he had dressed was Charlotte Corday. I heard that from his own lips; it was all he told me.

He did not say whether she was fair, nor of what colour was her dress. He merely related to me the above. He was not an educated man, and conversed but little: what seemed to have struck him most, and upon which he laid some stress, was that he had dressed her hair and *given it only a trifle of powder*, and that he had seen the knife upon the commode."*

* *

One may have noticed in the evidence we have here given, this phrase: "nor did *he tell me of what colour was her dress.*" Would that not lead us to suppose that Vatel had endeavoured to elucidate a question which to him seemed doubtful?

In fact, historians have very much discussed—the subject was attractive—the colour of the dress, or rather of the dresses, of Charlotte Corday. And as even the simplest detail may have its relative value, we will say what we know on the subject.

When Charlotte Corday called to see Marat, at nine in

* The poniard of Marat had a hilt of mother of pearl with the blade curved and the point turned upwards; it might be about eighteen inches long; the sheath had two little rings attached, through which a chain could be passed to suspend it.

Mdlle. Marat gave it to Mr. Bureau, Jun. of Argentan. She was often annoyed by the police and used to hide all weapons and other objects which had belonged to her brother: she deposited them in the hands of friends. (*Letter from Mr. Germain to Vatel*, of 24th Sept. 1862).

the morning of the 13th July 1793, she had on, according to Catherine Evrard, one of the witnesses of the drama— and, as Mr. Lenotre judiciously remarks, in matter of dress the testimony of a woman is indisputable.- Charlotte had on, we say, *a brown dress and a black hat.*" *

A portrait, formerly in the possession of Mr. Renaud

* When Charlotte Corday arrived at Caen, she wore the tall conical hat then in fashion: she had the same hat on when she went to see Marat. She also wore this tall black hat at her first hearing, as testified by the portrait of her that was sketched by Hauër. In the prison she had a cap made for her, with which she appeared before the Revolutionary Tribunal and which she still wore while mounting the scaffold. This cap, made at Paris according to the fashion of the day, is similar to that worn later by Marie Antoinette on the fatal cart. See the celebrated sketch made by David.

In the picture by the painter Scheffer, although he aimed at realism, the cap worn by Charlotte is not in accordance with historical truth.

The following is what Mr. Pourvoyeur an eye-witness of the drama related to a friend at Versailles, a Mr. Salmon, bookseller, on the 30th June 1866. We copy this from a note in the Vatel Papers.

"Mr. Pourvoyeur, an engraver, informed me that when a child he lived in the Rue de l'Ecole de Médecine, then des Cordeliers, in the same house with Marat, that he was present at the arrest of Charlotte Corday, and that she then wore a conical tall hat.

"He used to get vexed when he saw the picture by Ary Scheffer, saying:

"Is it possible to make such a mistake? Charlotte was not wearing a cap when she was arrested; it is possible that she wore one later, at the trial, but she certainly did not at Marat's."

He added that when she was being removed, one of those present would have attacked and maltreated her, but he was prevented by one of the others.

Pourvoyeur had first been a navy surgeon, but he afterwards took to his father's profession, that of engraver; it was he who engraved the celebrated picture representing the Review by Napoleon in the court of the Tuileries.

(of Caen), and of which Mr. Vatel had a wood engraving, represents her as follows: "The Knife in one hand, a fan in the other, and clad in a *a brown dress and on her head a black hat.*"

Towards evening, she returns to the Rue des Cordeliers; but in the meanwhile she had changed her dress.

Laurent Bas deposes as follows: "At half past seven in the evening, a person of the female sex, descending from a hired vehicle, wearing *a spotted morning gown* and a tall hat, with a black cockade and three black ribbons, and a fan in her hand, asked to be admitted to see citizen Marat..."

It is this spotted morning-gown that Mr. C. Clère has sought to represent in th[e t]ryptich he exhibited in the *Salon* of 1880.

*

But all the painters of the day, who were unacquainted with the declaration of Laurent Bas, have given to Charlotte a white gown: Hauër, Garneray senior, Pfeiffer, Monnet, Brillon, Joigneaux, d'Origny.

The engravers, on the contrary, have adopted a striped gown: at the bottom of page 105 of his *Mémoires sur Charlotte Corday*, Mr. Adolphe Huart writes:

"At the moment when she accomplished her courageous act, Charlotte Corday wore the following costume: *a grey striped dimity morning gown*, a tall hat, surmounted with a black cockade and green ribbons. I seem to remember that in the painting by Ary Scheffer, representing the arrest of Charlotte Corday, the dress is of white dimity. In the Museum at Versailles there is a portrait of Charlotte Corday by Jean Jacques Hauër, painted from nature at the time of her trial. She is represented sitting *dressed in white*.

In the number of the *Autographe* (of 1st October 1864), devoted entirely to Charlotte Corday the author, Mr. Chéron de Villiers is of the same opinion with regard to her costume.

To sum up, during the course of the drama Charlotte Corday wore several gowns, which must all be considered as authentic: the *brown* dress before the crime; the *spotted* one during its perpetration, and the *white* gown at the trial. To these three must be added the *red shirt* † which was the costume of her execution, the last dress of the "angel of assassination."

Vide *Figaro* of 20th and 24th August 1880 (Articles by Ad. Racot).

† In the sentence of death on Ch. Corday is the following:

"Pursuant to Article 4 of Provision 1 of the First Part of the Penal Code, which has been read, and is to the following purpose:

"Whoever shall have been condemned to death for the crime of murder, incendiarism or poisoning, shall be taken to the place of execution clad in a red shirt."

THE

PROLOGUE TO THE DRAMA.

CHARLOTTE CORDAY'S ADMIRERS.

I have marked
A thousand blushing apparitions start
Into her face; a thousand innocent shames
In angel whiteness bear away those blushes;
And in her eye there hath appeared a fire
To burn the errors that these princes hold
Against her maiden truth.

Much Ado, IV, 1.

II. THE PROLOGUE TO THE DRAMA. CHARLOTTE CORDAY'S ADMIRERS.

Most historians have endeavoured to find a personal motive for the murder of Marat. According to them, it was revenge which armed the hand of the heroine, who made the dictator of the Convention responsible for the death of her lovers. We purposely say her lovers, because several have been attributed to her, though wrongly, there being no sufficient proof to attribute a single one to her with any amount of truth.

There is a legend that while she was at the Abbaye-aux-Dames, Ch. Corday had many opportunities of meeting young Henri de Belzunce, second major in the Bourbon-Infantry Regiment, then in garrison at Caen, and that the intimacy between the young people had been facilitated by the lady Abbess herself, of whom the officer was a nephew. A few years later, Mr. de Belzunce was murdered by an infuriated mob, and his body horribly mutilated. This crime was asserted to have been the result of the preachings of Marat, in his sanguinary paper the *Ami du Peuple*.

Here again historical truth contradicts the legend; the assassination of de Belzunce took place on the 12th of August 1789, exactly one month before the appearance of the first number of the *Ami du Peuple*.

The lady Abbess of Caen, we may here remark, was only a distant relative of major Henri de Belzunce, and she died on the 3rd February 1787, more than two years before the arrival at Caen of Mr. de Belzunce, which was not until the month of April, 1789.

There exists besides, no positive proof of their having been any intimacy between the young gentleman and Charlotte Corday. Everything induces us on the contrary, to think that the young girl, who had early distinguished herself by ardent Republican opinions, would not have sacrificed her political faith to a passing caprice; particularly in favour of a young nobleman of such firm Royalist opinions as Mr. de Belzunce.

* *

It will be as easy for us to dispose of the opinion, more or less credited, that Charlotte Corday had a particularly tender feeling towards the Girondist Barbaroux. No doubt Barbaroux possessed physical advantages likely to make an impression on the young girl: his features were regular, his eyes full of fire, and altogether his physiognomy was most prepossessing.

Nor must we too readily believe those who have represented him as "a bloated, puffed-up fop," with "a more than ruddy face, fairly blotched." Let us be satisfied with a disinterested testimony, that of his colleague and friend Louvet: "Barbaroux, who was then 28 years of age, had the stoutness of a man of 40. He might succeed in captivating hearts, but only in a world where such triumphs are easy. He led besides, a life of dissipation and pleasure. He resided in the same hotel as a certain Marquise, anything but cruel, who was known by the name of Zelis or Zelia only, and whose fancy it was, notwithstanding her undoubtedly authentic titles of nobility, to proclaim the most advanced ideas.

Whatever fancy he might have had to do so, Barbaroux could not have found a discreet opportunity to pay court to Mdlle. de Corday. In such a small provincial town as was Caen at that time, such a thing would have immediately been noised about.*

* *

*. There can be no doubt that Charlotte had several interviews with Barbaroux, but these interviews took place before witnesses, generally at the *Intendance*, almost in public; the saloons of the Intendance were always crowded.

The first interview occurred about the 20th June; Barbaroux had been at Caen since the 15th.

Eight or ten days later, Charlotte Corday went again to the *Intendance* to visit the proscribed deputies. This second interview may have been about the 28th or 30th June.

The third was on the 7th July 1793, the date is given in Charlotte's own handwriting in her letter to Barbaroux.

"The idea of striking at Marat had been conceived by her since the 2nd June, but she had not fixed in her mind the date of its execution; she herself declares *that what quite decided her was the courage with which the volunteers came forward to enlist after the review of the 7th July.* The National Guard at Caen had been reviewed by General Wimpfen and his staff on the Cours-la-Reine, with the result that a battalion of volunteers was to be formed to join the federalist army at Evreux." Vide *Documents relating to the trial of Charlotte Corday before the Revolutionary Tribunal.* C. Vatel, advocate, 1861.

Ought we to pay more attention to Mr Boisjugan de Maingré, the nobleman who was shot in 1792, as an émigré, taken in armed resistance.

Mr. de Boisjugan may have met Charlotte at the house of her aunt Mme. de Brétheville, that is all that can be assumed, but no trustworthy evidence has been brought forward to prove that there was ever a project of marriage between the young people.

As for the fable, which we believe to have been imagined by Lamartine, of a young man of the name of Franquelin, supposed to have gone to Vibraye, in the Sarthe, there to die in despair after hearing of the death of Charlotte, we now know its origin.

It was, a Mr. de la Sicotière, who died some years ago, who first revealed it, and, according to all appearances, it was this story that the poet took as a canvas to embroider upon.

An old woman-servant, writes Mr. de la Sicotière, one day at Mans, entered a rich picture-gallery, where at the sight of a copy of Ary Scheffer's painting, she started and exclaimed:

"That is Charlotte Corday," pointing to the pale and noble features of the heroine . . .

"How do you know that?" asked her master.

And then the old woman related a strange tale. About the time when Charlotte Corday was executed, a young man came to reside with his mother at Vibraye; he was a native of Normandy, and his name was Franquelin. This young man was the prey to a continual melancholy; he was supposed to be consumptive, and it was not long before he died.

The old woman, who at that time was young, and,

who waited upon him, observed him often absorbed in the contemplation of a miniature, which never quitted him, or else reading a bundle of letters, over which he shed many tears.

One day she ventured to ask him the cause of his sadness.

"This portrait," he answered, "is that of the girl I loved, Charlotte Corday; these also are her letters, and, when I die, I desire that these letters and the portrait be buried with me!"

When he died, his last wishes were complied with.*

So that the secret of this admirer of Charlotte would appear to have been buried in the tomb! ...

Let us pardon the poet for having idealized the testimony of an old gossip, which, thanks to him, will thus be handed down to posterity.

* *

We should have rather more hesitation to pronounce an opinion with regard to the person who will next appear upon the scene.

When, on the eve of her execution, Charlotte Corday wrote to Barbaroux, she earnestly entreated him not to fail to communicate her letter to the "citizen Bougon."

Bougon, that is Bougon-Longrais, procureur-général syndic of the Calvados department, was a magistrate as amiable as he was grave, and was said to have been an intimate friend of Mdlle. de Corday. She is supposed to have written about twenty letters to him, mostly, it appears, on "literary and political subjects."

La Mosaïque de l'Ouest et du Centre, t. II, 1845–46, p. 360.

This correspondence, we hasten to say, has never been discovered. All that can be said is, that the letter addressed by Charlotte to Barbaroux, seems to attest nothing more than "friendship" towards Bougon; but as she knew that it was destined to be read by "all her friends who might wish to see it," it is possible that she may have been reserved.

"If," she adds, she has not written directly to Bougon, it is because "she is not sure that he is at Evreux," and more particularly that she fears he may be too much "afflicted at her death." These at all events are the motives that she gives, but are there not other motives or one in particular that she dare not avow . . . ?*

An impartial investigation of the facts leads us to recognize that Charlotte Corday has been the victim of calumny; we shall soon see how political passion could so far away her enemies as to lead them even to outrage her memory.

* * *

As we are now on the chapter of the *lovers* of Charlotte, it may be well to reserve this title to the man who most deserved it, employing the expression of course in its most limited sense.

History tells us that a love, at once enthusiastic, wild, and visionary, like every hopeless love, had followed

* I am convinced that if Charlotte Corday has *distinguished* or preferred any one, it is neither Belzunce, nor Barbaroux, nor Boisjugan de Mingré, nor any other, but Bougon-Longrais only. And even with regard to him I do not admit more than an affectionate sympathy." Vatel; *Dramatic Bibliography of Charlotte Corday*, t. 1. CCXI.

Charlotte Corday beyond the tomb. She died without having even suspected it.*

A young dreamy German, delegated to Paris by the town of Mayence as deputy extraordinary to the Convention, Dr. Adam Lux,—he was both doctor of medicine † and doctor of philosophy—had followed the fatal cart which conveyed Charlotte to the Place de la Revolution. He reluctantly dragged himself from the place of execution, murmuring before the astonished crowd: ‡ . . . *Greater than Brutus!*

This act of fanaticism has been variously judged, and some have not hesitated to attribute it to mental aberration.

A friend of Adam Lux, Dr. Wetekind, wrote on this

* In the well-known letter, addressed from her prison by Charlotte Corday to Barbaroux, mention is made of Bougon-Longrais, to whom the heroic maiden sends a remembrance at that supreme moment.

According to the intentions of Charlotte Corday, this letter was destined to be published, and one can understand the reserve of her expressions, at the same time it is easy to read between the lines that Bougon was far from being indifferent to her.

It is besides proved that Charlotte was in rather frequent correspondence with Bougon-Longrais, who had about twenty letters from his amiable friend, at the moment when he was himself arrested at Rennes.

It is not the less certain, on referring to a letter addressed by the same Bougon to his mother, the 5th January 1794, and for the first time published by Vatel (work previously cited, CCXIII to CCXV), that Bougon-Longrais entertained for her more than friendship, and, a real affection. Were these sentiments shared by Charlotte? The proof thereof may perhaps be found when the letter shall be discovered which was sold by auction at London in 1868, addressed, ("*the man she was in love with*" *according to the catalogue*). All that we know is that the letter was in the collection of Sir Henry Nottingham.

† Chéron de Villiers, *Marie-Anne-Charlotte-de-Corday*, p. 429.

‡ He had not practised medicine on account of an invincible aversion to anatomical studies, which were repugnant to his delicate nature.

subject in one of the journals of the period the following suggestive lines:

"There is at this moment in the prison of the Conciergerie, a German deserving of the pity of patriots, because his head has gone wrong and he has become absolutely mad ... Another circumstance has tended to increase this madness. Lux was deeply enamoured of his wife and although his temperament was particularly ardent, he has lived ever since he quitted her in a state of strict chastity. This new situation has augmented the disturbance of his senses, and at the sight of Charlotte Corday, the only woman that he had perhaps remarked since he has been in Paris, having produced an extremely strong physical impression upon him, has put the climax upon the confusion and dark melancholy which dominated his mind ... His imagination, thus overwrought, troubled, his reason, and he thought without reasoning ...

"All these facts have been made known to me by a physician of Mayence who knows Lux, and is of opinion that it would be better to shut him up in an asylum, or to send him off to America, than to guillotine him." *

Adam Lux protested indignantly against the assertions of Dr. Wetekind.

He wrote to the *Journal de la Montagne*, which published the 26th September 1793 his protest that "he was not mad enough to desire to live," and that it was a proof of wisdom to go forward to meet death.

He was left lingering for some time in the prison of

Revue Moderne, 1866, t. 39, pp. 126–127.

It may not be out of place to note that one of the daughters of Adam Lux, committed suicide.

La Force * and it was not until the 14th brumaire (10th October) 1793 that he was brought before the revolutionary Tribunal.

The same day, at five in the afternoon Adam Lux was executed on the same scaffold where the object of his adoration had perished.

It is related that on leaving the Conciergerie, he exclaimed, in a moment of supreme enthusiasm:

"At last, I am going to die for Charlotte Corday!" †

* * *

We think it will be our duty to produce here two letters which, as far as we know, have never yet been published, and which may serve to throw a curious light upon the mental condition of Charlotte Corday on the eve of her crime.

These letters are taken from the Vatel Papers from which we have already borrowed so many valuable facts.

The first is addressed by a Mr. or Mme. Rault * to Mr.

* We have discovered in the National Archives the following letter which we have every reason to think hitherto unpublished:

Letter from Adam Lux to the citizen Fougauld (sic).

At the Prison of La Force
20th September, 1793.

Citizen.

I am well aware that you are occupied with an immense amount of work. But being in this prison for the last two months, I have the honour to recall myself to mind, begging of you to decide if there is any cause of accusation against me and to hasten my trial

Adam Lux

Deputy extr. of Mayence.

† Chéron de Villiers, loc. cit., p. 425

Bourgeois, road-surveyor at Argentan.' It is dated from Saint-Gervais-les-Sablons (27th January 1847):

'The mind of this young girl was rather over excited, running quickly to extremes and enthusiastically adopting the opinions which happened to please her.

'First of all, she wanted to become a Carmelite nun, but her father withholding his consent, to make up for this refusal she used to live in her father's home just as if in a convent, wearing the habit of the Order, and following, as well as she could, the religious observances of the Order into which she had wished to enter.

'Later on her ideas were modified, and being at Caen at the house of one of her relatives, Mme. de Bretheville, she adopted rich toilettes and frequented society. It was then that she met some of the Girondists, lent a willing ear to their complaints and frequented their Club. One day she quitted them, hearing them murmur together: 'who will deliver us from such a monster as Marat?'

"'Before long,' she said, 'you shall hear men talk of me.' A few days later, Marat was no more...."

The second letter, far more important, and to our knowledge as yet unpublished, bears the signature of Mr. Gosnard-Desclosets, in reply to a request made to him by the historian of Charlotte Corday (Vatel) for information concerning her. This letter is full of anecdotic details of the highest interest.

. . . .

'Nothing in her conduct led the friends of Marie de Corday to foresee the projects to the execution of which she owes her celebrity.

'Always good, affable, devoted, her society was full of charm, and one felt attracted by sympathy towards this impressionable and ardent nature; her character was gay, and her conversation easy, often spiced with the least flavour of irony.

"Marie de Corday was fond of reading; and she expressed great admiration for the ancient republics of Athens, Sparta and Rome; when she touched on these subjects her conversation became more elevated in tone, and she regretted not have lived in such heroic times: but she had a horror of the Revolutionary tribunal, as well as of the Republicans of her day!

"Political questions sometimes exasperated her, and she then expressed her opinions with an amount of enthusiasm very foreign to her character.

"Mme. Gautier de Villiers has a thousand times told me that, in one of her political conversations, during a dinner at which General de la Rue was present (at Mme. de Bretheville's), she was witness to a circumstance which remained engraved upon her memory after the tragical ending of her friend. After giving, with her usual frankness, her opinion on the events of the day, Marie de Corday, excited by the contradiction she met with from the General, addressed these words to him: *If you were the last of the Republicans, I would poniard you!!!* at the same time showing him the knife she had in her hand.

"I was happy, Sir, to see you victoriously combat the idea, contrary to the truth and yet credited to a certain extent—that Marie de Corday had acted under the influence of a feeling of interest which she felt for one of the refugees at Caen, or that she wished to revenge an unfortunate lover.

"The resolution of Marie de Corday was inspired by no considerations of the kind; and I have often heard Mme.

11

Gautier de Villiers most energitically deny this imputation, which she declared to be a calumny.

"Madame Gautier even added that when people jested with Mdlle. de Corday on the subject of marriage she used laughingly to reply *that she never intended to marry, because there was no man born destined to be her master.*

"These details—coming from a friend of this celebrated woman—were of a nature to greatly interest a young man;—and I remember them the more faithfully, that during many years, I heard them repeated with that perfect lucidity of memory which Mme. Gautier preserved to the end of her life, that is to say, until 1848.

"After long conversations, in which aged people take such delight, I had at different times taken notes, which I have searched for in vain, and would have been happy to communicate to you: I should besides have accomplished—in quite an unexpected manner—the intention I had then in view, in the sole interest of historical truth.

"When my grandmother spoke of the devotedness of Mdlle. de Corday to her friends, and of how much she advanced in the esteem of Mme. de Forbin, to which she could testify,—she used to add that one day Mdlle. de Corday wanted to take her with her to the Intendance at the Place Saint-Pierre, where she went to see the representatives of the people who had taken refuge there.—But my grandmother feared to involve her family in disgrace and she went no further than the door, where she quitted her, saying *that Mdlle. de Corday being single was free to do as she pleased; but as for her, the mother of five children, she could not run the risk of compromising her family.*

"Mdlle. de Corday was besides escorted by Leclerc, her cousin's servant.

"My grandmother particularly liked to talk — which she did with great interest — about her last interviews with Charlotte Corday, and which she related even to the smallest details.

"Two or three days before her departure from Caen, Mdlle. de Corday had set out for Verson; she was accompanied by the Marquise de Fauville, who on such excursions often took the place of Mme. de Bretheville, who was not easily induced to quit her arm-chair.

"Mme. Gautier, who was the same day going to Caen, met these two ladies on the way, in their modest carriage; she brought them back with her, and they passed the rest of the day pleasantly at her house.

"Nothing transpired of a nature to indicate the terrible resolution that Mdlle. de Corday had no doubt already formed; and with regard to her approaching departure, she explained it by saying *that she had to undertake a journey*; merely adding, what the intimacy of the conversation may excuse, *that she had told her stupid cousin that she was going to see her grandfather* . . .

"They bade each other good-bye in the evening, promising to meet again the next day at Caen: Mdlle. de Corday took a shawl away with her, lent by Mme. Gautier—leaving with her a scarf and a fan which are still in our possession.

"The green paper forming the basis of the fan has altogether disappeared, and there remains only the wooden framework—its sole value being, that the gentle hand that made its light leaves flutter, was destined but a few days later, to wield the poniard that killed Marat.

"The next day, a circumstance happened which may have a certain importance in this matter.

"The young Emilie Gautier, a little girl, had for some

time past teased her mother to give her ear-rings, when Mdlle. de Corday, intervening in the affair, unhooked the *golden ear-rings* she wore, and gave them to the child, *telling her at the same time that she had others.*

'This would to some extent explain the character of Charlotte de Corday: kind and warm-hearted to those who were near to her, and, in the opinion of Mme. Gautier de Villiers, this seemed to be a convincing proof of a resolution irrevocably taken but of which no exterior token was visible, a sort of last testimony of affection to those whom she knew well she would never see again.

'Nothing—I cannot too often repeat,—could have seemed in these her last farewells to give the least indication of emotion or of wavering; nothing appeared to disturb the habitual equanimity of this young girl.

'You have, Sir, taken so close an interest in this historical question, that you will pardon me for entering into such minute details, but which, had it not been for your unexpected communication, would probably never have gone beyond the circle of my intimate acquaintances.

'I beg to add a few lines concerning the portrait of Marie-Charlotte de Corday.

'As well as I can recollect hearing, she must have been tall and well built, which did not prevent her being graceful; her features were not regular, but her complexion was *admirable*:—I preserve the word expressly—her hair was light chestnut; her eyes were blue, and very expressive: her hands were *very strong.*

'Mme. Gautier, who has never visited Paris, and had never seen the portrait of Charlotte Corday by Hauer, declared that all the portraits spread about were not at all life-like . . . . COSSARD-DESCLOSETS."

THE

EPILOGUE TO THE DRAMA

THE "BOUTISKAI" LIFTS HER HEAD

Oh, it is monstrous, monstrous!
Methought the billows spoke, and told me of it;
The wind did sing it to me; and the thunder,
That deep and dreadful organ pipe,
Did bass my trespass.

The Tempest, Act. III, Sc. 3.

III. THE EPILOGUE TO THE DRAMA.—THE BUFFET GIVEN BY THE EXECUTIONER'S ASSISTANT TO THE SEVERED HEAD OF CHARLOTTE CORDAY.

Sanson, the executioner who carried out the sentences of the Revolutionary tribunal, has related in his *Mémoires* the slightest incidents concerning the drama, the epilogue of which took place on the Place de la Revolution.

On leaving his office, Fouquier-Tinville met Sanson: "What, thou art still here?" said he, in a menacing tone. And as the executioner replied that he awaited the orders of the Public Prosecutor, he immediately signed the death warrant. The text was besides already printed: he had but to fill up the blanks.

Upon that, the chief clerk came up, bearing the original and the copy of the sentence.

He went immediately, followed by Sanson, to the Conciergerie.

The door-keeper, Citizen Richard, conducted them to the cell of the condemned heroine. The ushers of the tribunal entered first. The executioner waited outside. He then entered in his turn.

When Charlotte Corday perceived him, bearing in his hands a pair of scissors and the scarlet shirt, she could not help saying: "What, already!"

While requesting him to wait a moment—she finished writing the note addressed to the advocate she had chosen to defend her,* Doulcet de Pontécoulant—one of the ushers read aloud the sentence.

This formality completed, Charlotte took off her cap and seated herself conveniently in a chair.

Before the executioner had commenced his work, Charlotte took up the scissors and herself cut off a lock of her beautiful hair:† destined for Hauer, the painter, who had just finished her portrait. That done, she gave herself up without resistance to Sanson, who terminated his lugubrious functions. He put upon her the scarlet shirt prescribed by the law,§ and proceeded to bind the hands of the condemned.

The cords which had encircled her wrists when she had

* In this note she very unjustly accused Doulcet de Pontécoulant of cowardice, because he had not replied to her request: It was proved later that Charlotte's request did not reach him until four days after the execution.

† The hair cut off by Sanson, was given by Charlotte Corday to the door keeper of the prison, as a testimony of regard for his kindness towards her.

§ In the *Nouveau Paris* of Mercier, vol. II, Chap. 58, we read the following: "When the pretended prison conspiracies were invented, in order to massacre a greater number, the victims were called *cardinals*, because their shirts were red. Such a coloured shirt covered the modest charms of Charlotte Corday; and it is in remembrance of this courageous woman that many persons of her sex wore, and still wear, a red shawl."

first been arrested had been drawn so tightly, that she still bore the traces they had left.

Showing these marks to the executioner, she said to him.

"If you are not unwilling to let me suffer a little less before putting me to death, I would beg you to allow me to gather up my sleeves or to put a pair of gloves beneath the bands you are preparing for me." *

*

The fatal cart, destined to take her to the place of execution, waited in the court-yard of the prison. Charlotte mounted into it, the executioner following her.

Notwithstanding that she was requested by Sanson to sit down on a chair provided for her, she remained proudly erect, braving the insults of the populace howling threats of death.

The clamour of the mob was now mingled with the noise of thunder; for at this moment a formidable thunderstorm broke over Paris.

During the journey the calmness of Charlotte Corday never failed for a single moment. As regards that we have formal evidence, that of Doctor Cabanis, who has transmitted to us, in the following words, his impressions, or rather those of eye-witnesses who had communicated them to him: "I did not assist," says Cabanis, "at the execution of Charlotte Corday, nor at any other, for I could not have supported such a spectacle; but several persons of my acquaintance followed from the Conciergerie to the scaffold the cart which conveyed this woman who,

* Related by an eye-witness, Harmand (de la Meuse).

notwithstanding the evils of which she was the cause or of which she had at least given the signal deserved commiseration.

"They witnessed her admirable calmness on the way, and the majesty of her demeanour at the last moment. A medical friend of mine did not lose sight of her for a single minute. He has always assured me that her grave and simple serenity was always the same; she grew slightly pale at the foot of the scaffold; but it was but for a moment, and her handsome face soon shone forth in renewed beauty."

* *
*

Sanson vainly sought to hide the view of the guillotine from her, but impelled by a movement of feminine curiosity, Charlotte leaned forward to look. At the sight of the instrument she slightly trembled. But it was but momentary, and after having mounted the steps of the scaffold she showed no sign of fear, and gained the fatal platform.

Sanson roughly pulled off her neck-handkerchief which covered her shoulders, thus exposing her neck: a sudden access of shame reddened her cheeks. She bowed to the people surrounding the fatal machine and endeavoured to pronounce a few words; but time was not given her. She was thrust on to the plank, the knife fell and the head rolled down. It was then that one of Sanson's assistants according to Michelet, "a carpenter, an ardent Maratist," named Legros, seizing in his hands the decapitated head of Charlotte Corday, gave it a slap on the cheek.*

* Camet-Girouville asserts that the executioner's assistant Legros, gave "two or three slaps" to the head of Charlotte Corday.

Other historians say that she received several buffets, without specifying the number.

According to Doctor Süe:* "The face of the victim which up to that moment was pale, had no sooner received the slap from this cowardly cur, than both cheeks were seen to redden! All the spectators were struck with this change of colour and immediately demanded, with violent clamour, vengeance for such a cowardly and atrocious act of barbarity.

"It cannot be said that this reddening was the result of the slap, for however sharply the cheeks of a corpse may be smitten immediately after death, they never redden; besides the slap was given but on one cheek, and it was remarked that the opposite side blushed equally; this fact alone proves evidently that after the decapitation the brain and nerves still retained some traces of sensibility." †

* *

The opinion of Süe is worthy of consideration, for this physiologist enjoyed, in his time a considerable amount of credit in the scientific world. This opinion created a great sensation at the time, backed up as it was by the doctrines of a learned German, Sœmering, on the same subject. Sœmering, and after him, his translator, Elsner, did not hesitate to assert that consciousness existed after decapitation.

"Sentiment, personality, the *Ego*," wrote Sœmering from Frankfort, to the Editor of the *Magasin encyclopédique*, "still remain sentient for a certain time, and feel the pain by which the neck has been affected," and he quoted

* The grandfather of the novelist.

† *Magasin encyclopédique*, vol. IV, p. 170.

in that connection such authorities as Haller, and Weicard, a celebrated German physician, "who had seen the lips of a man whose head has just been cut off, move;" of Leveling, "who had performed the experiment of irritating the portion of the spinal marrow still adhering to a detruncated head, and declared that the convulsions of the head were horrible."

Cabanis,* who took a part in this scientific discussion while expressing the utmost reserve with regard to the fact itself, did not hesitate to declare that a person guillotined "suffers neither in the limbs nor in the head: that death is as rapid as the blow which gives it; and that if certain movements, regular, or convulsive, may be observed in the muscles of the arms, or the legs, or the face, they prove neither pain nor sensibility; they depend solely on a remainder of the vital faculty that has not been yet entirely annihilated in the muscles and their nerves, by the death of the individual, the destruction of the *Ego*."

* * *

Dr. Léveillé, then surgeon at the Hôtel-Dieu of Paris, refuting the opinions of Sue and of Sœmering, deliberately adopted that of Cabanis:

"The face of Ch. Corday reddened!" he says, "I don't believe a word of it. I may perhaps admit the possibility of this coloration, but I must seek an explanation else-

* Another medical man, of some fame in his time, also took a part in this discussion. In 1796, Dr. Gastellier, wrote his *Dissertation on capital punishment by the guillotine*, (published at Sens, an IV, 1796, in-8vo). He would himself have suffered the fatal punishment he so well described on the 17th Thermidor, had it not been for the death of Robespierre, which very fortunately for him took place on the 9th.

where, which at once presents itself, and to me seems purely mechanical. In reality, her head preserved, I will not say its *vital force*, but certainly its *vital heat*; for it is necessary to distinguish between the two modes of expression. The blood still in a fluid state contained in the small capillary vessels, flows out freely, when its escape is suddenly stopped by the violent impression of the hand. This atrocious act brought together the inner walls of the vessels, and the blood coming from above could not get past the compressed part: it collected therefore in sufficient quantity to cause a slight redness, which Mr. Sue, I think, erroneously attributes, to a remainder of *judgment* and of *sensibility*. The other cheek, it is asserted, reddened also. Oh! here the observation has gone too far! I beg to be allowed to give an absolute denial to this last statement. In fact, I do not either believe in the first, which I was perhaps wrong in endeavouring to explain." *

* *

What may appear still more extraordinary, was that in certain circles the question was seriously discussed, whether the face had reddened from *pain* or from *indignation*. At all events the following statement was made by a contemporary .... †

* A thing which seems surprising is the silence of Guillotin. There is nowhere to be found the least documentary evidence of his having taken part in this controversy. And yet his invention was in question, or rather the consequences of his invention, and one cannot but ask why he did not interfere. How is his silence to be explained? Is it to be supposed that he had fallen into such a state of physical and moral decrepitude as no longer to take any interest in the grave events taking place before his eyes?

† G. Duval, *Souvenirs de la Terreur*. Paris, Werdet, vol. 1842.

. . . "It is a long accepted fact that the executioner gave a slap to the head of Charlotte Corday, while he held it up before the people, and that the head was seen to redden, some say from pain, others from indignation; people are not agreed on the subject. I, who was at the entry of the Champs-Elysées, and therefore at a very short distance from the scaffold, saw nothing of the incident. Mind, I am careful not to deny the fact; I merely say that I did not see it.

"I may add that none of my neighbours saw it either, and it was only some days later that the report circulated in Paris. I do not know who invented it, or if you prefer, who first related it. With regard to the redness caused by *pain* or *indignation*, I leave it to physiologists to decide to what degree a head severed from the body can suffer the physical feeling of *pain*, and what would be still more extraordinary, the moral sentiment of *indignation*!

"What I say on the subject will not prevent this buffet on a dead cheek being recorded in history as an authentic fact, but I still adhere to my statement." *

Sanson was accused of having been guilty of this sacrilege; but he hastened to deny it in a letter published in the newspapers. He said that the buffet was given by one of the carpenters who had put up the scaffold.

Notwithstanding this protest from the executioner, after

* Perhaps it was only, as Michelet suggests, a reflection of the sun which at this instant caused such an extraordinary effect; or are we to accept another version concerning this strange fact, which I find in a letter written on the day following the execution, by a person who had evidently heard nothing about this legendary detail, who says: "The executioner's hands were covered with blood; and he left their impress on the cheeks of the decapited head." *Marie-Anne-Charlotte de Corday d'Armont*, by Chéron de Villiers, pp. 407—408.

the 9th Thermidor, there could be seen for sale on the quays, an engraving representing poor Sanson holding the head of Charlotte Corday with one hand, while with the other he gave it a slap!

Although he used his utmost efforts to refute this imputation, the memory of Sanson will long remain sullied by this stain.

After all, it matters little: this odious act could add but little to his sad notoriety.*

* The following hitherto unpublished letter from Sergent-Marceau, for which we have to thank Mr. Begis, shows that the act of the executioner was far from being generally approved.

"Citizen Sergent to the President of the Criminal Tribunal Extraordinary, sitting in Paris at the Palace of Justice the 13th July, in the year II of the Republic.

"*Citizen*,

"Among the ancient nations who were distinguished by a wise legislation, the criminals condemned to capital punishment were treated with respect when they were brought to suffer the penalty decreed by law. Our neighbours of England, who have given us examples worthy to be followed in criminal legislation, forbade the executioner the right to raise his hand upon the condemned man delivered unto him. The philosophy of humanity taught them that he who by the sacrifice of his life was about to give to society a great example of the respect due to the law, then became a being unhappily sacred. The people of Paris, *so much calumniated*, has also this character, and if any particular sentiment attracts it to the tribunals or to assist at the passing of criminals or to the foot of the scaffold, a majestic silence, interrupted only by the cry of *vive la République* at the moment when it sees the head of a conspirator fall, fully announces that it knows how to respect the man that is to suffer the penalty of the law. Let us preserve this delicacy which does honour to the people; for it is for that purpose that the legislators have abolished torture and the horrible penalties of the wheel and the stake.

"But yesterday, the man who is appointed to exercise the painful functions of executing your sentences was guilty in presence of the people, of reprehensible acts upon the mortal remains of the monster who had taken the life of one of the representatives of the nation. The people had seen that woman pass, had escorted her to the scaffold without insulting her last moments. Inwardly it applauded the sentence condemning her to the penalty due to her crime, and the more its indignation was strong and legitimate against this unhappy creature, the more did its calm attitude and countenance render it proud and generous. The people here again thwarted its enemies by the nobility of its conduct. How was it that the citizen charged with the execution of the law should have allowed himself to provoke excesses, by adding to the penalty outrages that nothing can excuse? Magnanimous people! Thou wishest only severe justice, no pardon, no mercy to traitors, nor to their accomplices, but thou seekest no base vengeance, which could but sully it.

"Vengeance is indicative of weak and ferocious souls, and thou art invincible and good!

"I demand of the Tribunal to repair the outrage made to nature, and philosophy, by that executioner who while exhibiting to the people, as required by law, the head of the girl Corday, permitted himself to bestow buffets upon it.

"This act, which would be disgusting on the part of another citizen, has appeared criminal to many persons when committed by the officer charged to scrupulously execute your sentences and the law. I therefore demand that he be publicly censured before the people at one of your sittings, and that you enjoin him to be more circumspect in future.

Your fellow-citizen
Sergent
Deputy to the National Convention."

THE

LAST INDIGNITY:

IN THE HANDS OF THE

"CHARCUTIERS"

IV. THE AUTOPSY OF CHARLOTTE CORDAY.

We have seen by what insinuations it has been sought to sully the memory of Charlotte Corday. We do not in the least degree plead extenuating circumstances for the crime she committed and which, according to our judgment is inexcusable, but we profess too great a respect for historical truth not to sacrifice to it our own prejudices or opinions.

The day after the execution of Charlotte Corday, the strangest reports had circulated. Not only were numerous lovers attributed to the heroine but the most odious assertions were launched against her.

We find an echo of these in a number of a journal of the period, the *Affiches et Annonces et Avis divers*, published at Caen, reproducing a letter dated from Paris the 16th July, the eve of the execution.

The following short extract will suffice to give an idea of the tone:

"As she (Ch. Corday) no doubt presumes that the provincial forces will be in possession of Paris before the end of a month, and that if her head does not now fall beneath the fatal knife, she will preserve her life, or rather that she will not allow her persecutors to sacrifice to their vengeance *even the fruit she bears in her womb, she has just now declared that she is four months gone with child* . . . ."

Now, according to all appearances, the unfortunate woman was a virgin! We say: according to all appearances, for a decisive document, which would settle the matter, is wanting: the official report on the autopsy has up to the present eluded all search, and in the absence of that document we can have nothing more than presumptions. All that we know at all precise, is that, according to a contemporary biographer,* the body of Charlotte Corday had been conveyed to one of the Paris hospitals—the Charité perhaps—to be examined.

Two doctors were charged with the operation. The report they drew up existed a few years ago, in a curious collection belonging to a distinguished physician.† It is not known what has since become of it.

* * *

We have in vain searched among the papers left by Vatel, the most complete biographer of Charlotte Corday, without succeeding in finding this precious document. In the absence of this testimony, which would have been decisive this is what we have discovered.

Under the title of *Iconographie* we met with the description of a drawing, representing: *Charlotte Corday after*

* Mr. Caille, advocate before the Royal Court of Paris, born at Caen the 2nd April 1767, son of Caille des Fontaines, advocate.

† Cheron de Villiers, loc. cit. p. 411. The work is dated 1865.

her execution, 17th July 1793, *an assembly of doctors attesting her virginity: N. fecit* (*sic*). Then follows the description of the drawing:

"The body, extended on a plank, is supported by two wooden props. The head has been replaced above the trunk; the arms are pendant; the body is still enveloped in a white gown the top of which is reddened with blood. A personage holding in one hand a light and in the other an instrument (a sort of speculum?) seems to be occupied in removing the garments from the body. Four other persons stoop and examine attentively. At the head of the corpse stand two other persons, one of whom appears to wear a tricoloured sash; the other extends his hands as if saying: 'Here is the body, look.'"

It may be that the artist meant to indicate two members of the municipality while the other persons assisting were doctors!

They are all wearing cocked-hats, broad skirted coats with facings, and top-boots.

There is also a fellow drawing to this one, evidently by the same artist, representing the fatal toilet; unfortunately it is also anonymous.

To this iconographical testimony must be added the following printed documents, which however are not very conclusive.

Harmand (de la Meuse), in his *Anecdotes sur la Revolution*,* writes this memorable phrase: "The medical men think they have discovered in the physical constitution of Mlle de Corday a quite particular cause for the mental excitement necessary to impel her to commit a

* This book was not published until 1824, and offers no guarantee of accuracy. (Note of Vatel).

murder. This physical cause may be called *moral chastity*."

Restif de la Bretonne, so greedy of such details, did not fail on this occasion to go and see: "The monster, said he, was a maiden, virtuous with the virtue of women, that is to say, she was *chaste*."

*

It has been written that David the painter wished also to assure himself that Charlotte Corday was a virgin. This fact was first noted in the following passage taken from the *Almanach des gens de bien*: * "After she had been executed, David, member of the National Convention, accompanied by some of his colleagues and by a surgeon, examined the corpse of the unfortunate young girl, expecting to find traces of loose conduct; but he was disappointed in his expectations; he convinced himself that she was a virgin." †

Another work which appeared about the same time, § publishes, in nearly the same terms, a similar version:

"To others, and in particular to Fouquier-Tinville, who ironically asked how many children she had given birth to, she replied, blushing: 'I have already told you, that I have never been married ...'"

* Paris, Picard, bookseller, Rue de Thionville. (*Calendrier pour l'an de grâce*, 1795, p. 85.) *Anecdotes pour servir à l'histoire, etc.* p. 35.

† Note in the Vatel papers.

§ *Portraits des personnages célèbres de la Révolution*, by François Bonneville, with historical table and note by P. Quenard, one of the delegates of the Commune in 1789 and 1790, to be had of the author at Paris, rue du Théâtre Français, 1796, year IV of the Republic. Vol. II. 45th portrait. See also: Mathon de la Varenne, *Les crimes de Marat*, an III, p. 122.

** This question is not recorded in the examination; it could not have

"Sacrilegious persons wished to convince themselves; they examined her mortal remains. She was a virgin!..."

None of these witnesses could be suspected of partiality towards Charlotte Corday. Nearly all of them may be counted among the most fanatical partisans and admirers of Marat. Would not this circumstance alone justify us in considering this evidence as absolutely trustworthy?

been published by reason of its nature; but some of the newspapers of the period asserted that Charlotte Corday had given birth to children. (Note by Mr. Vatel.)

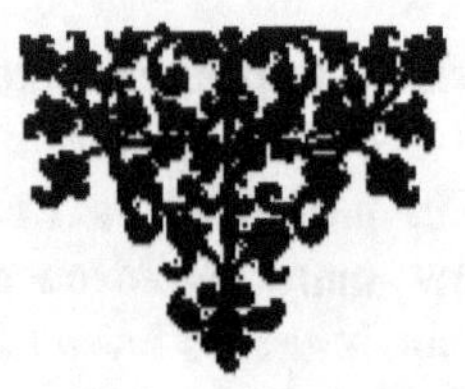

A CURIOUS

ANTHROPOLOGICAL NOTE

[illegible]

OUR HEROINE'S SKULL.

V. THE SKULL OF CHARLOTTE CORDAY.

Historians are generally agreed as to the place where Charlotte Corday was buried.

After the execution her body was taken to the cemetery of the Madeleine, situated in the Rue d'Anjou-Saint-Honoré. Her remains were deposited in pit No. 5, between that known as No. 4, containing the remains of the king, and pit No. 6, which not long afterwards received those of the ex-duke of Orleans.

Notwithstanding that the whole neighbourhood was infected by the putrefaction of the bodies buried there, it was not until February 1794 that Mr. Descloseaux, who had become owner of the ground, could obtain the closing of this cemetery. Most of the bodies were removed to Monceau, and the ancient cemetery was transformed into a pleasure-garden. *

* This may perhaps serve to explain the following passage in the very interesting novel *Le Roman de Dumouriez*, by Mr. Welschinger, who is so very exact in his historical researches: "It appears that at the extremity of the faubourg called *la Petite Pologne* (Little Poland), now the quarter of the Parc Monceau, at the angle formed by the

Mr. Deschseaux was careful to mark with crosses and even to surround with railings the tombs of the nobler victims of the Revolution.*

Cheron de Villiers, who has devoted a very closely written volume to the biography of Charlotte Corday, asserts that it was not until 1804 that Mr. Deschseaux had a cross planted on Charlotte's grave, and that her remains were exhumed in 1815 and removed to the cemetery of Montparnasse.†

This is the first error that we have noticed in the work that has been compiled with much care and from which we admit having borrowed some few extracts, which we however subjected to careful verification. But in order to be doubly sure we applied to the chief guardian in person of the Montparnasse cemetery to know if he could confirm the statement given by Mr. Cheron de Villiers. We here transcribe his answer word for word as we received it.

"Our registers do not contain the slightest indication that the remains of Charlotte Corday ever found a resting-place in the cemetery confided to my charge. See however, Mr. Cadiou, Chief of the Municipal Interment service, who will be able to give you more positive information."

* *

Rue du Rocher and the Rue de Valois(?), in a piece of ground forming a long square, the body of Charlotte Corday was buried. A few days later, there was deposited next to her the body of Adam Lux. Thus they were united in death." *Le Roman de Dumouriez*, p. 167 (Note).

* De Montegreaux, *Charlotte Corday*, p. 128.

† *Marie-Anne Charlotte de Corday d'Armont*, by Chéron de Villiers, p. 412.

Having visited this gentleman, he very obligingly, in answer to our question, gave us the following information:

"The bodies of those guillotined on the Place de la Révolution were buried in the cemetery of the Madeleine. It is highly probable that Charlotte Corday was interred there.[1] How long the body remained there it is beyond my power to state. At any rate, it could not have been removed to Montparnasse in 1815, as Chéron de Villiers has asserted, because *the cemetery of Montparnasse was not opened until* 1821."

"And what do you think of that other assertion of Chéron de Villiers?" we asked at the same time quoting to Mr. Cafford the following extract from the book mentioned above: "The Saint-Albin family, who were related to the de Corday family, obtained permission to retain possession of the skull of the unfortunate victim."

"To that point," replied Mr. Cafford, "I cannot reply with such certainty. If the autopsy took place as you say you can prove, it is extremely probable that any particular part of the body may have been abstracted, but here I repeat, I cannot speak with any certainty."

What Mr. Cafford could not tell us, we fully expected to learn elsewhere: and we therefore presumed that the present possessor of the skull of Charlotte Corday would hasten to relieve our uncertainty. But the actual possessor of the relic, Prince Roland Bonaparte (a) is not easy of access, and notwithstanding numerous letters and visits, we could not succeed in meeting him.

What we desired to obtain from Prince Roland was not only the favour of holding in our hands for a few

[1] See preceding chapter.

(a) Well known as a man of science and enlightened amateur.

moments the historical skull of which he is the possessor: the thing in itself is no doubt not devoid of interest; but as it appeared in the anthropological section of the retrospective Exhibition of the liberal Arts in 1889, all details concerning it are known. Learned men, such as Topinard, Lombroso, Benedikt, have studied, handled and measured it in every possible way, and it is easy to find in the scientific reviews the record of the discussion to which this anatomical fragment gave rise. *

What was far more important to us, and what we wanted to ask Prince Roland Bonaparte to show us, were the certificates which it was said indisputably established the authenticity of the skull. †

Prince Roland, instead of receiving us, sent a reply through his secretary, in which he informed us that the relic had come to him from Mr. George Duruy, and that if that gentleman consented to communicate its history, he, for his part, could see no reason to object.

* *

Mr. George Duruy at once placed himself at our disposal § with a readiness that we are happy to acknowledge, and without the least hesitation gave us his opinion concerning the relic which he had ceded, without much regret, to the Prince who seemed so proud of its possession.

"I must warn you," said this amiable gentleman, that

* For the details of this discussion, see *L'Anthropologie*, 1890, vol. I., N°. I; and the *Revue Scientifique* of the same year (article of Mr. Lombroso and reply by Mr. Topinard).

† G. Lenotre, *Paris révolutionnaire*, p. 254

§ The conversation with Mr. G. Duruy took place on the 10th November 1895.

in the matter of history my chief and only care—and you, who are an historian will understand me—is the search for truth, and to bring it to light I do not hesitate to state my firm convictions.

"Well! I must tell you without hesitation that there is nothing to prove that the skull I gave to Prince Roland, after he had expressed an intense desire to have it, is really the skull of *the angel of assassination* ....

"How did it come into my hands? Oh! simply enough.

"One day, paying a visit to a relation of mine, Mme. Rousselin de Saint-Albin, I perceived through the half-opened door of a cupboard, a skull!

"'Hullo! What's that?'

"'That, why it's the skull of Charlotte Corday!'

"'And you leave it there at the back of a cupboard?'

"'It is probable that if I were to put it in full view on a sideboard my visitors might pull a long face, and besides, it would not be a very pleasant sight for my children.'

"'But how did you get it? And what evidence have you that it is indeed the skull of Charlotte Corday?'

"'I inherited it from my husband, Rousselin de Saint-Albin, who used always to assure me that it was Charlotte's skull. It is a tradition preserved in the family. That is all I can tell you. Mr. Rousselin firmly believed it to be the skull of Charlotte Corday and I have no reason to doubt his word.'

"'Yes, but you must admit that your belief does not settle the question. Are there any proofs?'

"'There are,' she replied, 'documents connected with the skull, which prove its authenticity.'

"My venerable relative then handed me some papers that

were in the famous cupboard. As far as I can recollect, there was nothing very precise in them.

"In one of these documents, R. de Saint-Albin related how he had purchased the skull from a dealer of curiosities on the Quai des Grands Augustins, who had himself bought it at a sale.* It came, he added, from a fervent

* May it not have been at the Denon sale? We have found indeed, subsequently to our visit to Mr. Duruy, whilst searching among the unpublished Vatel papers, preserved in the Library at Versailles, the following curious note: "With regard to Charlotte Corday, a friend of mine, a man of letters and deputy, possesses in his study the authentic head of this heroine. This skull belonged originally to the learned Denon, of the Institute, who had obtained it from the executioner. I can testify as to its authenticity. (Signed) Bordot." (Letter addressed to Mr. Chesnard from Pont-l'Évêque, the 29th October 1861).

This would be at least a presumption in favour of the authenticity of the skull. And yet, is it not rather astonishing that not the slightest mention of it is made either in the Memoirs of Sanson, apocryphal or not, or in the carefully written notice, placed at the beginning of the edition of the engravings of Vivant-Denon, and due to the erudite pen of M. A. de la Fizelière? Nor does it appear in the catalogue of the sale of that eminent amateur's collection.

If the skull of Charlotte Corday had appeared at all in this catalogue of the Denon sale, it could only have been under the number 646 of the Description of art-objects belonging to the *collection of the late Baron Denon* (Paris, Tilliard, 1826).

Herewith we give, as a curiosity, the detailed description of this article of the catalogue: N°. 646. Copper gilt. A reliquary of hexagonal form and Gothic work, flanked at the angles by six turrets, connected by buttresses with a top-piece composed of a little edifice surmounted by a cross: the two principal faces of this reliquary are each divided into six compartments, containing the following objects:

Fragments of the bones of the Cid and of Chimene, found in their sepulture at Burgos.- Fragments of the bones of Héloïse and Abelard, taken from their tomb at the Paraclete. Hair from the head of Agnes Sorel, interred at Loches, and of Inès de Castro, at Alcobaça.- Part

admirer of Charlotte Corday, who had been able to have her remains exhumed and had kept the skull. I cannot exactly recall to mind the expressions used by M. de Saint-Albin, but I at least give you their meaning. Prince Roland might, if he liked, * show you all the documents

of the moustache of Henri IV, King of France, found when the bodies of the Kings of France were disinterred in 1793 at Saint-Denis.—Portion of the shroud of Turenne.—Fragments of the bones of Molière and of de La Fontaine.—Hair from the head of General Desaix.

Two of the side panels of the box are filled, the one with the autograph signature of Napoleon, the other with a portion of the blood-stained shirt, which he wore when he died, a lock of his hair and a branch of the willow-tree overshadowing his grave at Saint-Helena.—Lastly a gold ring, "in which is encased the half of one of Voltaire's teeth." Probably that which he had against Fréron. (a)

The catalogue enumerates also, under other numbers, several casts taken from the faces of historical personages: Cromwell, Charles XII of Sweden, Robespierre, Canova; a medallion, modelled from life, representing a portrait of Marat, the completion of which was prevented by his assassination by Charlotte Corday: this medallion was the work of Dreu; a lock of hair, cut from the head of General Desaix, previous to his burial in the convent of the monks of Mount Saint Bernard, in 1805.

But in all this conversation we find nothing relating to the skull of Charlotte Corday.

(a) To have a tooth against some one, means in French to have a grudge against him. (*Transl.*)

Prince Roland Bonaparte, being consulted on this subject by a reporter of the *Eclair*, made the following statement:

"Alas!" said his Highness. "I do not possess the certificates alluded to by Dr. Cabanès.

"One day my friend Duruy offered me a skull which he said was that of Charlotte Corday. He appeared," added the Prince laughing, "not to be sorry to get rid of this anatomical specimen which seemed rather to frighten Mme. Duruy.

"He added a manuscript note in which he said that the skull had been given to him by Mme. Rousselin de Saint-Albin, who herself had

I put into his hands when I gave him the skull; among others, there was a manuscript written by the same Rousselin, a sort of philosophical dialogue between himself, Saint-Albin, and the skull of Charlotte, which was extremely comical: Saint-Albin therein evokes the soul of the avengeress and seeks to discover the motive which impelled her to commit the crime!...

"You might have supposed that Rousselin de Saint-Albin had obtained from Danton, whose secretary he was,* authority to have the head of the heroine given to him

received it from her husband, who had always sincerely believed that it had belonged to the 'Norman maid.'

"As for Rousselin de Saint-Albin, there is no doubt that he always believed in its authenticity, as may be testified by the following anecdote, related to me by one of his friends.

"The father of this friend of his, then a minister of Louis Philippe, was one day invited to dine by Rousselin de Saint-Albin, who puzzled him considerably by promising him that there would be at table a great lady of the Revolution. At the dinner-hour the minister came; the guests entered the dining-room. No signs of the great lady! But underneath his table-napkin, my friend's father discovered a skull: it was that of Charlotte Corday, so the host affirmed.

"Unfortunately", continued his Highness, "there exist no conclusive proofs of the authenticity of the skull in my possession. Besides, it is not possible that any such should exist; for whatever number of certificates I might be able to produce, they could establish no certainty. An absolute proof cannot possibly exist, and we must content ourselves with the tradition.

"Further, even anthropological science leaves a large margin for doubt. For instance: in 1889 I showed the skull of Charlotte Corday to five phrenologists, without letting them know its origin, asking them if it was the skull of a criminal. Three of them answered affirmatively and the other two said, no: which are we to believe?"

* He was afterwards secretary to Bernadotte. See *Biographies de Michaud et de Didot.*

after her execution. But he became, as you see, possessed of the relic in quite a different manner."

"But how did Prince Roland know that you had it in your possession . . . ?"

"A few years ago, I met the Prince, who at that time took a great deal of interest in craniology. He pretended to be able, by the inspection of the cranium, to discover the sentiments of the person to whom it belonged. It was simply the doctrine of Gall grafted on modern anthropology.

"What if I were to show you," said I, "the skull of a murderer, or of a murderess? And for a little time I amused myself teasing him. However, to put an end to his perpexity, I told him what it was. He admitted to me that he did not consider himself quite competent to proceed to inductions which might be rather risky on his part, but he showed that it would be to him a great pleasure to add the skull of Charlotte Corday to his collection. And it was in response to that wish that I gave it him."

It would appear from this declaration of Mr. George Duruy that nothing proves that Prince Roland really possesses the skull of Charlotte Corday; and that in fact it may quite as well be only an ordinary specimen from a collection or from an anatomical museum.

The only thing which seems absolutely certain, according to what is said by the anthropologists, is, that the skull which figured at the Exhibition of 1885, had never remained in the earth, nor had it been exposed to the air.

And here arise, as Mr. Lenotre very judiciously observes, the following various hypotheses: Was there in 1793, a fanatic wild enough to have dared to risk his life, by going on the night after the execution to the grave-yard, to disinter the head of the heroine?

* Mr. Lenotre, the well informed historian of *Paris révolutionnaire*, has addressed a very interesting letter on this subject to our friend Mr. G. Montorgueil:

"Is the skull of Charlotte Corday, now in the possession of Prince Roland Bonaparte authentic or not?

"As you are good enough to mention my name, I answer *Yes*, I believe in its authenticity.

"Proofs? I can give you none; but I can give you presumptions.

"One evening, during the reign of Louis Philippe, Saint-Albin had invited to his table, under pretext of a sensational surprise, some friends known to be curious about matters connected with the Revolution. When desert was put upon the table, he ordered a servant to bring him a glass jar enclosed in a linen cloth: this was the surprise, and indeed sensational enough, as may be readily imagined, for the cover being lifted, the jar was seen to contain the head of Charlotte Corday. Not the skull, mind you, but the entire head preserved in alcohol, with its flesh and hair... the eyes were half closed.

"It had remained in this state ever since 1793; but Saint-Albin having decided to have it *prepared*--excuse these lugubrious details--wished before that operation to show to his friends this affecting spectacle. This explains why the anthropologists discovered that the said skull *had never sojourned in the earth nor been exposed to the air*.

"Rousselin de Saint-Albin thought fit to say that he had bought it from a dealer in curiosities. Well and good; but Saint-Albin knew the ins and outs of many things, and like all those who know a good deal, he said but little. He never would say through whom or how the head of Charlotte Corday had come into his possession; and that is all. Did not the father of Ledru-Rollin, have in his possession important fragments of the bones of Louis XIV, of Henri IV and of other Kings of France, given to him by an *anonymous* witness of the violation of the royal tombs at Saint-Denis?

"The executioner Sanson, it is said, was not the kind of man to

Or else, are we to believe that somebody had bought this bloody souvenir from the headsman himself?

Or, what is more probable, must we accept a tradition constantly denied, and having up to the present only the

lend himself to such a profanation? Is that quite certain? Has not the Sanson family its own secret, like all those intimately connected with the Revolution? Sanson was credited with being anything but partial to the Government he was actively serving: he may have rendered many services, have concluded many bargains, and have traded a little on the guillotine. Yes, traded! For his descendants were wealthy: the story of the guillotine being pawned in 1847 by his grandson, over head and ears in debt, is nothing more than a fable. Finding no possibility of being relieved from his functions, the last of the Sansons hit upon a pretext to provoke his dismissal. That is the plain truth. But he was far from being in low circumstances, the proof of which is that his daughter married, under a transparent pseudonym, a gentleman well noted in Parisian society ... Guess if you can.

"Leaving the executioner aside, if he did not dispose of heads, who sold them? For heads were sold! One evening in 1793, a woman fainted in the Rue Saint Florentin (a) she fell down; a parcel which she carried in her apron rolled into the gutter; it was a human head recently cut off. On enquiry, it turned out that the woman had just come from the cemetery of the Madeleine, where the head had been handed to her by one of the grave-diggers.

"The anecdote created some sensation at the time and became the subject of an engraving.

"And as for locks of hair of the condemned!.... they became the object of a trade which drew the attention of the Commune of Paris. It must be remembered that *this was taking place in 1793*: these dreadful things were a custom of the time. Did not Danton have the body of his wife exhumed that he might once more see the loved one who had died while he was in Belgium! This fact was published by Michelet without proof. It is true, and denied, as I well know. But

(a) A few steps from the Place de la Révolution (now Place de la Concorde), where stood the Guillotine. (*Trans.*)

value of an idle tale, and according to which, the Government of the day is supposed to have ordered the body of Charlotte to be taken to the dissecting-room to be carefully examined; can we not then suppose that the head might have been *prepared* by one of the surgeons and preserved by him as a curious specimen? *

No doubt all these hypotheses have their respective share of probability: but, as for the truth, who will ever reveal it to us? . . .

I can supply you with the proof: open the catalogue of the Salon of 1793, and you will find under Sculpture the following mention: Bust of the citizeness Danton, exhumed eight days after her death; the cast taken from the corpse by Citizen Deseine, a deaf-mute.

"To conclude, I do not know whether the skull now in the possession of Prince Bonaparte, is authentic, but what may be safely asserted is, that nothing, either in the facts themselves, nor in the manners of the period, nor in the habits of those who may have contributed to preserve this relic, are contrary to its authenticity.

G. Lenotre."

As Mr. Montorgueil judiciously observes there is nothing to disprove the authenticity of the relic, but there is nothing either to prove it. And with regard to old bones, too many proofs are hardly proof enough.

* G. Lenotre, *Paris révolutionnaire*, p. 255.

THE PRIVATE LIFE

OF

ROBESPIERRE.

Like madness is the glory of this life.
As this pomp shows to a little oil, and root.
We make ourselves fools, to disport ourselves,
And spend our flatteries to drink those men
Upon whose age we void it up again
With poisonous spite and envy.

TIMON OF ATHENS, I, 2.

THE PRIVATE LIFE OF ROBESPIERRE WHILE RESIDING WITH THE DUPLAY FAMILY.

History is, so to speak, a prolonged law-suit in which we are continually occupied in examining the papers to discover flaws. It is often in minor details that historians are convicted *flagrante delicto* of inaccuracy. To stop at such trifles may perhaps seem to be like exercising the right of criticism with a magnifying-glass in hand; and yet, is not the respect for truth in details, as it were, the surest mark of the historian's honesty?

Biographers principally, who make it a point of honour to study a personage from numerous points of view, are bound, more than any others, to preserve only evidence about which no possible doubt can be raised. They must at least inspire confidence themselves if they wish their word to be believed.

This is not said for the purpose of annoying Mr. Ernest Hamel, of whom it is justly said, that he is in a measure, "An official historian of Robespierre." We must render this justice to Mr. Hamel that he has made us more thoroughly acquainted with his hero than any of the historians who preceded him.

His work, the result of much research, is full of startling facts, piquant anecdotes, and unexpected revelations; in one word, it is full of curious information. And yet, Mr. Hamel, by not having "gone himself to see," has sinned by omission; and what is more serious, has committed some errors. Not that the offence is particularly grave, but it is so delightful to find in fault an author who has written a book which he assumes to be "definitive!" . . . Rather ask Mr. Sardou, that lucky ferretter out of facts, that hunter of rare documents, what a supreme pleasure there is in finding out the sins of the erudite.

As everybody knows, Mr. Sardou, has been for a long time preparing a book on *Thermidor*. That is to say that there is no one able to teach him anything new connected with Robespierre. It was therefore quite natural to have recourse to his inexhaustible kindness and to ask of him for some information on the subject which interested us.

*

As usual, the eminent Academician received us with courtesy mingled with good grace.

"You may flatter yourself with coming just in the nick of time, said he at once. You propose to make a study of the private life of Robespierre just before Thermidor, or in other words: *Robespierre at the Duplays*.

"Well! You now find me quite joyful at a discovery I have just made, and of which I am not a little proud: You have everywhere read that the house in which Robespierre passed the last days of his life had entirely disappeared. It is my old college chum, Ernest Hamel, who has put this legend into circulation, for it is but a legend.

"The house of Duplay, where Maximilien Robespierre lodged, exists, and nothing is easier than to assure yourself of the fact. Together with Mr. Th. Gosselin (our colleague G. Lenôtre) who will shortly publish a book on Paris of the Revolution, I visited the lodging of the *incorruptible*.

"The apartment is almost intact; the room occupied by Duplay, and those of his daughters are in a perfect state of preservation, just as they were in 1794. With plan and title-deeds in hand, I reconstructed everything again: the altered stair-cases, the little garden at the back of the dining-room. On the strength of Mr. Lebas' assertion, whose manuscript Hamel had had in his hands, the historian of Maximilien asserted that the house in question had been demolished.

"Listen to what he says about it: 'It would be useless to-day to seek for a vestige of this house; not a stone of it remains standing!'

"Nothing is more inaccurate. The house has been raised a storey, that is all. But Hamel did not think it worth while to trouble himself for so little. I was more curious than he, and I do not regret it. Thanks to the obligingness of the present owner, Mr. Vaury, I was able to explore Duplay's house in every corner.

"I have seen the chamber in which the unsociable Tribune -that is the word,- used to barricade himself. Ah! it was not easy to get access to him; he was well sheltered from troublesome visitors, look here . . ."

And, saying this Mr. Sardou, with a few rapid strokes of a pencil, drew up a plan of the house, and proved to us in the clearest manner, that it was almost impossible to reach the room in which Robespierre used to "earth" himself without disturbing the entire household: the children who slept in the next room, the joiners working at the back, etc ... And continuing his explanation of the plan, Mr. Sardou continued:

"The windows of the room are the same as in '93. The chimney-piece has been changed; the partitions have been taken down, but it is easy to reconstitute what has disappeared. There is one fact to be noted, and which sheds a particular light on the psychology of the man: the room of Eleonore Duplay, who used to be called Cornelie in intimacy, was situated at the other end of the house. This simple detail suffices to explain the nature of the relations that existed between Robespierre and she who was in turn pointed out as his mistress or as his betrothed. The topography of the place furnishes us with an unanswerable argument in favour of the purity of the morals of the tribune." *

* * *

Now that we are acquainted with the place, the moment has perhaps come to introduce its inhabitants. And first of all, how did Robespierre come to know the Duplay family?

Martial law had just been proclaimed at the Champ de Mars. On that day, the 19th July 1791, Robespierre had come to the meeting of the Jacobins, where a small

* This study appeared first in the literary Supplement of the *Figaro* for the year 1891. It was only in the following February or March of 1895 that the question arose between Messieurs Sardou and Hamel about *the house of Robespierre*. This question was in fact for us only of minor importance; but in order to properly know the man, it was necessary to say a few words about his lodging.

number of the friends of freedom had assembled. The court-yard, says an eye witness* from whom we borrow the following: "The court-yard was soon filled with artillery-soldiers and light infantry-men from the suburbs, blind instruments of the fury of Lafayette and of his partisans. Robespierre was trembling with fear as he crossed that yard to return home after the meeting, and hearing the imprecations and threats of the soldiers against the Jacobins, he was obliged, in order to steady himself, to take the arm of Lecointe, of Versailles, who wore the uniform of the national guard, and of Lapoype, since then General of division, at that time one of the Jacobins."

Robespierre did not dare to go home to sleep at No. 20 Rue Saintonge, where he resided at Humbert's, with Pierre Villiers, who then acted as his secretary. He asked Lecointe if he did not know any patriot, in the neighbourhood of the Tuileries, who could give him shelter for the night. Lecointe proposed Duplay's house, and took him there. From that day forward he never quitted it.

* * *

The house of which Maurice Duplay was the owner was No. 366, now 398, Rue Saint-Honoré. It has been sufficiently described by Hamel† so as to render further details superfluous. Suffice it to say that Duplay with his family occupied a retired building at the back of a court-yard, comprising: a ground floor with a dining-room opening out upon a garden; from the dining-room, a

* Note on Robespierre, by Fréron, published in the *Notes historiques* of Mr. A. Baudot, edited by Mme Edgard Quinet, 1894; L. Cerf, p. 277 and seq.

† Hamel, *Histoire de Robespierre*, t. III, p. 2[illegible]2.

wooden staircase led to the apartments above. Duplay and his wife occupied a large room on the first floor, and their four daughters were lodged just at the back of it. Robespierre's room looked towards the west, and next to him slept Simon Duplay, the nephew of the master of the house, who acted as the dictator's secretary, and Duplay's young son, Maurice, at that time barely fourteen years of age.

To the right and left of the door-way leading into the house, were two shops, one occupied by a restaurant, the other by a jeweller.

This detail is little known: a brother of the secretary of Condorcet kept, at No. 352 of the same street, on behalf of Mme. de Condorcet, a small linen-draper's and mercer's shop. The wife of the outlaw had on the entresol a studio where she painted, portraits and miniatures and, as it appears, her studio was particularly well frequented.*

Robespierre's new landlord Maurice Duplay, was barely over fifty, when he made the acquaintance of the dictator.

He was born in 1738 at Saint-Dizier-en-Velay, and was the son of Jacques Duplay, and his wife, *née* Marie Bontemps. Ten children were born of this marriage. Maurice followed the example of his eldest brother Mathieu, and became a carpenter. Whilst still a youth, he quitted Saint-Dizier-en-Velay (now St.-Dizier-la-Seauve in the Haute Loire) and seems to have walked over the greater part of France, before he finally settled down in Paris, where thanks to some lucky speculations, he acquired a respectable fortune.

It was not long before he became the proprietor of

* See in the *Correspondant* of 1880 an article by Mr. de Lescure entitled: *Les Femmes pendant la Révolution.*

three houses, situated in the Rue de l'Arcade, the Rue du Luxembourg and the Rue d'Angoulême. For the house he occupied in the Rue Saint-Honoré he paid a sum down of 1800 livres and a yearly rental of 200 livres to the Sisters of the Conception, who were the owners.

* *

Maurice Duplay had retired from business when the Revolution broke out. He does not appear to have taken any active part in the movement.

According to Lebas,* he had been called upon as a householder to be a member of the jury of the common criminal court, and he could not, notwithstanding his aversion, refuse to sit on the jury of the Revolutionary Tribunal.

It is not true that he was present at the trials of the Queen and Madame Elisabeth, for he seldom exercised his terrible functions. He often made the building work that he had contracted to do for the Government an excuse for non-attendance at the Tribunal. Most of the sentences on which his name is recorded were rendered in his absence. When Fouquier-Tinville was impeached, together with the members of the jury of the revolutionary tribunal, Duplay was the only one acquitted and indeed no serious charge was brought against him. In fact, Duplay was a thoroughly honest man. After forty years of work, he had barely amassed 10000 livres in house property. Political events soon disturbed to some extent the position he had so laboriously acquired.

It being no longer possible to let houses, Duplay found

* *Dictionnaire encyclopédique de la France*, article *Duplay*.

himself obliged to resume his trade. This we gather from the rough draft of a letter from Mme. Duplay to her daughter, Mme. Auzat, and which was found at Duplay's house when it was searched during Thermidor.

Maurice Duplay had married the daughter of a carpenter of Choisy (Mdlle. Vaugeois, imprisoned at Sainte Pélagie on the evening of the 8th Thermidor, together with her husband and her young son, and who was strangled by some of the women her fellow prisoners.

Four daughters were born of this marriage: Sophie, who became later on Mme. Auzat, by her marriage with a barrister of that name; Victoire, who did never marry; Elisabeth, born in 1773, who married in 1793 Lebas, a member of the Convention, and to whom we shall have occasion to refer; and lastly Eleonore, born in 1771, surnamed Cornélie, in allusion to the mother of the Gracchi, and who died during the Restoration.

Maurice Duplay had an only son: Maurice, born in 1769, First of all clerk in the central administration of the department of the Seine, he was later on in 1814, appointed administrator of the hospitals and asylums of Paris, which post he continued to occupy nearly until his death, in 1846.

To complete the genealogy of the Duplay family, we will say a few words concerning the descendants of Mathieu Duplay the eldest of the family, and the brother of Maurice, Robespierre's landlord.

Mathieu Duplay married in 1767, Marie Fournier, by whom he had several children. Of these, one alone deserves our attention; Simon Duplay, born in 1774, enlisted as a volunteer in 1792, and who had his left leg carried away by a cannon ball at the battle of Valmy, from which came his nickname of "Wooden-leg."

He was adopted by his uncle, and acted as secretary to Robespierre, who dictated all his letters, etc., to him. It should be added that he was very badly paid, Robespierre considering that he did him a great honour in selecting him as his amanuensis.

After Thermidor, the nephew of Maurice Duplay was arrested and his papers seized; another son, Auguste, died early, and the last, born in 1836, is Dr. Duplay, member of the Academy of Medicine and Professor of Clinical Surgery to the Faculty of Medicine of Paris.

*

In these latter days, numerous publications have given an insight into the private life of Robespierre while at the Duplays. But, as usual, it is necessary to distinguish the truth from among the many legends which obscure it. "Everything about him," says Buonarotti, "was equality, simplicity, morality, and sincere love of the people. He was austere in morals, of extreme sobriety, living quite retired, although much sought after in society."

Mme. Lebas says, in her manuscript, that he never quitted her father's house but once, when he paid a visit to his sister at Arras, probably in 1793. His sole recreation, on the rare occasions when he went out, was to take a walk in the Champs-Elysées, in the direction of the Avenue Marbeuf, at that time a fashionable rendez-vous. But he more frequently preferred to stop at home and work.

The room he occupied at Duplay's was as simple as possible. The furniture was quite modest. It was composed of a walnut bedstead, with blue damask curtains, with white flowers, made of an old gown of Mr. Duplay, a few cane-bottomed chairs and a common desk; a deal book-shelf suspended to the wall served him as library, and contained, among other books, the principal works of Corneille, Racine, Voltaire and Rousseau,— the dear companions of his waking hours ... This room had but one window, looking on the workshops, so that, during the day, Robespierre always worked to the sound of the plane and the saw. *

Robespierre always rose early; and his first step was to go into the shop to bid good morning to his landlord.

"He afterwards worked † for a few hours, taking no other refreshment than a glass of water. No one was then allowed to disturb him; then, he had his hair dressed and this operation usually took place in the court-yard, in an open gallery leading out from his bed-room. Immediately after this, numerous visitors came, since he had become so popular. But to these he paid not the least attention: being occupied with the perusal of the Gazette and the periodicals of the day, and he then took his breakfast, consisting of fruit, bread and a little wine. When not reading, his eyes were fixed on the ground; he often rested on his elbow, and seemed to reflect on important matters.

"After breakfast he returned to his work, until his public functions demanded his presence. He never received any visitors in the morning, unless they choose to see him while his hair was being dressed. He dined at his landlord's table, and it was always he *who said grace!*

* Hamel, *loc. cit.*, t. III. p. 256.

† These details are taken from a book published in Berlin in 1794, shortly previous to Thermidor, and dedicated to Robespierre himself.

"On one occasion, Mme. Duplay having hinted that the fare was perhaps not good enough for him, Robespierre became quite vexed. He did not latterly pay any more than he did at first, so that his landlord's family should not contract bad habits; and, even during a time of dearth, he did not pay them any more than usual, in order to oblige them always to observe the same line of conduct towards him. If he was invited out to dine he did not forewarn them, in order that nothing should be changed in their domestic arrangements. Willing however that these worthy people, who had shared bad fortune with him, should have a part in the advantages of his new situation, he did a good deal for their children. The son, also a joiner, was set up in business by him, or at all events he materially aided him; as regards the daughter, he promised her a marriage present, on condition that she should marry a citizen who had fought for his country.

"At table he partook of the simple fare of his host, and drank his *vin ordinaire*. After dinner he had coffee served him, remained another hour at home to receive visitors, and then usually went out. After he became the leader of the National Convention, he engaged a secretary; formerly it was an orphan boy adopted by the Duplays, and who used to do his errands.

"He came home extraordinarily late, and often worked until past midnight at the *Comité de Salut Public*; but even when he did not go there, he never came home before midnight. Where was he in the meanwhile? Nobody knew. Those who wished to see him in the evening had to wait until the following morning."

Perhaps this almost unknown description, borrowed from a contemporary, may appear rather romantic. All is not to be taken for granted without some reserve,* but much information, not devoid of value, may be gleaned from it. What the narrator says of the sobriety of Robespierre is but a confirmation of what we know already. During the last few years of his life, he drank water only, fearing that the use of wine might lead him to make some indiscreet revelations.

The only indulgence he allowed himself was to devour, during his meal, a quantity of oranges. They were careful to serve him for dessert a regular pile of this fruit; and that in all seasons. He used to eat them greedily.

It was easy to see which place Robespierre had occupied at table by the heap of orange-peel which covered his plate.

It has been asserted, and it is not of a nature to surprise us, that Robespierre sought thereby to cool his blood, which was full of acridity, and clear his complexion, rendered sallow by the bile which choked him. Was his aspect in reality so repugnant as some people have chosen to assert? Or had his physiognomy, on the contrary something seductive? It may be useful to elucidate this question, before handling a rather delicate subject, to which we have already briefly alluded: we refer to the nature of his relations with the eldest daughter of Duplay.

*

There exists but one portrait of Robespierre, representing him young, pleasantly plump, with the air of a hard

* Mr. G. Avenel, to whom we owe the translation of the pamphlet from which we have taken an extract (V. *Amateur d'autographes*, 1862–63) does not hesitate to say that it deserves to be taken into consideration because it was penned by a contemporary of Robespierre, who must have been of Parisian origin, and probably witnessed what he so well relates.

worker, but with a narrow mind. It is that painted by Boilly, and which is in the *Musée Carnavalet*.

In 1785, according to Beaulieu, Robespierre was a little man, "of mean aspect, and deeply pitted with the small-pox, his complexion was pale and leaden-hued, his glance dark and equivocal, and all about him expressed hatred and envy." *

Hamel asserts, without further testimony, that the head of Maximilien, though wanting in the leonine character of those of Mirabeau and of Danton, whose imposing ugliness was attractive, "was endowed with an indescribable sort of persuasive expression that at once seized upon the beholder. He had long chestnut hair (carefully powdered) thrown back, a vast forehead, open on the temples and slightly bulging, prominent eyebrows, the eyes deep and clear, full of thought, but unfortunately veiled by spectacles, rendered almost always necessary by his short-sight, the nose straight and slightly turned up, the mouth well formed, the chin firm, well accentuated: such was the portrait of the physical man." †

This portrait is singularly flattered, if we compare it with the testimony of those who were accustomed to approach our hero.

Dumont of Geneva, who had conversed with him, remarked that Robespierre did not look one straight in the face, and that he seemed to have a continual and painful blinking of the eyes.

The Abbé Proyart had already noted in Robespierre, while a youth, "something undecided in his glance, and that his eyes were deeply sunk."

* *Biographie Michaud*, ed. 1824, article *Robespierre*.

† Hamel, *loc. cit.*, p. 204.

In order to hide his blinking, he wore eye-glasses, which, Michelet says he used to handle with dexterity while speaking in public.

Miss Williams, in her *Souvenirs*, declares that he wore green glasses to rest his eyes, and sometimes also eye-glasses besides, through which he would examine his audience. So much for the physiognomy.

With regard to his clothing it was in the very best style. The writer who has delineated the tribune in the *Mémoires d'une Femme de qualité*, says that Robespierre wore fine linen, well cut clothes, and a number of rings on his fingers. This is true as to the linen and the clothes, but the story of the rings is a fable.* It is a fact that he was very natty in his dress, and that, in contrast to most of his colleagues of the Convention, he retained the custom of wearing ruffles and frills.

The painter, Vivant-Denon, who often had occasion to see him, clearly remembers having seen him 'powdered white, wearing a waistcoat of brocaded muslin with a light coloured border, and altogether got up in the most *recherché* style of a dandy of 1789.' †

* * *

After reading these various opinions one feels inclined to ask, if it were the physical charms of the dictator which made an impression on Mdlle. Duplay, or whether it was not rather the influence upon her mind of his intellectual superiority.

Robespierre was no lady's man; he was too much absorbed in his ambitious dreams to allow himself to be

* Hamel. *loc. cit.*, p. 245.

† *Biographie Rabbe*, art. *Denon*.

conquered by a woman. "He loved neither women nor money, and took no more care of his private interests than if all shopkeepers were his gratuitous and much obliged purveyors, and the houses, inns hired in advance for his use. In fact, he acted on this principle with his landlord." *

Robespierre allowed the eldest daughter of Duplay to pay attention to him, but he was not in love with her. Besides, Cornélie Duplay had a rather masculine face not calculated to inspire the tender passion.

"That pale young girl, with pinched lips, and glassy eye, sometimes lit up with a viperish glance, whose portrait exhibited at the Museum of the Revolution, struck one at once by its dry and cold expression; this absence of colour and of charm, of gaiety and smile, made this chlorotic and unsympathetic young girl the worthy betrothed of the proud and bilious Dictator, whose eye was as snake-like as her own. †

* *

With regard to Eleonore Duplay there are two versions: according to the one, she had been the mistress of Robespierre; according to the other, she was his betrothed. Charlotte Robespierre (his sister), who records these two opinions, sincerely believes that Mr. Duplay hoped to have Robespierre for son-in-law, and that she neglected no means of seduction to lead him to marry her daughter. Eleonore, herself, being very ambitious, did what she could to gain the heart of Robespierre. But, according to his sister, he never yielded, and the attention and

* Baudel. *loc. cit.*, p. 242.

† *Correspondant.* 18[illegible]. p. [illegible].

importunities of which he was the object only served to disgust him.

All this is problematical.

Robespierre in the Duplay family, felt himself surrounded with warm affections, and he could not have been otherwise than very grateful for the many attentions lavished upon him. In reality he was adored, and, when politics granted him a brief respite, he seemed to live again in this atmosphere of devoted attachment. It was generally after dinner, when they adjourned into the drawing-room, which was furnished "with heavy mahogany furniture covered with crimson Utrecht velvet," that Robespierre most liked the feeling of being at home. While the girls were engaged on embroidery or linen work, he used to read aloud passages from Voltaire or Corneille, or from Racine or Rousseau. Besides, he read with great expression, and much enjoyed the pleasure he gave to his hosts.

On Thursdays the evenings were not so private. For some time, during the *Constituante*, the brothers Lameth used to frequent the Duplays. Afterwards, at the time of the Legislative Assembly, Merlin (of Thionville), Collot d'Herbois, Panis, Camille Desmoulins (whose marriage-register Robespierre had signed as witness, which did not in the least prevent him from sending his friend to the scaffold), were assiduous frequenters of these evenings. There were also to be met some eminent artists: the painters Gérard and Proudhon; Buonarotti, a direct descendant of Michael-Angelo, played the piano. Le Bas, a fervent admirer of Italian music, which he could perform most agreeably, also contributed his talents to these very pleasant evenings, from which, by mutual consent, politics for the nonce were excluded.

Le Bas remained faithful to Robespierre, even unto death. And history records that when he was arrested along with his friend, he blew his brains out.

With regard to his wife, Elisabeth Duplay, she was dragged from prison to prison.

It was in the midst of such emotions, in the height of the Terror, that his son, Philippe Le Bas, was born, who was destined to be chosen afterwards by Queen Hortense to undertake the education of her son, Louis-Napoleon, known later as the Emperor Napoleon III ....

About 1854, Philippe Le Bas lived at Fontenay-aux-Roses, near Chatillon (a few miles outside of Paris). He used to come every Saturday to pay a visit to his mother, a respectable lady, venerated in the neighbourhood for her piety, benevolence, and charity. This saintly woman was the widow of Le Bas, the Conventional. One anecdote will suffice to portray this venerable matron, a worthy descendant of the Duplays. We borrow it from a colleague, one of the most charming gossips of the day, who used to relate it with exquisite humour.

Doctor Amédée Latour was a country neighbour of the widow Le Bas, and, as such, was in the habit of frequently visiting the good old lady.

"From the very beginning," he narrates, "my attention was drawn to a big parrot, for which Mme. Le Bas seemed to feel great affection.

It often happened that our conversation with the worthy dame was interrupted by the noisy bird, who, with a loud voice, would give us a strophe of the *Marseillaise.*

Allons, enfants de la Patrie,
Le jour de gloire est arrivé!

Or else this other song of the period:

Ça ira, ça ira,
Les aristocrates à la lanterne,

or the following well-known couplet:

Madame Véto avait promis (bis),
De faire égorger tout Paris (bis).

Mme. Le Bas used then to say: "Be quiet, you noisy bird, do."

But the parrot, according to his fancy of the moment, would either be silent or begin again.

One day I ventured to say to Mme. Le Bas:

"That's a very revolutionary parrot of yours."

"I should think so," she said, in an undertone, "it was the bird of *Saint Maximilien Robespierre.*" And as she said this, the worthy dame made the sign of the cross.

"Yes," she added, "this parrot was bequeathed to me by the Duplay family, who had been the devoted friends of *Saint Maximilien* (here another sign of the cross) until his death . . ."

Now here was a lady, of incontestable respectability, a fervent and devout Catholic, whose moral and intellectual faculties were above all suspicion, who had preserved for Robespierre the veneration due to a Saint, in fact to a god, for Mme. Le Bas placed Robespierre on the same level with Jesus-Christ, declaring him to have been equally the victim of the wickedness and perversity of mankind.

She never alluded to Robespierre otherwise than as *Saint Maximilien*, and when she uttered that name she made the sign of the cross.

To the vocabulary of the parrot, already very copious, —too copious,—she had added some very original variations.

One day she said to me. "Go near to the bird and pronounce the name of Robespierre!"

"Hats off, hats off!" cried the parrot, shaking its wings.

"Say: Maximilien," added Mme. Le Bas.

"Maximilien," I repeated.

"A martyr, a martyr," replied the bird.

"Say: *Neuf Thermidor*."

I shouted Neuf Thermidor! to the parrot.

"Go on and ask him: where is *Saint Maximilien?*"

To this question the bird promptly answered:

"In heaven, by the side of Jesus Christ."

* * *

Mme. Le Bas died at Fontenay about 1860, her son Philippe shortly afterwards. As to the parrot it may, perhaps, still be alive, these birds being said to live a hundred years and more...

At any rate does not this story of the Robespierre parrot seem worthy to occupy a place in the list of the legends about pigeons and canary birds which appear to be inseparable from all the biographies of the dictator.

THE

SUPERSTITIONS

OF

NAPOLEON THE FIRST

The king is but a man as I am; the violet smells to him as it doth to me; the element shows to him as it doth to me; all his senses have but human conditions; his ceremonies laid by, in his nakedness he appears but a man; and though his affections are higher mounted than ours, yet, when they stoop, they stoop with the like wing; therefore when he sees reason of fears, as we do, his fears, out of doubt, be of the same relish as ours are.

HENRY V, IV, 1.

THE SUPERSTITIONS OF NAPOLEON THE FIRST.

"It is a generally accredited fact," writes Baron Meneval in his *Souvenirs* of Napoleon, "that great men have been, or must be, superstitious. The vulgar man, who is in reality far more under the influence of superstition than those whom he reproaches, cannot realise that great men can accomplish great things otherwise than by supernatural means not granted to ordinary mortals; others consent only to pardon their superiority on the condition of attributing to them some of the frailties of common humanity."

Whatever sense may be attached to the word superstition, be it the belief in a certain power, or in supernatural means, in occult forces that our mind may imagine but that our senses cannot perceive, let this mysterious power, which directs our acts, without intervention of our judgment, be called *Fatality* or *Providence*, it will still appear that faith in necromancers or drawers of horoscopes is a symptom, perhaps only a slight one, of mental aberration.

"This mental aberration" according to the text of

Meneval, "ought not to be applied to the sentiment which, for instance, led Napoleon to pretend that he was an instrument of Providence to whom had been entrusted a special mission, and to walk forward without fear, sure of success, under this powerful shield." We should certainly not deny this, if Napoleon, who had the presentiment that he was charged with the accomplishment of a providential mission, as all his biographers are unanimous in recognizing, had limited himself to these outward manifestations, which were destined, in his mind, only to impose upon the masses. We must also recognize that he gave proof of most consummate political shrewdness when he recommended to his army in Egypt the greatest respect for the Mohammedan religion,* and when he himself thought it his duty to assist at their religious ceremonies; every time that he found it necessary for the success of his plans to make use of the public credulity, which he was partly inclined to share, in but which he was the more disposed to laugh at in others, the more he tried to conceal it in his own case.

*

The scrupulousness in religious matters of Napoleon may have been confounded, perhaps purposely, with his prejudices. The Emperor, whatever opinion he may have entertained of his own faculties, had the consciousness

* In the *Mémoires of Bourrienne* we read: "How can any one have had the idea of representing Bonaparte as disposed towards Mohammedism? It does not merit serious discussion. No, he never entered a mosque but from pure curiosity . . . What did he want? To gain a footing in Egypt. Policy and simple good sense dictated to him to avoid saying anything contrary to the religion of the people."

of the existence of a Supreme Being, to whom he considered himself subject. His confidence of help from on high in critical moments; his frequent appeals, in his proclamations, in his speeches, *to the sole arbiter who holds in his hands the combinations of all events;* the particular emotion he felt at the sound of church-bells,* which plunged him into endless reveries and ecstasy; the sign of the cross he made on the approach of danger, may have been, as it has been said, no more than reminiscences of his first education, of which religion, it is known, formed the basis.†

The future is in the hands of God was the maxim he most liked to repeat. He admitted that after he had made his best calculated dispositions for a battle, there was a moment when success no longer depended upon

* "I always loved the sound of bells," said he at Saint Helena. "There are two things that are to me the source of specially insupportable privation in this heretical, inhospitable island: no church-bells and mealy bread!" De Beauterne, *Sentiment de Napoléon sur le Christianisme*, p. 45.

"The sound of church-bells," says Bourrienne, "produced the most singular effect upon Bonaparte, which I could never explain: he heard it with delight. When we were at La Malmaison and used to walk along the avenue leading to the plain of Rueil, often did the sound of the village bell interrupt the most serious conversations. He would stop, so that the noise of our footsteps should not deprive him of the reverberation that charmed him. He used almost to be vexed with me for not feeling the same impression as himself.

"The effect upon his senses was, that he would then say to me in a voice full of emotion: 'That reminds me of the first years I passed at Brienne. I was happy then!' I have twenty times witnessed the singular effect of the sound of bells upon Napoleon."

† With regard to his religious sentiments see the work, mentioned above, of the Chevalier de Beauterne.

himself. It was then that fatality appeared upon the scene, and if he never despaired in the most critical moments, it was because, in spite of all, he had invincible confidence in his destiny.

This confidence never abandoned Napoleon under any circumstances.

When he informs the Directoire of the disaster of Aboukir, he writes: "The *Fates* have willed, on this occasion as on many others, to prove that if they grant us a great preponderance on the Continent, they have given the empire of the seas to our rivals. But however great this reverse may be, it cannot be attributed to the inconstancy of Fortune...." As early as 1795, writing to his brother Joseph, he says: "*If my hopes are seconded by that luck which never abandons me in my enterprises*, I shall be able to render you happy and to fulfil your desires;" as he afterwards wrote to Joséphine, in 1807, "Why these tears, this sorrow? Have you lost courage? *I should feel humiliated to think that my wife should have lost faith in my destiny*..." †

And is not this passage in the *Memorial* of Saint Helena still more significant: "All those who know me know what little care I took of my own safety. Accustomed from the age of eighteen to cannon balls and bullets, §

* Baron Meneval, loc. cit.

† Guillois, *Napoléon. L'homme, le politique, l'orateur*, Ch. I.

§ It is quite true that for himself Napoleon took no precautions and always displayed the most incontestable bravery. He was wounded three times, but he risked death twenty times, at Toulon, at Montereau, at Arcis-Sur-Aube, at Waterloo, and in many other battles.

Conversing at Fontainebleau with Mr. de Bausset, Napoleon said to him at the end of the conversation: "*See what is destiny!* At the battle of Arcis-Sur-Aube I did all in my power to find a glorious

and knowing the inutility of preserving my person from them, *I abandoned myself to my destiny*... Since then I have continued to abandon myself to my *Star*, leaving the care of all precautions to the police." *

* *

It may be inferred from these citations that Napoleon was a fatalist, and we would not venture to contradict this opinion, which seems to us to be quite incontestable. †

death while defending foot by foot the soil of my country; I exposed myself without the least care; the bullets whistled round me; my clothes were riddled by them and not one could touch me." *Bonapartiana*, p. 125.

In the eyes of his soldiers Napoleon was invulnerable. Lecœur heard it related in his youth that Napoleon charmed the bullets (*Esquisses du Rouergue*, II, p. 350).

The following passage from the Memoirs of Dr. O'Meara is another proof that Napoleon did not fear death. "As I was saying to Napoleon" (it is O'Meara who speaks), "that he ought not to hasten his death by refusing to take the necessary remedies, he replied: 'What is written above is written,' and raising his eyes towards the sky, he added: 'Our days are counted!'" Quoted by de Beauterne, loc. cit. p. 55.

As he was predicting his death, behold, a comet showed itself above Saint Helena. Napoleon at once thought of that of Julius Cæsar, and appeared to believe that it was a sign from heaven to make known to him that his own death would occur within a brief delay.

* Quoted by Guillois, loc. cit. pp. 171–172.

† In vol V of the *Mémorial de Saint-Hélène* this is implicitly admitted by the emperor himself.

"It must be agreed that during the latter part of my career, fatalities have accumulated upon me. My unfortunate marriage and the perfidies to which it gave rise; that Spanish canker from which it was impossible to draw back; that unhappy Russian campaign caused by a misunderstanding, the fearful rigour of the elements that swallowed up a whole army ... and then the whole world against me!..."

Nevertheless, Napoleon always energetically denied this imputation; but could he be an impartial judge in his own case?

He had legitimate pride in the belief that no commander had ever trusted in war more to his own intellect and will; but he none the less admitted that, "one worked vainly in war," and that, "the best is manifestly to be resigned to the chances of one's profession." Let us concede, at any rate, that Napoleon had a soldier's fatalism,* and it cannot be denied that in his military combinations, he left a large margin to chance and to the unexpected.

From chance to the marvellous there is but one step, and an ardent imagination like that of Napoleon would not be long in taking this step.

It has been said, to prove that Napoleon had no great faith in the marvellous, that he had always expressed contempt for charlatans and impostors, that he had overwhelmed with his contempt, Mesmer, Lavater, and Gall, that is to say all those people with improbable systems or ideas, whose Utopias were repugnant to his positive impressions. That is true, but what is not less so, is that,—and abundant facts shall be brought to support our theory,—Napoleon was full of prejudices: that he was superstitious

* In Egypt, Napoleon was in danger of being taken prisoner or murdered by a party of Mamelukes. He was proceeding considerably in advance of the army, accompanied only by a few guards and several officers of his staff. By chance he was not perceived by the Mamelukes who were only separated from him by a slight elevation of ground. Napoleon, who all his life, it is said, was a believer in fatalism, joked about the danger he had been in, saying: "*It is not written above that I should be taken prisoner by Arabs.*" (*Bonapartiana*, 1834, pp. 116–117).

to excess, which may not be very surprising in a Corsican in whose veins there flowed Italian blood. *

Besides how could he have failed to be superstitious this mortal over whose cradle good fairies would seem to have watched?

* * *

Has it not been related that the birth of Napoleon, like those of all heroes, was accompanied by most surprising prodigies? That, in the night of the 14th to 15th August 1769, the Abbé Martenot had remarked a new star in the constellation of Virgo; this star † which will present itself

* That is to say that he was doubly a Meridional and it is well-known how superstitious the Meridionals generally are.

† Before him, Constantine and Charlemagne had also believed in their star, and also, after the taking of Damietta, the pious King Saint Louis thanked God for showing him the star *Antaris*. The following are the reflections inspired in a celebrated alienist, Dr. Brière de Boismont, by the *Etoiles des grands hommes* (The *Stars* of great men): "The faith of genius is rare. Celebrated men who have faith, believe in the supernatural. They persuade themselves that their destiny is linked to some sensible sign they perceive in the air: in such wise many have believed in the existence of a *star*, of a tutelary genius, and such marvellous apparitions have not always found them incredulous. The explanation appears to us to be simple enough: the mind, continually concentrated towards one end in view, attains its highest degree of enthusiasm in that state which may be called *ecstasy* or *illumination*, but which is none the less one of the inmost faculties of our being, from which spring the animated creations of genius, and in which thought, in order to make itself understood, clothes itself with the attributes of the body." *Union médicale*, 1853 p. 213.

Of course we insert this explanation for what it may be worth, without vouching for its correctness.

to him in the most memorable circumstances of his life,[1] and which his eyes will seek for in hours of anxiety.

This at least, is a strange coincidence; in the night of 15th to 16th August 1769, Frederick the Great, being at Breslau, had a dream, which on awakening on the morning of the 16th, he thus related to one of his Aides-de-Camp: "Could you," said he to him, "interpret a dream which troubles me much? I saw the star of my Kingdom and my genius shining in the firmament, luminous and resplendent. I was admiring its brilliancy and its lofty position, when above mine there appeared another star which eclipsed it as it descended upon it. There was a struggle between the two, for a moment their rays were confounded together, and my star, obscured, enveloped within the orbit of the other, fell to the earth, as if pushed down by a force which seemed likely to extinguish it. The struggle was long and obstinate; at last my star got free, but with much difficulty. It rose again to its place and continued to shine in the firmament, whereas the other one vanished." And the Chevalier de Beauterne, who relates the anecdote, adds the following comment: "In-

[1] Napoleon, being at Bayonne, had given some very important despatches to the captain of a corvette, with orders to set sail at once. However the next day the Emperor was informed that this captain was still in the town. Angry at his disobedience, he sent for him and asked him in the severest tone the cause of his delay: "Sire," said the captain, greatly troubled at such a reception, "the English are blockading the port, and I feared to set sail, not on account of my ship, nor of myself, or my crew, but for the safety of the despatches you have deigned to confide to me."

Napoleon, mollified by this explanation, answered: "Fear nothing, captain, start; *my* star will guide you."

This prediction was accomplished, for the officer escaped the vigilance of the British cruisers." *Bonapartiana*, pp. 41—42.

credulity may deny the mysterious connection between this dream * and the existence of Napoleon; but it cannot contest the truth of the fact itself, † nor the coincidence

* The dream of Charles Bonaparte, the father of Napoleon, is not less curious. A few days before his death, Ch. Bonaparte had a sort of supernatural revelation, for, in a moment of delirium, he cried out: "that all exterior aid would be unable to save him, since *this Napoleon, whose sword would one day conquer Europe*, would in vain endeavour to save his father from the dragon of death which was tormenting him." (Fact related by Mr. du Casse in his *Histoire anecdotique de Napoléon Ier*. Paris, Paul Dupont, 1869.)

† After the battle of Jena, Napoleon, who had twice beaten the Prussians, said to the poet Wieland, who had solicited a private audience of him: — "You know the dream of Frederick?" "Yes, Sire." "Well," continued the Emperor, "do you believe in the constellations?" "The dream is true, Sire, that is all I can say." "There is a strange menace, Sir, in this dream! There is something sinister in it for us." "How so, Sire?" said the poet. "Yes something sinister, for *the star of the dead man is to overcome the star of the living*," said Napoleon in a peculiar tone as he called to mind the dream of Frederick.

This star was to show itself to him on two other different occasions.

In 1806, General Rapp, returned from the Siege of Dantzig, having an urgent necessity to speak with the Emperor, had entered his cabinet without causing himself to be announced. He found him so deeply absorbed that he could not say a word to him. Seeing that he remained still motionless, Rapp thought that he was unwell and purposely made some noise. Napoleon, turning round at once, clutched the General by the arm and said to him: "Do you not perceive it?... It is my star!... There, yonder... before you... brilliant:" and becoming gradually more excited, he exclaimed: "It has never abandoned me, I see it in all great occurrences; it commands me to go forward, and is to me a constant sign of good luck."

Towards the end of the year 1811, Cardinal Fesch adjured the Emperor to cease warring against religion, against nations and against the elements: "Do you see that star above?" said Napoleon suddenly, drawing him towards an open window?

of the dates, since it is all to be found in several biographies, and in the histories of Frederick II, published in Germany before and after the death of that sovereign, at a time when Napoleon was no more than a pupil at the military school at Brienne, or an officer of artillery."

* * *

It was in fact during his residence at the college at

"No, Sire."

"Look well!"

"Sire, I see nothing."

"Well then! I myself do see it," replied Napoleon, who could not brook contradiction.

The above anecdote has been related somewhat differently by Mr. Passy, who made it known to M. Augustin Thierry, after the latter's communication to the Institute concerning the vision of Constantine (Vide *Union médicale*, 1858, loc. cit., p. 311).

From another source in the number for the 18th August 1896, the *Gaulois* published the following paragraph:

"Mr. Arthur Levy, the well-known historian of *Napoleon in private life*, has, during the course of his researches, discovered a pretty piece of German servile flattery, which is quite *à propos* on the approach of the 15th August

FREDERICK THE GREAT AND NAPOLEON.

"Frederick the Great was in Berlin during the summer of 1769. The orderly officer, sitting up in the King's antechamber, had orders to awaken His Majesty at five in the morning. At this hour the King was plunged in a profound sleep, and no one dared to wake him, because he had gone to bed in a very bad humour. The officer alone, faithful to the orders he had received, approached the bed of his sovereign, who, contrary to the anticipation of all those around, woke up in good spirits. 'Do you know how to interpret dreams?' asked the King. 'No, Sire,' answered the officer.—'Never mind, listen

Brienne and consequently at the very outset of his career, that Bonaparte had the first presage of his extraordinary career, as is witnessed by this anecdote which we remember seeing somewhere. When he was First Consul, he sent word to Mme. de Montesson that she was to come to the Tuileries. As soon as he saw her, he advanced to meet her, and told her to ask for whatever she liked.

"But General, I have no right to avail myself of your offer."

at all events and pay great attention to the dream I have just had, and we shall some day see what event is connected with it; in my dream I saw a brilliant star descending towards the earth, its resplendent light so enveloped me that I had the utmost difficulty in extricating myself from it and in making myself visible.' So spake the King. The officer paid great attention to the dream and to the date. It was the night which preceded the birth of the emperor Napoleon!" (Gazette de Munich, of 15th March 1810.)

We begged Mr. Arthur Levy to give us some additional information and he was obliging enough to send us in reply the following interesting letter:

"19th October, 1890.

"Sir,

I found the dream of Frederick II, in the National Archives under the letter A. F. IV, N°. 1505, in the extracts from foreign newspapers which formed part of the collection of the office of the Secretary of State. It is neither preceded nor followed by any comment; you have it in the *Gaulois* just as it is in the Archives, minus the last phrase which I have suppressed: '....It was *the same night* that witnessed the birth of the Emperor Napoleon,' because that is untrue.

"My opinion is that it is a servile piece of German flattery, thousands of which were inspired by Napoleon, and issued to our neighbours across the Rhine. It was quite in this sense, if I remember rightly, that I gave it to the *Gaulois*.

"Regretting a thousand times my inability to further enlighten you, I beg, Sir, etc., etc.

Arthur Lévy."

"You forget then, Madame," he said, "that I received my first laurel crown from your hands. You came to Brienne to distribute the prizes, and when you placed on my head the wreath that was the forerunner of so many others, you said, 'May it bring you good fortune.'"

Madme. Montesson was about to reply, but Bonaparte interrupted her. "I am," he said, "a fatalist. Therefore it is easy to see why I have not forgotten an incident that you do not remember."

At a later period, Napoleon loaded Mme. de Montesson with gifts and honours, and bestowed upon her a pension of 60,000 francs a year.

On leaving the school at Brienne in 1785, Napoleon, after passing his examinations brilliantly, had been appointed second sub-lieutenant to the La Fère regiment, then in garrison in the Dauphiné. After remaining some time at Grenoble, he came to reside at Valence. As soon as he was installed, he sent for his brother Louis, nine years younger than himself.

Both lodged with a Mdlle. Bon. Louis occupied a modest attic over Napoleon's bed-chamber. Napoleon used to wake him in the morning by knocking with a stick on the ceiling. One day young Louis was late in coming down. Napoleon was about to knock again with his stick when his brother appeared:

"Why, what is the matter this morning. We seem to be rather lazy?"

"Oh, brother! I had such a lovely dream!"

"And what did you dream?"

"I dreamt that I was king."

"And what then was I? . . . Emperor?" said the young sub-lieutenant, shrugging his shoulders . . . "Come along, let us get to work!" and the daily lesson of mathematics was as usual given to the future king by the future Emperor. *

Bonaparte had doubtless forgotten that incident when, nine years later, in January 1794, passing through Marseilles, he for the first time had recourse to a fortune-teller. This woman had often been consulted by Napoleon's sister, the widow of general Leclerc, the beautiful Pauline, who was probably more curious to learn the issue of her amorous intrigues than to know her future; † Bonaparte was more anxious about his future elevation. The gipsy said to him in the following exact terms: "You will cross the seas; you will be victorious; you will return and become greater than ever."

It was this same fortune-teller who, one evening that she was performing in the open air at la Tourette, remarked in the crowd which had gathered around her, the sisters of Napoleon, Pauline and Elisa, accompanied by a rich Marseillaise republican who was extending hospitality to the Bonaparte family: "You shall one day be a queen, my pretty child," said the gipsy to Pauline.

When, later on, Pauline had married for the second time, taking for husband the Prince Borghese, she came to reside at the chateau de Saint-Joseph, at an hour's distance from Marseilles. The Republican who had accompanied her several years previously, and who had at one moment been her *fiancé*, reminded her of the adventure with the

* *Bonapartiana*, p. 151. This scene occurred in presence of Mr. Parmentier, surgeon of the regiment in which Napoleon was second sub-lieutenant.

† Vide, General de Ricard. *Autour de Bonaparte*, Paris, 1891. pp. 114–115.

fortune-teller: "She did not altogether tell the truth," answered Pauline, "for I am only a Princess."

It is to be supposed that Fortune is a woman, for if Pauline saw but one part of the prophecies realised which concerned herself, her brother was destined to see realised all and far more than had been foretold to him.

* * *

One of the predictions which produced the greatest impression upon the mind of Napoleon was that which was made him for the first time in Egypt,* under circumstances which have been often, if not very exactly, reported.

Bonaparte was one day taking a walk in Cairo, with his officers, when an old woman, of sordid appearance, came up and barred his way, and, without further preamble, offered to tell him his fortune. Without waiting for an

* On board the ship which was conveying him to Egypt, "How often," writes Mr. Turquan, "when surrounded by Monge, Berthollet and other savants, did he propound the question of the truth or falsity of presentiments and of the interpretation of dreams! No matter what these learned men could do or say, he never could prevail upon himself to believe that presentiments had no real signification regarding the future."

Thus, a little later, when in Egypt, being informed that the best sloop of his Nile flotilla, the *Italie*, had been taken and destroyed by the Turks, after a most heroic defence on the part of the crew, he was much struck by the event, exclaiming: "Italy is lost to France! my forebodings never deceive me." His secretary, Bourrienne, observed to him that there could be no connection between Italy and a small armed boat to which the name of that country had been given, but nothing could rid Bonaparte of the notion. But what is most curious in the matter is, that his presentiment was destined shortly to be realized. Italy was in fact evacuated by the French armies after a series of defeats which were put a stop to only in 1800 by the thunderclap of Marengo.

answer, the sorceress built up a pyramid of variously coloured shells, and according to the arrangement and tint of the shells she drew his horoscope.

"You will have," she said to Bonaparte, "two wives; one, you will *most wrongfully* repudiate. The second will not be inferior to her in great qualities. She will bear you a son. Soon, great wars and dark intrigues will be raised against you. You will cease to be happy and powerful. All your hopes will be overthrown. You will be driven out by force, and banished to a volcanic land, surrounded by the sea and by rocks. Beware of counting upon the fidelity of those nearest to you; your own blood will rise against your rule."

The mind of Bonaparte was the more struck by this prediction that the pythoness was ignorant of the rank of the personage to whom she addressed herself. Turning to one of the officers of his suite, he caused twenty-seven sequins to be given to the old woman, all the money that the officer had about him, and went away much troubled.

When he returned to France, he must have been haunted—if indeed the legend of the Egyptian fortune-teller be not apocryphal—by the memory of this adventure, when he signed, before the notary Raquideau, his marriage contract with the widow of General de Beauharnais, who was destined to make such clever use of the superstitious beliefs of her husband.

* * *

The quite accidental circumstances which led to the first intimacy between Bonaparte and Joséphine are pretty well known.

After Vendémiaire, Eugène Beauharnais, then but still a

child, went to the commander-in-chief of the army of the interior (General Bonaparte) to solicit from him the sword of his father. The aide-de-camp, Lemarrois, introduced the boy, who, on recognizing his father's sword, burst into tears. The commander-in-chief, touched by this show of feeling, overwhelmed him with caresses. When Eugène related to his mother the reception he had met with from the young General, she hastened to pay him a visit of thanks. "It is known," the Emperor used to say when alluding to this subject, "how much she believed in presentiments, and in sorcerers. In her childhood a great future had been predicted to her, that she should become a sovereign. Her finesse is also well known, and she used also often to repeat to me, that it was after the first accounts given to her by Eugène, that her heart had begun to throb, and, that from that moment, she had foreseen a shadow of her destiny."*

All historians have repeated that, in the early days of her marriage with Bonaparte, Joséphine had heard it predicted by a gipsy "that she would become greater than a queen, and that notwithstanding she would die in an hospital." †

* Constant says, in his *Mémoires*, that Joséphine took pleasure in repeating to Napoleon: "They talk of your star, but it is mine that influences you; it is to me that high destinies have been predicted." And the Emperor wished nothing better than to be so convinced.

* Vide. *Souvenirs de l'Empereur Napoléon* Ier, p. 175.

† According to Constant (Mémoires, t. 1, p. 310), this prophecy had been made to Joséphine at the moment of her leaving Martinique. A sort of gipsy is said to have told her: "You are going to France to get married; your marriage will not be happy: your husband will meet with a tragical death: and you will yourself, at that time be exposed to great danger: but you will triumph over that; you have

The first part of this prediction was accomplished by her marriage with Napoleon. With regard to the second, it was equally verified, for she died in her property of La Malmaison, which, it is said, had been originally an asylum for sick people. *

When the ascendancy exercised by Joséphine upon Napoleon is taken into consideration, it may easily be explained how she may have brought him, without much effort, to participate in her faith in divinatory powers. †

before you the most glorious of destinies and, without being queen, you will be more than queen."

She added, that being very young at the time, she paid but little attention to this prediction, and she remembered it only when Mr. de Beauharnais was guillotined; she then mentioned it to several ladies who were imprisoned together with her, during the time of the Terror, but that now she saw it in each point accomplished.

* Lord Holland, in his *Diplomatic Souvenirs*, p. 174, says that he had often heard this prediction repeated in 1802, "consequently before the death of Joséphine, before her elevation to the dignity of Empress and when it was still possible to doubt whether the wife of the First Consul had already actually accomplished the first part of the oracle."

† Baron Meneval, who pretends that Napoleon never had recourse to "the ridiculous practices of necromancy," admits, however: "It is to be possible, that in the great ardour of his love for Joséphine, he may have allowed himself to be induced to assist at a consultation with a fortune-teller, and that he made this sacrifice solely to gratify the impressionable mind of the woman he so tenderly loved."

What we can add is not of a nature to invalidate this very plausible opinion. Mdlle. Lenormand has pretended that she was called for the first time only to la Malmaison in 1801 (2nd May), but that, during this interview, Joséphine had told her, that in 1795, Bonaparte had consulted *a person in the Faubourg Saint-Germain*[a]; and it was at the moment when he was asking leave to quit France and to go to Constantinople: "You will obtain neither the one nor the other."

a The Rue Tournon, where Mdlle. Lenormand resided, is in the Faubourg Saint-Germain. (*Transl.*)

After being so much in the company of Joséphine, Napoleon had come to believe that he himself was gifted with a certain prophetic talent, * and one day indeed he took a fancy to try his hand at fortune-telling. It was during a soirée at Joséphine's, who had not yet become his wife, and whose heart hesitated between the choice of three aspirants to her hand: Hoche, Caulaincourt, and Bonaparte. The latter, who was in disguise, resolved to play the part of a chiromancer; the mistress of the house was alone admitted to his confidence.

After having foretold the future to each of the guests, it came to be the turn of Hoche. Examining the palm of the future general, he gravely predicted to him "that his mistress would be stolen from him by a rival, and that he would not die in his bed."

When later the news was spread that Hoche had died prematurely of poison, there were malignant tongues which

said the sibyl, "but you will marry a woman of dark complexion, the mother of two children, whose father will have honourably accomplished the duties of his military career."

Hardly had she said these words — it is Mdlle. Lenormand who speaks — than Bonaparte entered and recognized in the sibyl his fortune-teller of 1795. And Mdlle. Lenormand adds, in relating this anecdote, that Joséphine had particularly recommended her not to reveal this, for, she said: "The great do not like to let the public know that they are subject to the same weaknesses as the vulgar crowd."

* He had also some pretensions to medical knowledge, and often called all the physicians of his day, quacks, ignoramuses, etc. Even Corvisart did not find favour in his eyes. He liked very much, at any rate, to give advice; and what he prescribed was naturally .... *old grandmother's remedies.* For instance, writing to the Prince Eugène, on 20th August 1806, he said: "Take care of yourself in your present state and try not to give us a daughter. I can give you a recipe for that, but you will not believe me: "*it is to drink every day a little pure wine.*" *Mémoires of Mme. de Rémusat*, t. III, p. 177.

did not fail to call to mind this prediction. Let us hasten to add that this was a calumny on Bonaparte, which is amply refuted by the official report (*procès-verbal*) of the illness, and the account of the last moments of Hoche.*

* * *

In divesting Napoleon of the divine aureole of his glory, to lower him to the level of the humblest mortals by attributing to him some of the weaknesses to which poor humanity is subject, we had no intention to systematically depreciate his glory: those who think so would misinterpret our intention. But historical veracity obliges us to own that this great genius had some blemishes which have tarnished his Cæsarian fame.

One of Napoleon's secretaries, one of those who has undertaken his defence with the most passionate zeal, has endeavoured to persuade us not only that he did not participate in the superstitious beliefs of Joséphine †, but

* We shall explain in detail the true causes of the death of Hoche in our work, to be published shortly, on the *Mysterious deaths of history*.

† To that assertion we will first oppose the following passage from the *Mémoires of Mme. de Rémusat*, t. I, p. 102:

"When, after leaving his study, Bonaparte used to come in the evening to the drawing-room of Madame Bonaparte, he would at times cause the wax candles to be shaded with white gauze; and, after requesting us to remain perfectly silent, took a pleasure in telling us, or in hearing us relate, ghost-stories."

Then again, this passage of the *Mémoires de Constant* (t. I, p. [illegible]): "She (Joséphine) says that he is superstitious; that one day, being with the army in Italy, having broken in his pocket the glass which covered her portrait, he was in despair, being persuaded that it was an omen that she was dead; and he had no rest until the return of

that he omitted no occasion to turn them into ridicule. He was present when Napoleon forbade his wife to consult

the courier whom he had despatched to obtain information." It is true that in a note is added, that "the Emperor was then still enamoured of Joséphine."

We subjoin, simply as a curiosity, the following passage from t. III of the *Apocryphes* of *Cambacérès* p. 347 et sequitur:

"After the great campaign made by Napoleon in Spain in 1808 and in the beginning of 1809, he remained but a short time in Paris, the war with Austria having immediately recommenced. In the meanwhile, we went to spend a few days at Fontainebleau. One day that I entered the Emperor's cabinet, at the same moment that the Prince of Benevento (Talleyrand) was coming out, His Majesty said to me:

"'Prince, do you possess the talent of Daniel?'

"'Which, Sire?'

"'The interpretation of dreams. This is what I dreamed last night: I was in bed, someone knocked at the door; I sat up in bed; I saw enter a man of gigantic stature, clad in magnificent but rather barbaric attire; in one hand he held a long and broad sword, and in the other a sceptre surmounted by an eagle; his brow was decked with the Imperial crown. This phantom said to me: Sleep not, thou must fight again: thou shalt conquer, but on condition that thou dost respect the weak. He was still speaking when I saw another monarch enter crowned with lilies and loaded with fetters. After him, there came a third whom I recognized by remembering one of the masterpieces of Titian. This was Francis I, and the other doubtless, King John. Both took away Charlemagne with them, and the noise of the door in closing awoke me.'

"This vision," continued the *Prince*, "was related to me with more details than I give you, gentlemen. It very much troubled the Emperor, and although Charlemagne had predicted victory to him, yet as it was but under the condition that he should spare the weak, which Napoleon, perhaps, had not the least intention to do, all his attention was concentrated on the two other monarchs, both defeated and both made prisoners. I endeavoured to divert his mind from these sad thoughts.

"'I know,' he said, 'that dreams are only illusions, but there are

Mdlle. Lenormand, whom he afterwards had arrested and subjected to a regular cross-questioning. He adds, that

cases when God employs such methods to communicate with us. Without referring back to the Old Testament, I see, in the New, an angel reproving the jealousy of Joseph; a dream determining the flight into Egypt; the wise men, returning from their journey to Bethlehem, turned aside from the nearest road by a dream; then again the dream of the bad rich man; ... all this makes one reflect. Nothing is easier than to laugh, to doubt, to deny; but is it reasonable? I should like to know the meaning of my dream. The principal point is that Charlemagne is led away by two prisoner Kings. I have half a mind to go and consult Mdlle. Lenormand, or else Moreau ... No, not the first, she might gossip; I will go to Moreau. Will you go there with me?'

"'This was said laughing, and gaily. I replied that in my quality of arch-chancellor of the Empire my duty was to follow my Emperor everywhere.

"'Well,' said he, 'we shall see about it ...' I was surprised when, later, I learned that the Emperor had been to see this Moreau; I supposed that it was with the Marquis de Lenlanges, for whom he had a particular affection, or else with the Count Louis de Narbonne, whom he noticed on account of his genuine royal descent.

"I am not aware," continued the Prince, "that the Emperor ever went with any other persons than myself to see Moreau; with regard to that visit, we made it together with the Dukes of Frioul and of Rovigo. Napoleon called for me one opera evening, for a joke, cautioning me to don

...... The brown overcoat,
And the midnight cloak of real mouse-colour,

"I guessed the reason of the injunction, and disguised myself in accordance. The place of meeting, for I was not to go to the Tuileries, so as not to arouse the attention of its inhabitants, was on the Quai Saint Nicholas, close to the Louvre, where a hired coach was waiting.

"I got into the coach, in which was the Emperor; the vehicle

Joséphine surrounded with the deepest mystery her connection with this adventuress, and the comptroller of her

stopped at the corner of the Quai de Gesvres and of the Pont Notre-Dame.

"There we got out, well enveloped in our overcoats; a footman led the way, and we arrived at the lodging of Moreau; I spare you a description of the room, it was in conformity with the usual habitations of magicians. Moreau, the sly rogue, guessed who we were; the dream was related to him, but Charlemagne had been transformed into a contractor for blankets, and the Kings John and Francis I, his two sons who, having badly succeeded in business, were in prison at Fort-l'Evêque; Napoleon was supposed to be the actual director of the manufactory.

"Moreau listened to all we had to tell him; he then sorted his cards, consulted his whites of eggs, his coffee-grounds, promised marvels, endeavouring to gloss over the predictions of captivity. The Emperor brought him back to it, upon which he said:

"'Yes, the cards speak of prison, but that concerns those who trouble the actual proprietor of the establishment.'

"He was telling a lie, that is sure. It was now my turn, he scrutinized me, and recognized me, related all my private life and finally announced that I should marry a near relation to the manufacturer (the Emperor), having a similarity to me in point of taste and age. This allusion to Madame *Mère* was not very successful.

"'And I,' said Rovigo?

"'You will go to prison, and more than once.'

"'And I?' asked Duroc.

"Moreau examined his hand and remained silent.

"'Speak,' said the Duke of Frioul.

Continued silence.

"'Will you speak?'

"'If I must, I charge a cannon ball to carry my answer.'

"Things began to turn out badly; we went away sad, anxious, and we could barely compliment Savary on his various captivities, which seemed to be all the less probable that his special and permanent mission was to run other people in. (a) I remember this incident in

(a) Savary was Minister of Police. (*Transl.*)

privy purse never knew what sums she expended in payment of the latter's predictions. *

We shall be able, by examining the memoirs of contemporaries, to estimate the value of his assertions.

* * *

Mdlle. Avrillon, first lady of the chamber to the Empress Joséphine, declares that the predictions of Mdlle. Lenormand

connection with the adventure of Mallet, and I mentioned it then to Savary, who seemed particularly anxious: the terrible death of Duroc (a) added to his veneration for Heaven; and how often, in 1814, did he not remind me of this dream of the Emperor, of his two captivities, represented by the two Kings: the one was already realised, what would be the other? Saint Helena has proved to us that the Emperor was right when he inclined to believe that heaven sometimes made use of dreams to communicate with Kings."

* Baron Meneval, *loc. cit.* During the Consulate, the 2nd of May 1803, as we have said above, the sibyl was summoned to La Malmaison by Joséphine. She announced to her among other things that the First Consul would fail in his attempt to invade England. Bonaparte, hearing of this, caused her to be arrested and taken to the prison of the Madelonnettes, where she was confined from the 16th December 1803 till the 1st January 1804. On that day she sent the following lines to Fouché (the Prefect of Police):

Si le préfet veut bien en ce moment
Par un bienfait commencer cette année;
S'il m'ouvre enfin ce triste appartement,
Je lui prédis heureuse destinée. (b)

(a) Duroc was killed by a cannon ball at the battle of Wurtschen, on the 22nd May 1813. Bonaparte, in his bulletin of that battle, mentions a very remarkable conversation he had with his favourite in his dying moments. If we are to believe this bulletin, Duroc said to his master, "that he awaited him in heaven, but he trusted that it would not be until after thirty years, so that he might have achieved the welfare of France." Vide Michaud, *Biographie Universelle*, t. XII, p. 111. (*Transl.*)

(b) "If the Prefect will but hear,
And let me out of this dismal cell;

were nothing but a tissue of falsehoods; † that Joséphine knew very little about her, and, that as for Napoleon, he never consulted her.

She relates how one day she was impelled by curiosity to visit the pythoness of the Rue Tournon, whom she

† Nevertheless the "falsehoods" of Mdlle. Lenormand were credited among the "upper ten," for it seems positive that the sibyl was consulted by Barras, Talleyrand, Tallien, David, General Moreau, Denon, the Duke of Berry, the tragedian Talma, the singer Garat, besides many others. With regard to Napoleon this is what we can reply to the testimony of Mdlle. Avrillon. First of all Napoleon, while at Saint Helena, is supposed to have spoken as follows to an Englishman, of the name of W. Killian, who has published it in a book entitled the *Prophecies of Napoleon*. The book in question being however of very questionable authenticity, we quote the following with the reserve that is usual under such circumstances:

"Mdlle. Lenormand showed me Saint Helena, and made me a sketch of the island on the wainscot of an apartment still existing in the Rue Tournon.

"She wrote thereon in different places:

Plantation-House.

Hut's gate (*sic.*)

Longwood

Marchand

Bertrand

The Tower and Hudson Lowe."

Were these prophecies made after the facts? That is quite possible, the book not having been published until 1830.

Can greater faith be placed in the assertions of Mdlle. Lenormand herself, who has published in her *Souvenirs d'une sibylle*, a consultation which, according to her, she gave, to an emissary from the Emperor, "a country girl... who had been charged with the mission by an unknown person."

At the beginning of this new-year;
His future happiness I foretell.

The request was listened to and Fouché released his prisoner.

very picturesquely describes as, "dressed in a dark coloured cloth riding-habit," the form beneath which was so huge

Though this document is rather long we thought it better to reproduce it, if only as a curiosity. It is, besides, but little known, the book in which it appeared being now out of print.

In 1807, Mdlle. Lenormand had drawn the horoscope of the perjured husband. She published this extraordinary prophecy in extenso in her 'Souvenirs of a sibyl':

'The consulter is born under a lucky star; at his birth all the stars were in favourable conjunction. The Sun, Mars, and Jupiter showered their blessings on him.

'He was born in an island, which is now an integral part of France.

'His father is dead, he has four brothers and three sisters. Two of his brothers have been married twice.

'His mother now resides in the capital, she owes a great deal to him.

'The character of the consulter is firm, decided; sometimes pensive, more serious than gay, he holds much to his opinion, he does not like to be governed, even by women, particularly avoiding giving them too much ascendency; he grants his confidence with difficulty, he fears to have his plans guessed, which makes him hide his smallest actions; he is sensitive to offence, forgiving it with difficulty; he hates ingratitude.

'From his earliest days he was destined for the military profession, he has been instructed in the best principles, those indeed which concern artillery. He was formerly attached to a respectable corps, and was once even in a town besieged by water.

'He has been all over beautiful Italy, and has entered the capital of the Christian world; at one time he was there much thought of.

'The consulter has visited a country which in ancient times was the cradle of a religion; he must have been charged with a command from which those who arranged to send him on this voyage did not expect him to return; even his wife was losing hope; it had been predicted to her and to his relations, that he would return, and hardly had he been back three weeks or three months, than he was invested with great powers (he was even twice exposed to great danger, once by an explosion), and finally dictated laws to his greatest enemies.

'His wife is a foreigner; she is a very amiable woman, and thoroughly

that she had much difficulty in "not taking her for a man dressed up as a woman."

possesses that grace, that amenity which always causes those to whom it is given to be sought after.

"She is gentle, and has a sensitive and good heart; her soul is great and generous; she really loves him; she is doubly annoyed at the present moment; she fears, and with just reason, that he does not think enough of her... that idle gossip, repeated by the vulgar, may later turn to certainty.

"The consulter must have made the acquaintance of this amiable lady in quite a strange manner; a man in place may have given advice, but it was in the destiny of both that they should be united; there are incredible things in life. She was the widow of a fair man, esteemed in the army and who left her two children, a son and a daughter.

"This lady had lost her first husband in a terrible manner; by the steel; she was herself shut up in a place which had formerly been a palace but in those unhappy days had become a prison: to-day, this beautiful monument has been restored to its original purpose.

"This wife, for more than one reason, should be dear to him; she carries good fortune to all around her: she has but to wish you good luck and it comes to you. In short, with her everything must succeed.

"Her son is married to a German of good family; he resides in a country where the people love good music; her daughter has married a member of the consulter's family; she even bears his name.

"This young lady must have already resided in a country where navigation and commerce form the wealth of the inhabitants; she has two sons, one is dead; a third is on the way and will come happily. (Prediction accomplished.)

"My consulter is very uneasy; I see him even uncertain, which with him is rare; for he knows how to take a decision at once. A proceeding that his wife is about to take (and which he advises her) will astonish many people, inwardly he cannot but be thankful to her. Nevertheless this lady will meet with some obstacles which later will be removed. This proceeding will take place, but after a certain time (2? moons at the most); and the consulter will one day learn most painfully what this separation will have cost him.

She was satisfied on that day with the *petit jeu* (small game, in which the whole pack of cards is not required) and retired leaving on the table a crown-piece.

"The consulter's blood is heated, he even requires a little rest, which hardly agrees with his ardent character. Moderate exercise becomes necessary to him, as also uninterrupted perspiration. He sometimes has pimples which appear on the surface of the skin. Even at the present moment there are a few. (*a*)

"The name of the consulter will be repeated to the extremities of the world: it will even be looked for not far from the country of the great wall. (*b*) He will co-operate in great events. He will be the mediator of great interests. It is predicted to him that he will be a man unique of his kind.

"I have already said that he had seen part of Europe, and even of Asia, but he will want to go still further...

"Consulter is a statesman, he often works in the secret of his cabinet and will speak to the mightiest. He has three kinds of friends: some true ones attached to him by gratitude; others attracted by his present fortune: others again are watching his slightest actions. As for himself, the man must be very clever who can read through him. He will rise to the greatest honours to which a mortal can aspire: but if in seven years time from now he consults me, and remembers my past predictions, all the better for him...

"For I see so many events for this consulter, that I should require a folio to write them all..."

I was ignorant of the rank, and what was the fortune of the person who consulted me; in drawing up this singular horoscope, in which I have left even the faults of style, and of which I give here but a brief extract, I remarked such astonishing and even striking events, that I stopped myself, fearing to go too far; nevertheless for my own safety, I kept myself within just limits, and I gave latitude to my thoughts only as far as did not carry me away from the rules of prudence.

---

a. Good Josephine used to dress his irritated skin every day at the time I was penning this prediction; its singularity and justness astonished them both; the fact was afterwards imparted to me by eye-witnesses.

(*b*) Persia.

When she got back to the palace, Joséphine pressed her with questions concerning her interview with Mdlle. Lenormand; and Mdlle. Avrillon concluded that, unless the Empress was possessed of a great amount of dissimulation, it seemed evident to her that until then Joséphine had never had any connection with the sibyl.

Mdlle. Avrillon adds, that it was not until shortly before the divorce that Joséphine decided for the first time to consult Mdlle. Lenormand, and then only by correspondence, and through the intermediary of one of her ladies of the palace, "who believed more in these predictions than in an article of faith." The reply was brought to Joséphine by the lady in question.

Mdlle. Avrillon admits that after the divorce Joséphine summoned Mdlle. Lenormand to La Malmaison, and that she was charged by the Empress to conduct her there. On this occasion Mdlle. Lenormand very obligingly offered to Mdlle. Avrillon to tell her fortune, this time gratuitously, and with the *full game*, but the latter thought fit to decline this offer.

* * *

More than six months afterwards, a person gifted with every virtue, a perfect model of filial love, Mademoiselle S. H. (of whom death has so prematurely bereft her friends), gave me a copy of the celebrated thesis, (a) telling me that the messenger chosen to bring me the month, day and hour of the birth of Bonaparte, was simply a country wench, knowing neither how to read nor write, and who, furthermore, was deaf....; she had been charged with the commission by a person unknown to her, so much was it dreaded that she might have some notions of the rank and importance of such a personage. *Souvenirs d'une sibylle*, pp. 463–469.

(a) It was deposited in the Bureaux of the police on the 11th December, 1808.

From the above narration there is but one thing to be gathered, that Joséphine did really communicate with Mdlle. Lenormand. Mdlle. Avrillon assures us that Joséphine had not visited the pythoness; but on this point again we shall contradict her by the evidence of a relation of Joséphine, who had also occasion to be often near her, and who, in consequence, was likely to be cognizant of her most trivial sayings and doings.

Joséphine, writes the Princess of Canino (widow of Lucien, the brother of Bonaparte), was at that time in continual dread that the First Consul, anxious to have children, which she was no longer able to give him, might seek for a divorce. The question had been mooted on his return from Egypt, not under the pretext of sterility but of lightness of conduct.

It was at this moment that the incident of the broken snuff-box occurred, which incited Joséphine to consult Mdlle. Lenormand concerning the future before her.

The First Consul, in a moment of irritation against his brother Lucien, who had been reproaching him, allowed his temper to carry him so far as to say to him: "I will crush you as I crush this box!" At the same time hurling to the ground a gold snuff-box, on the lid of which was the portrait of Joséphine painted by Isabey.

The box was not broken, because there was a thick carpet on the floor, but the portrait was detached from the lid. Lucien picked up the box and the portrait, and handed them to his brother, saying in a bitter tone: "That is a pity; it is the portrait of your wife that you have broken, before you break with the original."

Mme. Bonaparte, on being informed of the incident, manifested much anxiety on hearing that her portrait had detached itself from the box: "Oh!" she cried, "it is all over! it is a sign of divorce! Bonaparte will separate himself from me as the snuff-box separated itself from the portrait!" It was after this incident, that Joséphine, full of confidence in Mdlle. Lenormand, already a famous fortune-teller, went to consult her, and thereby, not a little contributed to the latter's celebrity.

She proposed to cover the portrait which had risked destruction, with another absolutely identical, painted also by Isabey. And the Princess of Canino adds: "We are told that the snuff-box with the double portrait is at present in the possession of the Duchess of Braganza, granddaughter of the Empress Joséphine, by her father Eugène de Beauharnais, a Prince of Leuchtenberg. In 1819 and 1820, Queen Hortense used still to relate at the house of her mother-in-law Mme. Letizia, in Rome, how greatly Madame Bonaparte had been alarmed at this incident, so insignificant in itself.

* * *

A few days before the coronation, Joséphine had the presentiment of an impending misfortune. She suddenly fell into a state of melancholy that nothing could dissipate.* For some time she had flattered herself that Na-

* She is said to have wept bitterly during the whole of the ceremony which took place at Notre-Dame (*Souvenirs d'une sibylle*, p. 280). Bausset has written in his *Mémoires* that on the day of the coronation, when Their Majesties got into the coach which was to convey them, they made a mistake and sat down on the front seat. "This observation is doubtless rather finical, but I know not why, I have never been able to drive away the remembrance of it. Someone more superstitious than myself would have attached greater importance to it." Bausset, t. I, p. 29, quoted by Alb. Lombroso.

poleon loved her too dearly ever to abandon her.* She was bitterly undeceived.

. . . .

When the divorce was pronounced and the sad ceremony was over, the Emperor was escorted to his private apartments, where he remained the rest of the evening without receiving anyone; that night the palace was silent as a tomb.

People accustomed to take notice of everything remarked, that, during the ceremony, and notwithstanding the season, a fearful tempest broke over Paris. Torrents of rain and terrible blasts of wind struck terror into the minds of the timorous; it seemed as if the heavens manifested their reprobation of the act which put an end to the happiness of Joséphine; and, by an extraordinary coincidence, the same phenomenon occurred on the same day and at the same hour at Milan. †

We now come to the 1st January 1813. On that morning Joséphine was under the influence of real terror.

"Have you noticed," said she to those about her, "that the year commences on a Friday, § and that it is the year

* She was convinced that not only Napoleon, but his soldiers also considered her as the Emperor's "luck-bearer". Turquin writes on this subject in his *Mémoires* (1902, p. 204):

"The name of Joséphine was often on our lips at the time of our disasters. Speaking of the Emperor, they (the soldiers) used to say: *he ought not to have quitted the old woman, she brought him good luck and to us as well.*"

† *Anecdotes du temps de Napoléon* I, pp. 141–142.

§ "Joséphine, whose mind had been impressed ever since the Friday, first day of a year bearing the number 13, was much distressed at the news of the death of Bessières, and her terrors were reawakened. As for Duroc, as she did not like him, she paid but slight attention to his loss" (Turquan, *L'Impératrice Joséphine.*)

one thousand eight hundred and thirteen. This is a presage of great misfortunes."

It was useless to remark to her that these signs, if they really announced[*] misfortune, must prognosticate it equally to the whole world; to other countries as well as to France; it was useless to explain to her that she had no more cause for alarm than any one else: nothing could remove her singular prepossession. During the entire day she was still under the influence of this superstition and she could not forbear from endeavouring to make every one else partake in her fears.

Her daughter, Hortense, to whom she had given as a New-Year's present a splendid ornament of variously coloured gems, which had cost 50,000 francs shared her superstitious terrors. The evil days came and Joséphine did not fail to attribute them to the malign influence of the Friday and of the number thirteen; she could not understand that they were rather the fatal consequences of the Emperor's obstinacy in not consenting to conclude peace when he could still have done so honourably, and also to

she was more affected at the death of Lannes, whose end she had as it were foreseen. Mdlle. Avrillon has related that when he was on the point of starting for the campaign in Austria, in which he was destined to meet so tragical a fate, Marshal Lannes, whether from presentiment or for some other motive, had the utmost difficulty in parting from his family, delaying his departure as long as he possibly could. When he paid a visit to Joséphine, the Empress, noticing his dejection, could not refrain from making a remark on it.

"That is true," he answered; "for the first time I have a painful feeling for which I cannot account, and I never before felt it so hard to quit my family."

When the news of his death arrived, Mdlle. Avrillon reminded Joséphine of the interview she had not long before had with the Marshal. She did not fail to see therein a prophetic warning.

his bad management of the campaign in Germany. But, that, of course, she could not know.

* * *

This justice must be rendered to Napoleon, that, either by calculation or by foresight, he possessed a power of divination far superior to that which Joséphine attributed to herself. He seemed to have a prevision of what was about to happen to him, and the hesitation with which he has sometimes been reproached had no other causes than inward warnings, which often providentially saved him from a peril which he did not seem to wish to avoid.

It is well known that one of the greatest dangers that ever menaced the life of Bonaparte, at the outset of his career, was the explosion of the infernal machine, in the Rue Nicaise, on the evening of the 24th October 1800. An oratorio was to be performed. Joséphine and some of his intimate friends pressed him strongly to go there; he evinced the utmost repugnance to go out. He was fast asleep on a sofa; they were obliged to drag him from it, one brought him his sword, another his hat, and in fact they had to hustle him out.

Was not this repugnance rather a presentiment of the catastrophe, than the result of chance?

* * *

At Burgos, in 1808, the first information brought to Napoleon, on his arrival, was a piece of bad news, and

* Joseph Turquan. *l'Impératrice Joséphine, loc. cit.*

that was sufficient to cause him to be haunted by the most sinister forebodings.*

When he married Marie Louise, in 1810, † he was painfully impressed by hearing of the burning of the Schwartzenberg palace; to him it was an evil omen, and the exclamation that escaped him, at the battle of Dresden, at sight of the disorder which a ball from one of his cannons had caused in the Austrian staff, shows that this idea had fully taken possession of his mind. "Schwartzenberg," said he, with an air of evident relief, "*has purged off the fatality.*" This shows evidently that he had considered the presage as addressed to himself. §

The whole of Napoleon's staff, accompanying him on that day, 23rd August 1813, heard the expression. **

In the same year 1813, Napoleon made another remark, which again shows the peculiar dispositions of his mind: "It is remarkable," said he, "that Saint-Priest was mortally wounded by the same gunner who killed General

* Vide Marco de Saint-Hilaire, *Histoire de la garde impériale*, Brussels, 1846, t. I, p. 35; quoted by Mr. Alberto Lumbroso in his curious *Bibliographie de l'époque Napoléonienne.*

† He did not either conceal from Marie-Louise that he considered her to be the cause of all his misfortunes.

One afternoon as he returned on horseback from Saint-Cloud, and the archduchess preceded him in her carriage, her cashmere shawl, which was of a fiery red colour, fluttered from the window and frightened the Emperor's horse which threw its rider. The carriage stopped and the Emperor quickly got up again unhurt. Marie-Louise expressed the greatest regret; but he gave her the following harsh answer: "Madam, since you have been with me nothing but ill luck attends me." The Empress burst into tears. (*Bonapartiana*, pp. 98—99.)

§ Guillois, *loc. cit.* p. 190.

** Vide de Ségur and the *Manuscrit de 1813*, by Baron Fain.

Moreau. There is reason to exclaim: Providence! O Providence!"

On the other hand, the coincidence of the death of Desaix with that of Kleber caused him no particular astonishment. *

Speaking of General Laharpe, whom he styled: "a grenadier in height and in heart," Napoleon used to say, that during the entire evening which preceded the death of this brave man, his anxiety and lowness of spirits had been remarked. "He issued no orders, and was seemingly deprived of his ordinary faculties, and dominated by a fatal presentiment." †

* * *

But it was particularly in 1812, at the time of his fatal

The death of Lasalle, the hero of Wagram, and that of Cervoni made more impression upon him.

General Montholon, in his history of the captivity at Saint Helena, attributes the following words to the Emperor:

"Paul I had soul, but all his moral faculties were kept under by that same instinct of fatality that I have often observed among my own soldiers: Lasalle, for instance, who, in the middle of the night, wrote to me from the bivouac on the battlefield of Wagram to ask me to sign at once the decree of his title and estates as Count, and send it to his wife's son, because he felt that he was to die in battle next day, and the unfortunate man was right.

"It was the same with Cervoni, who was at my side at Eckmühl, exposed to fire for the first time since the war in Italy: 'Sire, you have obliged me to quit Marseilles which I loved, by writing to me that, for soldiers, the grades in the Legion of Honour could only be earned before the enemy: here I am, but it is my last day;' and a quarter of an hour later, a cannon ball carried his head off...."

† Guillois, *loc. cit.*, p. 191.

campaign in Russia, * that Napoleon had a real prophetic warning of the misfortunes awaiting him. †

On the 23rd June, the eve of the passage of the Niemen, before day-break, Napoleon arrived at the border of the forest of Polwiski. The Emperor, who had come hither in his carriage, mounted his horse and started off at a gallop, with General Haxo and a small escort, to reconnoitre the river in person. ‡

As usual, Napoleon proceeded at full gallop: suddenly his horse stumbled, and rolled into a ditch, carrying his rider with him. Everyone rushed forward, but the Emperor had already gained his feet, complaining only of a slight bruise on the hip.

In such circumstances he used generally to get angry, and to impute to those about him the blame of his own awkwardness. On this occasion he did not speak a word, agitated probably by fatal presentiments, for as one of those who accompanied the Emperor said concerning the incident: "in such great circumstances, on the eve of

* A Pole, perfectly acquainted with Russian history, told Napoleon one day that there existed a *saying* among the Russians "that the French would not come to Moscow as long as the cross remained on the steeple of the church of *John-Veliki*." Bonaparte had this cross taken down in order to justify the arrival of the French, proving thereby to the Russian nation that *his destinies were being accomplished*." The *Anti-Napoléon*, by a Corsican, p. 12.

† On three different occasions Napoleon could have escaped from Saint Helena, as we read in the book called: *Les Prophéties de Napoléon* (p. 11)..., he refused to leave Saint-Helena: "*It is not my destiny*, said he. *On the evening of the battle of Austerlitz I knew that I should die in this atrocious island, of which an honourable dog* (*sic*) *would not consent to be King*."

‡ Dumas, *Le Maître d'Armes*, Paris, 1866; p. 6, quoted by Mr. Alb. Lombroso, *loc. cit.*

grave events, one becomes superstitious in spite of one's self."

At the end of a few moments, Caulincourt felt his hand gripped by Berthier, who was galloping by his side, and who said: "It would be better for us not to cross the Niemen; this fall is of evil omen." *

The Emperor appeared all the next day to be preoccupied with this event, and his accident certainly caused him more annoyance than the slight lameness which resulted from it.

Baron Denniée, on his part, in another account of this campaign writes: † "Some citizens of Kowno had been brought before Napoleon . . . He learned that the Emperor Alexander assisted at a ball where, by a singular coincidence, the flooring of the principal saloon gave way towards midnight, at which hour the bridges had been thrown over the Niemen. It may easily be understood that all sorts of conjectures were made about this event, to give it a favourable interpretation!" §

Revue des Deux Mondes, 1894, p. 271, article by Mr. Alb. Vandal.

† Denniée, *Itinéraire de la Campagne de 1812*, Paris, 1842, p. 17.

§ Once only perhaps, did Napoleon have a fortunate presentiment. It was a few days before his entry into Berlin: Napoleon was surprised by a storm, on the road to Potsdam; it was so violent and the rain was so furious, that the Emperor was obliged to take refuge in a house. Wrapped in his grey overcoat, he was surprised to see there a young woman, who was visibly startled at his presence: she was an Egyptian, who had preserved for him that religious veneration that all the Arabs had for Napoleon. She was the widow of an officer of the army of the East, and fate had taken her to Prussia, to this house where she had been taken care of. The Emperor gave her a pension of 1200 francs a year, and took charge of the education of her son, the only inheritance left her by her husband: "This is the first time," said Napoleon to his officers, "that I dismounted to seek shelter from a storm; I had a presentiment that a good action was awaiting me here." *Bonapartiana*, p. 29.

To judge by the events which followed* it would seem as if Napoleon had indeed now exhausted the credit of lucky days which had been plentifully granted to him by Providence.

Our study of the *Superstitions of Napoleon* would be incomplete, were we not to add that Napoleon had a dread of certain dates, † of certain days, and of certain letters.

* Dr. Foissac relates the following anecdote, which well depicts the forebodings of the Emperor as to the fatal issue of the campaign of 1815.

Together with General Corbineau, he was one morning walking along the banks of the Sambre, and approached the fire of a bivouac. A pot was boiling, full of potatoes; he asked for one, which he began to eat, appearing to meditate, and then, not without a certain sadness, he pronounced the following broken words:

"After all, it's good, it's supportable ... with that one might live anywhere ... the moment is perhaps not far off ... Themistocles ..." and he resumed his walk.

The name of Themistocles is also mentioned in his letter to the Prince-Regent, and it is impossible to see in this remembrance of the name of the illustrious proscribed Athenian a mere play of the imagination; but his mind found in this ancient misfortune an analogy with his own, a presentiment of that which destiny reserved him. (*La Chance et la Destinée* pp. 634 and 635.)

† Mr. Guillois cites the characteristic letter written by Napoleon to Talleyrand, on the 25th December 1805, concerning the conclusion of peace with Austria: "If there are no means of signing at once, wait and sign at the New Year: for I have a few prejudices and I should be glad if the peace were to date from the renewal of the Gregorian calendar; which presages, I hope, as much happiness to my reign as did the old one. (Guillois, *loc. cit.* p. 100.)

There was in Napoleon's career a coincidence of dates which is at least strange: little Napoleon, the eldest son of Hortense, whom the Emperor loved so much and whom he would perhaps have made his heir, in which case the divorce would not have taken place, died of croup on the 5th of May 1805, exactly fourteen years day for day before the Emperor.

In this connection, when at Saint Helena, he called to mind that it was on a Friday * that he entered the school at Brienne, and that on seeing his father depart he burst into a flood of tears. "Born," said he, "with a strong propensity to superstition, I never undertook anything on a Friday without apprehension; moreover, I do not know whether it was by pure chance or by reason of the unfavourable state of mind into which the Friday put me, but the enterprises which I commenced on that day always

On the other hand there are other dates, the 15th August for instance, which rather brought him luck, of which Las Cases adduces as an example the extraordinary favour with which fortune gratified Napoleon during the voyage to Saint Helena: in the evening a game of vingt-et-un used to be played; Admiral Cockburn and some other Englishmen would sometimes join in. The Emperor used to withdraw when he had as usual lost ten or twelve napoleons; that happened to him every evening, because he always played doubling his stakes. One evening his napoleon brought him in one hundred; he won every time and wished to continue; but he perceived that Admiral Cockburn whose deal it was wished the game to cease. Everyone marvelled at this extraordinary run of luck, when one of the Englishmen present drew attention to the fact that it was the 15th August the birthday and the *fête* of the Emperor.

He was fond of recapitulating the fortunate dates of his career: Austerlitz; the anniversary of his coronation; Friedland; Marengo.

On the eve of the battle of Friedland, he thus addressed Marbot (*See Mémoires de Marbot*, t. I. p. 384):

"Have you a good memory?"

"Tolerable, Sire."

"Well then! What anniversary is it to-day, the 14th of June?"

"That of Marengo."

"Yes, yes, that of Marengo, and I am going to beat the Russians as I beat the Austrians."

* He took very good care never to fight a battle or to sign a treaty on a Friday (Pilot, quoted by Sébillot in the *Revue des traditions populaires*, 1891, p. 280).

succeeded badly. For instance, among others, I remember that the night of my departure from Saint Cloud for the campaign in Russia, was a Friday night."

It was a superstition regarding dates that in 1815, on his return from the Island of Elba, made him wish to re-enter Paris on the 20th of March,* the anniversary of the birth of the king of Rome. And yet, it was in the night of the 19th to 20th March (1814), that being at Fontainebleau, he perceived before him a broken mirror: soon afterwards he was defeated at Waterloo. † The

* No date brought more souvenirs to his mind than the 20th March. As a fact, the ephemerides of the 20th March in the life of Napoleon, are particularly remarkable.

It was on the 20th March 1779 that Charles Bonaparte, the father of Napoleon, came with his son to Paris for the purpose of placing him at the military school at Brienne.

The 20th March 1785 Napoleon was informed of his father's death.

20th March 1794 Napoleon arrived in Nice as Commander in Chief of the army of Italy.

20th March 1800, battle of Heliopolis.

20th March 1804, the Duke of Enghien was shot in the night at Vincennes.

20th March 1808, abdication of Charles IV of Spain.

20th March 1809, battle of Abensberg.

20th March 1811, birth of the King of Rome.

20th March 1814, taking of Toul.

20th March 1815, return of Napoleon to Paris.

20th March 1821, Napoleon wrote the last codicil to his will at Saint Helena.

† While he was at Saint Helena, Mr. de Montholon had a daughter: he asked the Emperor if he would deign to be her godfather, and Napoleon consented. When Mr. de Montholon had gone: "Alas! I did not dare to tell him," exclaimed Napoleon, "that his daughter was born on an unlucky day: to-day is the anniversary of Waterloo." (*Prophéties de Napoléon*, p. 88.)

remembrance of the broken looking-glass came back to him after the battle; suddenly he interrupted the dejected silence of those around him with this exclamation: "D....d mirror! I had indeed foreseen it!" *

The number *thirteen* always caused him an apprehension that he could scarcely combat. M. d'Hédouville relates how attentively he listened to the account he gave him of the death of d'Esménard, the author of the *Poème de la Navigation*. Exiled *pro forma* to Italy, Esménard was preparing to return to France. On the eve of his departure from Naples, he took part in a banquet given in his honour by some Frenchmen among whom was Mr. d'Hédouville. All at once he noticed that they were thirteen at table and became quite troubled. First of all the others joked about the matter, and then tried to reason with him; but nothing could divert him, nor dissipate his sad presentiments. He started the next day, and his carriage being upset near to Fondi, he fell over a precipice and was killed: or, as some suppose, he was assassinated by brigands. †

* * *

Napoleon did not only attribute a cabalistic influence to days and dates.

By what seems an inexplicable bizarrerie he always considered the letter *M* as fateful.

This prepossession was not quite so unjustifiable as it at first may seem to be.

Mortier had been one of his best generals.

* See la *France Nouvelle*, 10th September 18[illegible].

† Cited by Dr. Foissac in *La Chance et la Destinée*.

Three of his ministers were named Maret, Mollien, Montalivet.

The name of his first chamberlain was Montesquiou.

The Duke of Bassano, Maret, was his favourite adviser.

Six of his marshals had names commencing with the letter *M*: Massena, Marmont, Macdonald, Mortier, Moncey and Murat.

Marbeuf was the first to recognize his capacities at the military school.

But Moreau was a traitor to him, † Mallet conspired against him, Murat abandoned him; as also did Marmont.

Metternich had beaten him on the diplomatic field.

It was to Captain Maitland that he surrendered on board the *Bellerophon*.

Marengo was, it is true, his first victory, gained over General Melas, a predestined name! He also gained the battles of Montenotte, Millesimo, Mondovi, Montmirail, Montereau.

On the contrary, he was completely crushed at Mont-Saint-Jean (Waterloo).

Milan was the first city he entered as a conqueror; Moscow was the last.

He lost Egypt with Menou, and it was Miollis who, by his order, took the Pope prisoner.

At Saint Helena, two of those who remained faithfully attached to him, were his valet de chambre Marchand, and General Montholon.

* On another occasion, in 1814, the resistance of Soissons might have saved the Emperor, by securing for him the result of his flank march on the allied forces: the name of the General commanding in that town was *Moreau*; he opened the gates too soon, and Napoleon, seeing his plan fail, exclaimed: "That name Moreau has always brought me ill luck." (Guillois, *loc. cit.* p. 190).

Finally was it not at La Malmaison that he passed the only few hours of calm and happiness that he enjoyed during his chequered existence.

* * *

It was at La Malmaison that the following adventure is said to have happened to him and with the account of which we shall terminate this study.

It was shortly after his coronation. The Emperor had in his hands a very old book, which had just been brought to him.

The book bore the title: *Livres de Prophéties* by Master Noël Olivarius, Doctor of medicine. "Here," said Napoleon, handing to the Empress this parchment covered book yellow with age, "see what it is and read it to us."

And Josephine read aloud:

"*Prediction of Master Noël Olivarius.*"

"Well?" said the Empress.

"It is said that I am spoken of therein" replied the Emperor.

"What? in a book published in 1542?"

"Well, read it."

The Empress tried to read it; but as the language was old French and the characters badly formed, she took some moments to first read over to herself the three pages composing the chapter, and then with a firm voice she commenced as follows:

"Italian Gaul shall see born not far from her bosom, a supernatural being: this man will come early from the sea, will come to learn the language and manners of the

Celtic-Gauls, will open to himself, though still young, and through a thousand obstacles, a career among soldiers, and will become their greatest chief. This sinuous road will give him much trouble, he will wage war near to his native land for a lustre and more....

"He will wage war beyond the seas with great glory and valour, and warring once again throughout the Roman world.... Will give laws to the Germans, will spread trouble and terror among the Celtic-Gauls and will then be called King, but afterwards will be called *Imperator* by an enthusiastic people.

"He will wage war everywhere throughout the Empire, driving out princes, lords, and kings, for two lustres and more....

"He will come to the city, commanding many great things: edifices, sea-ports, aqueducts, canals; he will alone by means of great riches accomplish as much as all the Romans, and all within the domination of the Gauls. Of wives he will have two.... And but one son only.

"He will go on warring until where the lines of longitude and latitude do cross fifty-five months (*sic*). There his enemies will burn a great city and he will enter there and go out again with his men from beneath the ashes and great ruins, and his men having neither bread nor water, by great and killing cold, will be so unfortunate that two thirds of his army will perish, and further one half of others, then no longer under his domination.

"Far away, the great man abandoned, treacherously forsaken by his own, hunted out in his turn, with great loss in his own city by great European population: in his place will be put the old King of the cape. (*a*)

(a) King Capet? (*Transl.*)

"He compelled to be in exile in the sea whence he came so young, and near to his native land, living there for eleven moons with a few of his own true friends and soldiers, who were only seven times two in number, as soon as the eleven moons are run, he and his men take ship and land in the country of Celtic-Gaul.

"Driven out once more by European trinity, after three moons and one third of a moon, is again replaced by old King of the cape, whereat he is thought to be dead by his soldiers, who in these times will press Penates to their heart....

"And he, saving the ancient remains of the old blood of the cape, rules the destinies of the world, dictating, sovereign counsel of every nation and of every people, fixes basis of everlasting fruit and dies...."

Joséphine, surprised at what she had just read, closed the book and asked Napoleon what he thought of this strange prediction. But the Emperor not wishing to appear to attach any importance to the prophecies of Master Olivarius by commenting on them, contented himself with replying: "Predictions always say what you exactly want them to say; though I admit that this one has much astonished me." And he changed the conversation.

* * *

What is most singular is that the history of this prophecy was not written afterwards, as might be supposed.

The first person who unearthed the book of Olivarius, was François de Metz, cousin of François de Neufchateau and secretary general to the Commune of Paris.

One day in June 1793, a great many libraries had been

pillaged; the big hall in which these papers were collected was full. François de Metz and several employees were busy sorting the manuscripts, for on that day but few printed books had been brought in.

Most of the books came from the libraries of palaces or from monasteries. The demagogues had brought them there in heaps: some were preserved and others were burned. Up till that moment the employees of the Commune had only catalogued books of little importance, when a small 12mo volume attracted their attention.

It was the Book of Prophecies composed by Philippe Noël Olivarius, "Doctor of medicine, Surgeon and Astrologer." The book contained several other prophecies, without the name of the author, but this one was signed. On the last page was the word *Finis* in Gothic letters, and lower down: 1542, in XVIth century figures.

François de Metz read it through, but failed to make out the sense, as he admitted to his daughter Mme. de M. . . . Nevertheless, on account of the singularity of the book, he copied it and added it to several others which were afterwards found among his papers. The textual copy of the prophecy of Olivarius, in the hand-writing of François de Metz, is dated the year 1793; there can be no doubt on the subject.*

* * *

* The *Mémorial de Rouen* of 1840 having inserted the prophecy of Olivarius in one of its numbers, a lady residing in Rouen, in the Rue Beauvoisine, went to the office of the paper, and asked to see the number in question, in order to compare it with a copy she had herself taken from the book of Olivarius before the Revolution, and long before Bonaparte was thought of. With the exception of two words the two copies were exactly similar. (See *Mémorial* of 1st October 1840.)

Bonaparte had smiled when in 1800 he read this prophecy: but in 1808, he could not read it again without turning pale. It is said,* that at that time he consulted a theologian of the seminary of Saint Sulpice, asking him whether religion obliged one to believe in prophecy. The priest answered, without much compromising himself, in the words of the creed: "The Spirit of God spake through the prophets."

This prophecy was printed in 1815, and afterwards inserted in the *Mémoires de Joséphine* (Editions of 1820 and 1827). It is said to have been lastly published in a book that we have been unable to discover: the *Recueil de prophéties* published by a bookseller named Bricon.

When this prophecy is examined with a certain amount of attention, it may be noticed that all which relates to the reign of Napoleon and to the return of the Bourbons came to pass exactly. But by torturing the text, it is equally possible to discover therein the troubles of 1827, the plots of the Liberals and… even the Revolution of 1830!

* * *

We will waste no more time over these dreams mixed up with extravagancies, but we judged it proper to avoid at least the reproach of not being armed with sufficient authorities (they may be, in fact, styled almost redundant) in order to prove that Napoleon had a marked leaning towards the supernatural.

Notwithstanding all, and having arrived now at the end of this study, we must admit with some embarrassment that we hesitate to draw conclusions. Napoleon was

* *Almanach Astrologique*, 1840, pp. 104–109.

at once the intuitive man and the man of action; let us admit that this faculty of intuition was pushed so far as to enable him to guess the future, to give him that *far insight* which will sometimes reveal to him beforehand events still hidden in the undefined haze of a distant future, and we shall be enabled to explain those presentiments, those prophecies, which a superficial examination would have so easily induced us to liken to idle dreams. If to that is added that he was gifted with a most fertile imagination and immeasurable ambition (which prodigious good fortune had not a little contributed to develop), besides what has been so happily styled the intoxicating madness of power, will there be cause for astonishment that he should harbour the illusion to believe and proclaim himself divine, — much more a god than a prophet?

* * *

Napoleon had faith in Providence and in an immortal soul, and this admixture of fatalism and of spiritualism is not so contradictory as it would at first sight appear. He believed not only that the soul was separate from the body; but that it could live a life of its own in an atmosphere special to itself, which is a domain that our senses do not permit us to explore, the domain of the occult and of the marvellous.

"Chance, so often alluded to," said he in 1816, "chance of which the ancients made a divinity, which every day astounds us, falls upon us at every moment; chance, after all only appears so singular to us, so fantastical, because we ignore the secret and quite natural causes which have brought it about, and this occult combination it is that suffices to create the marvellous and to breed mysteries." * Does not that signify, that for Napoleon chance was a factor which it was necessary to take into account, as well as everything that produces great things, although our human intelligence naturally limited, does not always succeed in giving us a satisfactory explanation.

As for justifying his superstitious *manias*, the task would be too *arduous* for us to attempt to undertake it.

Far from judging too severely the diverse conceptions of a brain which may have had moments of weakness from intense overwork, we prefer adopting the opinion expressed by one of the most rational of Napoleon's panegyrists: that man is necessarily imperfect, and that however high he may rank in the hierarchy of intelligence, there will always be found in him, by reason of psychological predispositions, the characters of weakness that remind him of the common and inferior origin of the human creature. †

* Guillois, *loc. cit.* p. 150.

† Id., *Ibidem.*

THE CASE

OF

MADAME RECAMIER

...Yet this rule I advise you, that you communicate vulgar secrets to vulgar friends, but higher and secret to higher and secret friends only. Give hay to an ox, and sugar to a parrot only; understand my meaning, lest you be trod under the oxen's feet, as oftentimes it fell out.

The ABBOT *of the* MONASTERY *of* HERBIPOLIS *to* CORNELIUS AGRIPPA, *the astrologer of* CHARLES V. (*Ann.* 1510.)

THE "CASE" OF MADAME RECAMIER.

It is a source of astonishment to all writers who have taken an interest in Mme. Recamier, that this queen of beauty should have ruled hearts and minds by the power of her charms alone.

This rare gift was possessed by Mme. Recamier in the highest degree. There were other women more beautiful, none was ever more seductive; and this fascinating power did not help her only to conquer a number of adorers, but also to keep them as so many devotees prostrated at the feet of their Divinity.

By her side, love changed into friendship without leaving the least malice in disappointed hearts; it seemed as if what had been hoped for was too exalted, and the little she granted was still a greater boon than the love of other women.*

Could it then be possible that "her heart was inaccessible to any but placid sentiments," and that, like a salamander, she had the privilege of passing through flames unscathed?

Correspondance littéraire, 25 Dec. 1859, article by Mr. Vallier.

Ought we to give her the merit of that virtue which historians have been pleased to recognize in her?

Would it be too hardy to attribute it to a vice of physical organisation which would suffice to explain what might otherwise have been mistaken, very wrongly, for more or less calculated reticence?

When the number of those who succumbed to the incomparable fascination of this siren is taken into consideration, without a single one of them having been able to flatter himself with having conquered her; when the talent is observed which she engaged to spare so many susceptibilities, "ready to revolt at a smile, a word or a more or less trifling attention," is it to be imputed to delicacy, to exquisite tact or, rather to a complete absence of physical sensation?

* *

It is in the *Souvenirs* which retrace the life of Mme. Recamier that we are tempted to seek the solution of this strange mystery. Others before us have felt the same temptation, and their anticipations were not completely thwarted: hardly are the first pages of this memorial opened than the enigma is almost easy to decipher.

"When, in 1793, M. Recamier asked for the hand of Juliette, he was himself forty-two years old, and she was only fifteen. It was, however, quite voluntarily, without fear or repugnance, that she accepted his offer... M. Recamier never had any other than a paternal relationship to his wife; he never treated the young and innocent child who bore his name otherwise than as girl whose beauty charmed his eyes, and whose celebrity flattered his vanity."

A lover of forty-two is rather old; but he is not yet reduced to the part of the heavy father of comedy.

But, it has been remarked,* between the lover and the father, there was another place, that of husband; why was it not occupied?

From which side came the resistance? From the husband? but he was much in love; and, besides, he had not yet come to the age of voluntary abdication.

Therefore would not the fault seem to be imputable to the wife?†

* *Correspondance littéraire*, loc. cit.

† The following unpublished letter, addressed by Ballanche to one of his correspondents, M. Sauvage de Saint-Marc, on the occasion of the death of M. Recamier, sheds a new light on the nature of the attachment professed by Mme. Recamier for her husband:

"30th March.

"Sir, and dear friend.

"I begin by announcing painful news to you. M. Recamier had been unable to quite recover from the malady which he had while you were in Paris. Did he perhaps venture out too soon, or was it that he ought to have taken more care of himself? But the fireside was too tedious for him; that is easy to understand in a man who was so accustomed to an active life out of doors. Perhaps also, it may have been that his age no longer permitted him to successfully resist that chronic catarrh, from which I have always known him to suffer, and which caused him frequent attacks of pneumonia. On Sunday evening he was suddenly stricken by an access of that nature. His strength was exhausted, and he expired the following day, that is to say on Monday, at half past three in the afternoon. In the morning it was hoped that he might get better, or at all events that with great care his life might be prolonged for some months. Doctor Recamier saw no immediate danger. It was only towards three o'clock in the afternoon that the symptoms of his malady became alarming, at half past three he was dead. So you see the end was neither long nor painful. But we were all of us affected by this unexpected blow. He died in the presence of Doctor

Then again it is difficult to form a very precise opinion,— to judge, at all events, only by the confidences of the interested party, or rather by those who were the closest witnesses of her life.

If we question the latter, that is to say Mme. Lenormant, the author of the best informed work concerning Mme. Recamier, of whom she was the niece, they give us the following answer, which serves but to increase our embarrassment:

"She was wanting in those affections which are the true felicity and the real dignity of woman: *she was neither wife nor mother*, and her arid heart, hungry for tenderness and devotedness, sought its nurture in a passionate homage the language of which was pleasing to her ears."

This *want of love* would seem to have been able to meet with satisfaction, on a certain occasion: this was at Coppet, when she listened to the sentimental declarations of Prince Augustus of Prussia.

On this occasion, at all events, the angelic creature consented for once, to don her terrestrial envelope.

Recamier and of another physician who had accompanied him. He expired while the priest was administering to him extreme unction. Mme. Recamier, who had not quitted him, was also there. Mme. Lenormant was in the next room, without being aware that the end was so imminent. But she knew that the final catastrophe could not be long delayed. Mme. Recamier had been unwell for the last few days; Mme. Lenormant also was not very well. She was rather fatigued by a pregnancy the term of which was approaching. However there is every reason to believe that she will this time come safely to port. Mme. Recamier was more cast down than any of us, because she had never believed that M. Recamier's health was so much shattered as it was in reality. She relied upon his strong constitution which, according to her, would still give him several years to live . . ."

Mme. Recamier had been positively touched and moved by the impassioned accents of the Prussian prince.

"For a moment she accepted his offer of marriage; a proof not only of the sincere passion, but of the esteem of a prince of royal blood, strongly imbued with ideas of the privileges and dignities of his rank.

"Promises were exchanged. The kind of bond which had united the lovely Juliette to M. Recamier was of that nature which the Catholic religion itself declares null. Ceding to the emotion of the sentiment she inspired in Prince Augustus, Juliette wrote to M. Recamier asking him to consent to the rupture of their union. He replied that he would consent to the annulling of their marriage, if such was her desire, but appealing to all the sentiments of the noble heart to whom he addressed himself, he reminded her of the affection he had entertained towards her since her infancy, *he even expressed a regret for having respected certain susceptibilities and repugnances without which the thought of such a separation could never have arisen;* but he added, that if Mme. Recamier persisted in her resolution, to break their union, he begged that the separation might take place, not in Paris, but in some place out of France, to be fixed upon between them."

An appeal to such noble sentiments was heard, and M. Recamier continued to be the husband of the lovely Juliette.

* * *

But Prince Augustus was not the only one to occupy the *Souvenirs* of Mme. Recamier. We can also read in this martyrology the names of: Ballanche, "an innocent and tender soul, to whom abnegation was never a sacrifice;" Duke Mathieu de Montmorency, "an ardent heart, tempered by faith;" and lastly, Chateaubriand. They did not all die, but they were all wounded.

Among the lot, however, is there not one, who could boast of having taken possession? Not one; not even Chateaubriand, inclined as he was to the sin of vanity.

In this connection, it is related, that one day Mme. Hortense Allard, the blue-stocking who wrote her living reminiscences under the singular title of: *Les Enchantements de Prudence*, reproached the author of the *Mémoires d'Outre Tombe* (Chateaubriand), her lover for the nonce, with his infidelities with the goddess of L'Abbaye-aux-Bois (Mme. Recamier).

"My dear Hortense," replied Chateaubriand, in order to calm her, "you make me laugh with your jealousy. Mme. Recamier is for me neither a love, nor a friendship, *a custom in fact that is nothing more than a habit.*"

It may suffice to add that at that time Chateaubriand was a septuagenarian, in order that our readers may know what sense may be attached to this affirmation, which otherwise might be interpreted differently.

Chateaubriand, at his age, would have been but badly fitted to play the part of Cherubino. If he ever had that foolish notion, the following quatrain, had it chanced to come before his eyes, ought to have sufficed to confine his pretentions to their proper limits:

> Juliette et René s'aimaient d'amour si tendre
> Que Dieu, sans les punir a pu leur pardonner,
> Il n'avait pas voulu que l'une pût donner
> Ce que l'autre ne pouvait prendre.*

* Juliette and René loved each other so,
That God, compassionate for mortal's woe
Would not permit the one to bestow
A pleasure the other could never know.

The mystery clears up singularly, and we are very near seeing through it.

Artifices of language in vain seek to hide the truth; it still will break forth.

Guizot had the ability to clearly hint at a thing without saying it in so many words, but his periphrase allows the veiled meaning to appear so clearly that the question is whether anything could possibly be added:

"Madame Recamier," writes this subtle diplomatist, "wanted two things which alone can fill the heart and the joy of a woman... the joys of family love and the transports of passion. Are we to seek the cause in her destiny or in the very ground of her nature?"

A writer who uses less ceremony, although he was the pupil of one who was a master in the art of saying every thing without transgressing the rules of propriety, A. J. Pons, who had been one of the secretaries of Sainte-Beuve, has said, more explicitly than Guizot:

"Nature forbade her to give herself up wholly, and none of her adorers could pass the *bar* which defended her virtue."

It is not impossible, to say more clearly that it was a fault of conformation that gave Mme. Recamier full latitude to give herself up to flirtation which she knew could not compromise her?

A lively poetaster, still more irreverent, has written that the lovely Juliette could no more go to happiness than she could lead others there, because, says our quidam,

The streamlet of love was dammed across.

For a man who most probably had not been there to see, this was an audacious affirmation.

* * *

We would not like to be accused of greater temerity, in going beyond the field of permissible hypothesis. It is therefore only an hypothesis that we will risk in comparing together the *case* of Mme. Recamier with the *case* of queen Elizabeth of England,* and also with that which

* Queen Elizabeth presented an .. anomaly nearly similar. This is what we read on that subject in the *Curiosités de la littérature*, (t. 2, p. 582):

"No one doubts that Queen Elizabeth of England had experienced the passion of love in its highest degree, particularly for her favourite the Earl of Essex; but all our readers are not aware that this passion never could receive satisfaction; physical reasons opposed it; *the satisfaction of her love would have entailed the loss of her life.* She was so strongly convinced of the truth of this, that one day, when she was warmly pressed by the Duke of Alençon to marry him, she replied that she did not think herself so little loved by her subjects that they should wish to see her die a premature death."

The curiosity of the reader will find food for observation in some strange anecdotes concerning our Virgin Queen, in MARIE REINE D'ECOSSE VENGÉE, by Mr. Whitaker. "She could neither," he says, in rather too pronounced language, "fulfil the duties of a wife, nor taste the pleasures of a prostitute: she was constantly seeking to extinguish a fire which consumed her."

PIERRE BAYLE, in his *Dictionnaire*, 5th edit (1734) vol. II., page 731, a work now little consulted, but very valuable still for its out-of-the-way and really profound enquiries, has the following concerning the physical formation of Queen Elizabeth.

"Je ne sai pas si tout ce que l'on a dit ou écrit des amours et des amans de la Reine Elizabeth est bien vrai; mais il est certain qu'elle n'avait point de vulve; et que la même raison, qui l'empêchait de se marier, la devait empescher d'aimer le déduit. Elle pouvait bien aimer, et elle aima en effet passionnément le Comte d'Essex; mais de la manière qu'elle était faite, elle ne pouvoit connoitre charnellement aucun homme, sans souffrir d'extrêmes douleurs, ni devenir grosse; sans s'exposer inévitablement à perdre la vie dans le travail de l'accouchement. Et elle en était si persuadée, qu'un jour qu'elle fut priée avec des instances importunes, de vouloir

one of our most distinguished colleagues * has described at length in a novel which had its hour of celebrity, and which has permitted all women afflicted with the infirmity of Mme Recamier, to be treated as the *eternally wounded.* †

épouser le Duc d'Alençon, qui la recherchait avec passion, elle répondit, qu'elle ne croioit pas être si peu aimée de ses sujets qu'ils voulussent l'ensevelir avant le tems."

Amelot de la Houssaie (Lettres d'Ossat vol. III., p. 390).

We may explain that Amelot de la Houssaie is commenting on the letter CARDINAL D'OSSAT had written from Rome, 1st February, 1595, with reference to a Discourse of POPE CLEMENT VIII regarding the state of England at that time and the possibility of its being reconquered, and it is under "Remark III" anent the probability of a successor to the Queen of England that the passage cited occurs.

We subjoin a translation of this passage for those unable to read the original.

"I know not whether all that has been said or written concerning the loves and the lovers of Queen Elizabeth be quite true; but it is certain that she had no union, and that the same reason which hindered her from marrying, prevented her having any inclination for the pastime. She could love, and indeed she passionately loved Essex; but by reason of the way she was made, she could have no carnal knowledge of man without suffering excessive pains, nor become pregnant without inevitably exposing herself to lose her life in the labour of bringing forth. And she was so convinced of this, that one day when the Duke of Alençon who, ardently in love with her, was urgently importuning her to marry: she answered him, that she did not believe that her subjects cared so little for her as to wish her in the grave before her time."

* Mr. Vigné d'Octon (Dr. Paul Vigné).

† We recommend those of our readers whom the subject may interest, to consult the learned *Traité de Gynécologie* (3rd edition) of our master Dr. S. Pozzi, in the chapters: *Sténoses et atrésies de la vulve et du vagin*, p. 1165; *Vaginisme*, p. 1072—1057; *Malformations*

The following note has been furnished us by a medical friend; we decided to insert it because it shows that the *Récamier* case is not so isolated as may at first appear.

"While a student in a German University, some years ago, I was intimately acquainted with a young doctor who had just been appointed resident surgeon to a military hospital. He decided to marry, and being young and handsome, had no difficulty in finding a willing partner. His choice fell upon a charming young lady whom he had long admired and who reciprocated his feelings.

"The marriage took place and joy seemed to await the fortunate pair; but alas! there was a *bar* to their mutual happiness, an impediment of so sturdy a nature that intromission was impossible, or could only have been gained by an effort of cruel brutality. Under these circumstances surgical intervention was resorted to as the only means to overcome the difficulty. A colleague having been called in, a careful examination was made of the case, and an operation decided on. The patient having been chloroformed, a rapid cruciform incision removed the objectionable barrier, and thenceforward the nights of the honey-moon glided smoothly on and presented no further difficulties. Ultimately the lady lived to see crop up around her several charming little pictures of herself."

FICTITIOUS VIRGINITY.

The following has been sent us by a West End doctor of wide travel, who vouches for the truth of the practice.

du vagin, p. 1217; *Absence de la vulve*, p. 1182; and *Malformations de la vulve*, p. 1178.

Doctor Ricard, Professor, and Fellow of the Paris Faculty of medicine, has given, in his lectures on surgical pathology, in 1896, some curious cases of malformation of the genital organs.

"The Chinese, who are a very ingenious people, have discovered a way of forming a new virginity when by some accident that object has gone astray. The method consists in astringent lotions applied to the parts, the effect of which so draws them together that a certain amount of vigour is required in order to pass through, and if on a nuptial night, the husband is convinced of having overcome the usual barrier. To make the illusion more complete a leech-bite is made just inside the critical part and the little wound is plugged with a minute pellet of vegetable tinder, with this result that the effort made by the husband to overcome the difficulty displaces the pellet and a slight flow of blood ensues.

See also MANTEGAZZA "*I Riti e le Feste Nuziali*"; he states:

"*Una celebre etera parigina dei nostri tempi si vantava di aver venduto ottantadue volte la propria verginità.*"

Many and diverse are the tricks resorted to by the women of different countries to simulate a virginity lost and the literature on the subject is fairly large.

See PLOSS. "DAS WEIB in der NATUR und VOLKERKUNDE." (Leipzig 1884, B.I.)

GUÉRARD, *Sur la valeur de l'existence de la membrane hymen comme signe de virginité.* (Ann. d'Hyg. 1872, 2e serie, t. XXXVIII, page 409).

BERGERET, *Des fraudes dans l'accomplissement des fonctions génératrices*, PARIS, 1873.

TAYLOR'S *Medical Jurisprudence*, 3rd Edit. p. 807.

The Slavonians, it appears, hold virginity in the highest esteem. In South Russia the bride, "*prima di dare al marito le prove autentiche della propria verginità deve mostrarsi affatto nuda a testimonii, onde mostrare che non ha nascosto qualche artifizio per simulare ciò che non ha. Si suole anche chiamare un altro a sverginare* (to devirginate) *la sposa nella prima notte del matrimonio, nel caso in cui lo sposo non possa farlo.*"

MANTEGAZZA, *Gli Amori degli Uomini* (p. 95 vol I). *Mil.* 1892.

Some peoples, on the other hand, set no price on this commodity as is shown by the communication of JAGOR to the BERLIN ANTHROPOLOGICAL SOCIETY. In the Canary Islands there used to exist, what may be termed, *stupratio officialis*, and perhaps, I cannot do better than quote the exact text. "On ne connait point d'exemple d'une coutume aussi barbare que celle qui s'y était établie, d'avoir des officiers publics et payés même fort chèrement, pour ôter la virginité aux filles, parce qu'elle était regardée comme un obstacle aux plaisirs du mari. A la verité il ne reste aucune trace de cette infâme pratique depuis la domination des Espagnols . . . Mais aujourdhui même un Bisayos s'afflige de trouver sa femme à l'épreuve du soupçon parce qu'il en conclut que n'ayant été désirée de personne, elle doit avoir quelque mauvaise qualité qui l'empêchera d'être heureux avec elle."

In that curious old book "GYNAECOLOGIA HISTORICO-MEDICA HOC EST CONGRESSUS MULIEBRIS CONSIDERATIO, etc.;" (*Dresden*, 1730) page 418, SCHURIGIUS gives a remarkable instance of a custom prevalent in India, of deflowering young brides by means of an enormous priapus in the temples.

Schurigius quotes from WALTHER SCHULTZENS' *Ost-Indi-*

anische Reise, (fol. *Amsterd.* 1676), and we cannot do better than quote his words:

"Ehren die Einwohner des Koenigreichs CANO-NOR den PRIAPUM als einen Gott, und richten sein Bildniss oeffentlich in ihren PAGODEN auf, wohin sich die angehende Ehe-Leute verfügen müssen. Durch diesen PRIAPUM wird denen Jungfern, auf eine schmertzliche Art und mit Gewalt, und mit Hülffe derer gegenwaertigen Freunde und Verwandten ihre Jungferschaft genommen, worüber sich alsdenn der Bräutigam erfreuet das der schaendliche und verfluchte Abgott ihr diese Ehre bewiesen, in der Hoffnung, er werde nun einen bessern Ehe-Segen erhalten."

For further details see "UNTRODDEN FIELDS OF ANTHROPOLOGY". (*Paris*, 1897).

"PADLOCKS AND GIRDLES OF CHASTITY" (*Liseux*, Paris 1892) gives some curious information in connection with this subject.

DR. PAUL MANTEGAZZA * gives the following curious case which is well worth quoting because it throws, combined with his remarks, a flood of light upon the subject of our enquiry.

In cases of nymphomania or female aphrodisia, several physicians have recommended amputation of the clitoris, but I am altogether opposed to that mutilation. It is very rare that a moral, hygienic, and therapeutic cure does not succeed in overcoming no matter what genesic fury, and one ought not, by a cruel and irreparable operation, deprive a woman of an organ which procures her the

* IGIENE DELL' AMORE (*Milan*, 1888).

most lively enjoyments. A very eloquent fact convinced me of this: it is the case of a woman who underwent clitoridectomy at the hands of one of the most celebrated Italian surgeons, Peruzzi di Lugo, and in which the amelioration lasted but a very short time.*

This unfortunate, virtuous, and very pious woman had all her life to fight against this ungovernable lust; the mere rubbing of her shift against her genital parts, and, in her most ardent age, the least movement of her thighs or that of a coach would provoke a venereal excitation. She admitted to me that she had a pollution even during the operation at the moment of the section of the clitoris, and I believe it, for when I examined her, several months after the operation, all upset with the dread of a re-appearance of the nymphomania, beneath my eyes, at the sole contact of my hands, whilst crying and cursing at her nature, she was seized with a fearful voluptuous spasm. And yet she was a virgin and assured me that she had never consented to marry because she would not make another victim share her misery. She further added: "I know that I should have killed him!"

When Peruzzi published this observation, which we subjoin in a note, he thought that she was cured, but I saw her again a prey to her former malady and I encouraged her to place great hope in the cessation of her menses, the signs of which had already manifested themselves. Since then I have lost sight of her: she was of dark complexion, with a slight mustache. She was poor.

1. The following is the history of this case published by PERUZZI in the *Hippocratique*:

"N.M., aged 50 years, has her menses regularly. In

* IGIENE DELL' AMORE (Milano 1889).

her youth she gave herself up to masturbation until the age of 12 years, at which period reason and a moral education caused her to abandon this habit. While a young girl she had to withstand several assaults upon her virtue, but she repelled them with energy and courage. However her senses had been strongly excited thereby, but only momentarily. Towards her 24th year, these voluptuous excitations now repeated themselves, often even without being provoked by the presence of individuals of the opposite sex, and they persisted until a spontaneous pollution (I beg to be pardoned this improper expression) would put an end to this sexual erothism; after which she was exhausted, dejected and ashamed.

"This state continued for 26 years, becoming constantly more serious and more insupportable. The most insignificant causes provoked these fits; ordinary shocks, the inevitable contacts produced by the cares of cleanliness, the bed-sheets even by their pressure were the cause of excitation, and at last the pollutions were several times repeated during the twenty-four hours.

"*Subjective symptoms.*—Besides those already noted, pains in the lumbar regions, in the buttocks, in the epigastrium, a sensation of twitching along the inner sides of the thighs, burning during frequent emission of urine, defecation difficult, great prostration, dizziness, buzzing in the ears, anorexy and even profound aversion to food with continual thirst.

"*Objective symptoms*—Nothing in the urethra, nor in the bladder, nor in the vagina, the uterus, or the rectum; the hymen intact, the clitoris developed and congested, promptly erected at the least contact; the big *labia* are turgid and purple in colour, leucorrhœic flux from the genitals, remarkable general emaciation.

"I diagnosticated a nevrosis of the genital organs against which the best conducted therapeutical treatments had been unavailing (bromide of potassium had for a long time been administered in proper doses). On reflecting that the irritation started from the clitoris and was thence irradiated to the adjoining parts, and bearing in mind the lessons of Lallemand and of the celebrated Baker Brown,(a) I proposed as a last resource to resort to clitoridectomy. The operation was accepted by the patient in perfect knowledge of its nature; the physician who attended also approved of it.

"My colleague and friend, Doctor V. Liverani, who was at Lugo on the 2nd of May, was kind enough to consent to assist me in the operation, in which I decided to follow the precepts of Baker Brown, unless some unforeseen circumstance should make me act differently.

"Doctor Baker Brown recommends to seize the clitoris and to freely section it with scissors and bistouri, to plug the wound with graduated linen pledgets so as to prevent any secondary hemorrhage, and then to leave it afterwards to cicatrisation by second intention which, according to him, would be obtained after about thirty days.

"I therefore endeavoured to seize the clitoris between my two finger-ends, but either on account of the tumefaction of that organ, or because of the movements of the woman, who was continually flinching, I was forced to fix it with an ordinary pair of pincers, grasping at the same time the two *nymphæ* corresponding to the *frænum.* I then entrusted the pincers to my assistant and I cut with a scissors into the stretched mucous folds close along the upper edges of the instrument, with the object of uncover-

a.—*On the curability of certain forms of insanity, epilepsy, catalepsy and hysteria in females.* London, 1866.

ing the clitoris and to lay bare the whole of its under surface, after which, holding it solidly with a *tenaculum*, by means of a second cut with the scissors I proceeded in the same manner from below upwards in the neighbourhood of its root to the point of the mucous membrane which covered it above, and then laterally. This second cut was at right angles with the first. It was necessary to tie a small artery which bled profusely. On with-drawing the pincers, I perceived that by a slight traction upwards I could join together the edges of the wound resulting from the section of the *nymphæ* (which however remained united above) to the edges of the wound caused by the section of the clitoris and of its envelopes; which I effected by means of two points of suture tied on the side and of one above. The only treatment prescribed was cold fomentations.

"During the first twenty-four hours it was necessary to sound the patient; on the second day there was complete apyrexy and spontaneous emission of urine; on the fourth the points of suture were removed: *immediate union*. On the twelfth day, the patient returned to her home, perfectly cured of the effects of the operation and of her malady. In fact, she no longer felt any excitation, either spontaneous or provoked by the manœuvres indispensable to the treatment and for the cares of cleanliness.

"I saw her about one month afterwards; she was in quite a satisfactory condition. The lumbar pains had disappeared as also all other incommodities, the appetite returned, which caused an improvement in the general health. The moral condition recovered. All seems to indicate a definitive cure, without it being however possible to guarantee the same after so short a time.

Lugo, 15 July 1870."

That clever and eccentric old Frenchman, Dr. NICOLAS VENETTE in his profound book entitled LA GENERATION DE L'HOMME, ou TABLEAU DE L'AMOUR CONJUGAL* (Paris, 2 vols, 1751), has the following observations on the narrowness *pudenda muliebri*, which are so curious and apposite that we give them *in extenso*:

DES DÉFAUTS des PARTIES NATURELLES DE LA FEMME.

Je suis persuadé que la femme a moins de chaleur que l'homme, et qu'elle est aussi sujette à beaucoup plus d'infirmités que lui. La stérilité, qui en est une des plus considérables, vient le plus souvent plutôt de son côté que de celui du mari, car entre cette infinité de parties qui composent ses parties naturelles, s'il y en a une qui manque ou qui soit défectueuse, la génération ne peut s'accomplir, et une femme qui est ainsi imparfaite ne peut espérer l'honneur d'être appelée de ce doux nom de mère.

Je n'ai pas résolu ici de parler de toutes les parties qui concourent du côté de la femme à la formation de l'enfant, il me semble en avoir assez dit au chapitre précédent. Mon dessein n'est présentement que de découvrir les défauts des parties naturelles de la femme qui peuvent empêcher la copulation, et qui peuvent être guéries.

Je ne m'étonne pas si les Phéniciens, au rapport de saint Athanase, obligeaient leurs filles, par des lois sévères, de souffrir, avant que d'être mariées, que des valets les déflorassent; et si les Arméniens, ainsi que Strabon le rapporte, sacrifiaient les leurs dans le temple de la déesse Anaïtis, pour y être dépucelées, afin de trouver ensuite des partis avantageux à leur condition; car on ne saurait dire quels épuisements et quelles douleurs un homme souffre dans cette première action au moins si la fille est étroite. Bien loin d'éteindre la passion d'une femme, souvent on lui cause tant de chagrin et de haine, que c'est pour l'ordinaire une des sources du divorce des mariages. Il est bien plus doux de baiser une femme accoutumée aux plaisirs de l'amour, que de la caresser quand elle n'a point encore connu d'homme, car comme nous prions ici un serrurier de faire mouvoir les ressorts d'une serrure neuve qu'il nous apporte, pour éviter la peine que nous prendrions le premier jour; ainsi les peuples dont nous venons de parler avoient raison d'avoir établi de semblables lois.

Jeanne d'Arc, appelée *la Pucelle d'Orléans* étoit du nombre de ces filles étroites; et si elle eût prostitué son honneur, ou qu'elle eût été mariée, comme les ennemis de sa vertu et de sa bravoure le publient encore aujourd'hui, jamais Guillaume de Cauda et Guillaume des Jardins, docteurs en médecine, n'auroient déclaré, lorsqu'ils la visitèrent dans la prison de Rouen par l'ordre du Cardinal d'Angleterre et du comte de Warwick, qu'elle étoit si étroite, qu'à peine auroit-elle été capable de la compagnie d'un homme.

Ce n'est pas ordinairement un grand défaut à une femme d'avoir le conduit de la pudeur trop étroit, à moins que cela n'aille, comme il arrive quelquefois, jusqu'à s'opposer à la copulation et à la génération même. Le défaut est bien trop commun quand ce passage est trop large, et il ne faut pas toujours mal juger des filles qui ont naturellement le conduit de la pudeur aussi large que les femmes qui ont eu plusieurs enfants.

Bien que ce défaut n'empêche pas la copulation, cependant on ne voit guère de femmes larges qui conçoivent dans leurs entrailles, parce qu'elles ne peuvent garder longtemps la liqueur qu'un homme leur a communiquée avec plaisir.

Le conduit de la pudeur est naturellement un peu courbé: il ne se redresse que lorsqu'il est question de se joindre amoureusement: car il étoit bien juste que d'un côté la Nature le roidit, puisque de l'autre elle roidissait les parties génitales de l'homme, pour favoriser les conjonctions de l'un et de l'autre et pour faciliter la génération.

L'amour tout seul n'est point capable de redresser ce canal quand il est endurci. L'imagination n'a point assez d'empire sur cette partie pour la ramollir, et les esprits s'émoussent et perdent leur vigueur quand ils agissent sur sa dureté. Il faut des humeurs douces et bénignes, que la Nature y fait passer tous les mois pour adoucir et redresser ces parties endurcies; à moins de cela, elles ne se rendent point capables de faire leur devoir en contribuant à la production des hommes.

Si nous suivions, en France ce que Platon nous a laissé par écrit pour une république bien réglée, nous ne verrions point tant de désordres dans les mariages, que nous en observons quelquefois. On se marie en aveugle, sans avoir auparavant considéré si l'on est capable de génération. Si, avant que de se marier, on s'examinoit tout nu, selon les lois de ce philosophe, je suis assuré qu'il y aurait quelques mariages plus tranquilles qu'ils ne le sont, et que jamais Hammeberge n'eût été répudiée par Théodoric, si ces lois eussent été alors établies.

A voir une jeune femme bien faite, on ne diroit pas qu'elle a des défauts qui s'opposent à la copulation. Quand son mari veut exécuter les ordres qu'il a reçus en se mariant, il trouve des obstacles qui s'opposent à sa vigueur. L'hymen, ou les caroncules jointes fortement ensemble, occupant le canal des parties naturelles de la femme, s'opposent à ses efforts. Il a beau pousser et se mettre en feu, ces obstacles ne cèdent point à la force; et quand il auroit autant de vigueur que tous les écoliers du médecin Aquapendens, jamais il ne pourroit dépuceler sa femme qui est presque toute fermée. Toutes les femmes en cet état et qui vivent après quinze ou dix-huit ans, ne sont pas entièrement fermées; elles ont un petit trou, ou plusieurs ensemble, pour laisser couler les règles, et pour donner quelquefois entrée à la semence de l'homme. Car bien que ces femmes ne soient pas capables de copulation, elles peuvent pourtant quelquefois concevoir; et c'est ainsi qu'engendra Cornelia, mère des Gracques, à qui il fallut faire incision avant que d'accoucher.

L'accouchement est quelquefois accompagné d'accidents si fâcheux, que les femmes se fendent d'une manière étonnante, et j'en ai vu une dont les deux trous n'en faisaient qu'un. Ces parties se déchirent d'une telle façon, et la nature en les repoussant y envoie tant de matière, qu'il s'y engendre plus de chair qu'auparavant: si bien qu'après cela l'ouverture en est presque toute bouchée; et quand ces femmes sont un jour en état d'être embrassées par leurs maris, elles sont fort surprises de n'être pas ouvertes comme auparavant.

For those of our readers not conversant with the style of old French we append the following translation.

ON THE DEFECTS IN THE NATURAL PARTS OF WOMAN.

I am convinced that woman has less heat than man, and that she is subject to many more infirmities than he.

Sterility, which is one of the most considerable, proceeds more often from her side than from that of the husband; for if, among the infinity of elements which compose her natural parts, there is one that is wanting or defective, generation cannot be effected, and a woman thus imperfect cannot hope for the honour of being called by the sweet name of mother.

I have not resolved to speak here of all the parts which contribute on the woman's side to the formation of the child; it seems to me that enough has been said on that subject in the last chapter. My present object is merely to discover the defects in the natural parts of woman which prevent copulation, and which may be cured.

I am not surprised if the Phenicians, according to Saint Athanasius, obliged their daughters, by severe laws, to suffer themselves before marriage to be deflowered by valets; or also that the Armenians, as Strabo relates, sacrificed their daughters in the temple of the goddess Anaitis, with the object of being eased of their maidenheads, so as to be able afterwards to find advantageous marriages suited to their condition; for one cannot describe what exhaustion and what sufferings a man has to undergo in this first action, at all events if the girl is narrow. Far from quenching a woman's passion, she is thereby caused such grief and hatred, that it is ordinarily a source of divorce. It is far sweeter to have connection with a woman accustomed to the pleasures of love, than to caress one who has not yet known a man: for, as we ask a locksmith to ease the wards of a new lock he brings us, to save us the trouble we might have the first day; so the nations of whom we have been speaking had good reason for establishing such laws.

Joan of Arc, called *the Maid of Orleans*, belonged to the category of narrow girls; and if she had prostituted her honour, or had been married, as the enemies of her virtue and of her bravery publish even to-day, Guillaume de Canda and Guillaume des Jardins, doctors of medicine, who, by order of the Duke of Warwick and the English cardinal, visited her in the prison at Rouen, could never have declared, as they did, that she was so narrow that she would hardly have been capable of having commerce with a man.

It is not alway a defect for the duct of shame in a woman to be too narrow, unless, as sometimes happens it is too narrow for copulation or for generation. The fault is more usually in the other direction when this passage is too large, and girls should not always be judged unfavourably because they have it as large as women who have had several children.

Although this defect does not hinder copulation, yet women that are large seldom conceive, because they cannot long retain the liquor that a man has communicated with pleasure to them.

The passage of Venus is naturally slightly curved; it straightens up only in the amorous conjunction, it being quite natural that on the one hand Nature should stiffen it, because on the other hand it had stiffened the genital member of the man, in order to favour the conjunction of the one with the other and to facilitate generation.

The passion of love alone is not capable of straightening out this canal, when it has become hardened. The imagination has not sufficient power over that part to soften it, and the spirits are blunted and lose their vigour when it is a case of its hardening. For that, soft and benign humours are required, which Nature sends through them every month to soften and raise up again these hardened parts; without that, they are no longer capable of fulfilling their duty in contributing to the production of humanity.

If we followed in France the precepts which Plato has left us in writing for a properly regulated republic, we should witness fewer of those marriage troubles which we sometimes have to observe. With us marriage is contracted blindly, without first considering whether we are capable of generation. If, previous to marriage, we could examine each other stark naked, in accordance with the laws of Plato's philosophy, or that there were persons appointed specially for that duty, I am assured that there would be some marriages more satisfactory than they are at present, and that had these laws been then established, Hermenbergia would never have been repudiated by Theodoric.

On looking at a well-made young woman, it is impossible to say that she has defects which oppose copulation. When her husband wishes to fulfil the duties he contracted to perform when he married, he encounters obstacles which oppose his vigour. The hymen, or the caruncles strongly jointed together, occupying the canal of the woman's natural parts, oppose his efforts. It is useless for him to shove and to get himself on fire, these obstacles do not give way to force; and had he even as much vigour as all the scholars of Doctor Aquapendens, he would never be able to take his wife's maidenhead, which is almost entirely closed-up. All the women that are in this state and who are older than fifteen or eighteen years, are not entirely closed up; there is always a little hole, or several together, which permit the outflow of the menses, and sometimes to allow the semen of the man to enter.

For although these women cannot copulate, they may, notwithstanding sometimes conceive; it was thus that Cornelia the mother of the Gracchi engendered, and she had to be incised before being delivered.

The accouchement is sometimes accompanied by such unhappy circumstances that some women rip open in an astounding manner, and I have seen one where the two holes were confounded in one. These parts tear asunder in such fashion, and Nature in healing them, supplies them with so much matter, that there grows more flesh than there was before: so that afterwards the orifice becomes almost closed; and when some day these women are in a condition to receive the caresses of their husbands, they are quite astonished to find themselves not so open as they were before.

It would have been strange indeed if this subject had escaped either the notice or wit of old BRANTOME, and we extract the following from LES DAMES GALANTES, a book that Octave Uzanne called "The Breviary of Love." The courteous reader will pardon us for omitting the English translation, for these lines rendered into the tongue of Albion would make our pages turn red with shame!! And recollect that Brantôme cannot claim with outspoken Venette the licence of a doctor.

"J'ay ouy parler d'une dame grande, belle et de qualité, à qui un de nos rois avoit imposé le nom de "Pan de C...," tant il estoit large et grand: et non sans raison, car elle se l'est fait en son vivant souvent mesurer à plusieurs merciers et arpenteurs, et que tant plus elle s'estudioit le jour de l'estressie, la nuict en deux heures on le lui eslargissoit si bien, que ce qu'elle faisoit en une heure, on le deffaisoit en l'autre, comme la toile de Penelope. Enfin, elle en quitta tous artifices, et en fut quitte pour faire élection des plus gros moules qu'elle pouvoit trouver.

Tel remède fut très bon, ainsi qui j'ay ouy dire d'une fort belle et honneste fille de la cour, laquelle l'eut au contraire si petit et si étroit, qu'on désespéroit à jamais le forcement du pucellage; mais par avis de quelques médecins ou de sages-femmes, ou de ses amys ou amyes, elle en fit tenter le gué ou l'efforcement par des plus menus et petits moules, puis vint aux moyens, puis aux grands, à mode des talus que l'on faict, ainsi que Rabelais ordonna les murailles de Paris imprenables: et puis par tels essays les uns après les autres, s'accoustuma si bien à tous, que les plus grands ne luy faisoient la peur que les petits auparavant faisoient si grande.

Une grande princesse estrangère que j'ay cogneue, laquelle l'avoit si petit et estroit, qu'elle aima de n'en taster jamais que de se faire inciser, comme les médecins le conseilloient. Grande vertu certes de continence, et rare!

A ROMANCE WITH THREE ACTORS.

Look in my face; my name is Might-have-been;
I am also called No-more, Too-late, Farewell;
Unto thine ear I hold the dead-sea shell
Cast up thy Life's foam-fretted feet between;
Unto thine eyes the glass where that is seen
Which had Life's form and Love's, but by my spell
Is now a shaken shadow intolerable,
Of ultimate things unuttered the frail screen.

ROSETTI.

THE LOVE-ROMANCE OF THREE CELEBRITIES.

(Alfred de Musset, George Sand, and Doctor Pagello.)

A GREAT stir was made in the world of letters, when, in the principal French Review, * there appeared an article, of a not very respectful nature, which claimed to give all the particulars of a romance of real life.

Elle et Lui, was the story, penned by the survivor, of a love drama with three actors, the first of whom had just quitted the scene. This "official report of a necropsy" as it was justly called by Maxime du Camp, produced a great sensation. The critics of the period had no difficulty in recognising in this romance an apology, the sincerity of which was legitimately open to suspicion. In it, George Sand overwhelmed her "big baby" with maternal scoldings, the remonstrances of an elder sister, prescribing to the invalid sick in body and mind, whose cure she had undertaken, "an entire physical and moral regimen."

From the moment of the publication of *Elle et Lui*, it

* *Revue des Deux Mondes*, 1859.

was easy to guess that beneath borrowed names, were concealed persons of flesh and blood, and from all sides efforts were made to solve the mystery: "I hear everywhere," said Prévost-Paradol, in the *Débats*: "that it is the pleading of Thérèse against Laurent, or rather the funeral oration of Laurent fulminated by Thérèse; that this Laurent was not a painter, but a great poet now fallen, of whom it had been wittily said, before his death, that he was *a young man with much behind him.* It was added, that in this trip to Italy, and it is the plain truth, Thérèse had in fact sacrificed both her purse and her tranquillity; that on his side Laurent lost his illusions and his health. Palmer is the only one who remains in the back-ground and whom the vulgar public persistently fails to recognize." *

At the time when Prévost-Paradol wrote the above lines no one could guess at the real history of "*Elle et Lui*": the events were too recent, and besides there was only the testimony of a single witness.

* * *

The reply of Paul de Musset, on behalf of his dead brother, while voluntarily revealing certain facts, which had been left in the shade in the plea composed by George Sand, could not entirely rend the veil.

* * *

Lui et Elle † was a brutal reply, and it is the gravest

* *Journal des Débats*, 3rd March, 1859.

† Published first in the *Magasin de Librairie*, in 1859.

We mention merely as a reminder the various publications which appeared after the works of G. Sand and of Paul de Musset.

First of all *Lui*, by Louise Colet, which appeared for the first time in the *Messager de Paris*, in 1859. It is easy to guess that *Lui* is Alfred de Musset, *She* has resisted him in order to remain faithful to

reproach that could be addressed to him; at all events, the romance which served him for excuse, gave him the advantage of good faith.

Paul de Musset had a duty to fulfil, if not a right, he could not be permitted to flinch from his duty. That he may have exaggerated certain points, that he may have wrongly interpreted the sentiments of his brother, of whom he was the surest and most devoted confidant, must be attributed only to an excess of affection.

Blinded by passion, neither the one nor the other uttered the unreserved truth.

Was she culpable? was she implacable? It is difficult to decide, after reading both works composed with equal art, wherein *He* appears as a big spoiled child, sensitive, to excess, terribly suspicious; where in *She* appears more calm, more indifferent, "Without either virtue or temperament" as she has so well been described.

* *

In reality, the necessary documents are wanting to enable us to form an opinion. These would be the letters exchanged between the two lovers—between Lelio and Fantasio.

Would it not have been perhaps risky to prolong and embitter a quarrel which had already lasted too long, by

lécoute whom *She* loves, and who can be no other than Gustave Flaubert.

In *Eux et Elles*, M. de Lescure has summed up in a few brief witty points the whole of this literary orgie:

"*Elle et Lui* is a calumny against a dead man; *Elle et Lui*, is a violent attack against a woman; *Lui*, mere coquetry.

"*Elle et Lui* attacks, out of revenge a reputation, which, pride defends in *Lui et Elle*, and *Lui* compromises all parties by excess of vanity."

laying bare, before the eyes of contemporaries, the foibles of two geniuses. But now, to-day, are we not "the posterity that judges?"*

The *liaison* between de Musset and George Sand, is it not the great passional romance of the XIXth century, as was that of Jean Jacques Rousseau with Mme. de Houdetot in the last century?

The account of this liaison does it not belong to literary history by the same right as the *Confessions* of J. J. Rousseau?

Since Rousseau, disclosed to public gaze his most secret infirmities, how many are there that have dared to open wide the doors of the sanctuary of their private life, lacerating their flesh and soul just to make copy for the printer!

The heroes of this drama, the phases of which we will unroll, are they not depicted by themselves in most of their works, and their amorous adventures have they not been so many pretexts for beautiful strophes or admirable periods?

The following phrase, which might indeed serve us as epigraph, is it not from the pen of George Sand:

"There is always a forced personality in the books which we write, for what could we put into our books, if it were not the experience of our lives?"†

* * *

* *Revue Bleue*, 15th Oct. 1892.

† This is what M. Marcel Prévost has himself expressed in excellent terms: "Let us congratulate ourselves that, during her lifetime she had met with enough real love to give passion to twenty master-pieces. For none other has ever made more literature out of her own life.

For those who know the flesh and blood romances of our time, which have so often tended to turn to the tragical rather than to the idyllic can there be a surer source of information than the actual writings of the persons most intimately engaged therein?

As has been remarked, in terms as elegantly concise as they were eloquent, by one of our most eminent colleagues, the story which we have undertaken to relate is commonplace enough, but is it not precisely for that motive that "it touches to the quick every human being" and that in this drama in which two lives are opposed, peculiarly exceptional on account of the rare expression they gave to the common sentiments of humanity, and in which, far from seeking the glare of scandal, we look more for an insight into ourselves?

The actors, besides, have neglected nothing to draw attention to themselves, so much were they tormented by the desire to divulge their affairs to the world; and which is already the symptom of that special quality of passion which cannot find satisfaction within itself.

True as their sentiments may be, however their sensa-

She was the type par excellence of the novelist: an intellectual organism which receives reality, assimilates it, and by a mechanism as mysterious and also almost as involuntary as that of the stomach, gives it out again in the form of a romance. Latouche, who knew her well, said, speaking of her: 'She is an echo which amplifies the voice.' She could indeed amplify it to such an extent, that the meanest reality, transmuted by her, became a poem."

Let us not forget a delightful detail, noted by M. Jules Claretie. The most beautiful phrase perhaps in *On ne badine pas avec l'Amour* was borrowed literally by Alfred de Musset from a letter addressed to him by George Sand.

As M. J. Lemaître judiciously remarks, a man of letters has nothing to lose!

tions may vibrate, they have lost the modesty of them. They feel bound to tell them, to depict them and to dramatize them for everybody; and each of them, in the depth of his or her soul, is glad when dreadful stains are disclosed in the other, for the instruction, perhaps for the consolation, of those who, always hoping and always deceived—have never seen their dreams realized. How many have there been, unknown to us, who have perhaps suffered most tragical hours without being able or even willing to ease their hearts by an artistically composed confession.

Such was not the case with George Sand and Alfred de Musset. They have spoken, they have shed tears, sang, shouted, and called upon the whole Universe to witness the state of their soul. Let us listen and judge, since they request us to do so.*

* * *

But, it has been objected, writers belong to the public only by their works. When we scrutinize their private life we commit an act of unwholesome curiosity and show envious mediocrity. "We cannot console ourselves with not being on a par with their genius, when we see them in the most compromising situations."

But is this not the best way for the moralist and the psychologist to form an exact and complete notion of a work, to make himself intimately acquainted with the sayings and doings of the author?

And, besides, all those memoirs, correspondences of which the private character is maintained, which it is wished to

* M. G. Clémenceau, in an article in the *Journal*.

preserve from *violation*, had they not been carefully ticketed, and classed by their authors and destined, in their minds, to a posthumous publicity?

For our conscience and relief we may say, under the cover and authority of M. Jules Lemaître, that all these "ecstasies, tortures, cries and sobs of George and of Alfred, and this marvellous story of three actors in a romance, so absolutely "*lived*" that it and all the rest had been wisely made into first class copy, being in fact that of *Jacques* and of the *Lettres d'un Voyageur* of the *Nuits* and of *On ne badine pas avec l'amour*, awaiting the *Confession d'un Enfant du Siècle*.

This reminds us that the basis of some of the best books, is but a blurred and insignificant reality. This, at all events, can reassure us regarding the case of those, who having experienced this adventure, have been able to draw from it both prose and rhyme. And it warns us not to put too indulgent faith in their complaints, and rather to reserve our pity for the really unfortunate.

* * *

This preamble has seemed to us not without utility in order to answer the critics who accepted the primitive version * of the episode which we will now again relate.

The circumstances are at present well known which are connected with the first rencontre of George Sand with Alfred de Musset, who had hitherto never had occasion to meet together: it was at a dinner given by the *Revue des*

* This first version has appeared in the *Revue Hebdomadaire* of 1st August and 24th October 1890.

deux Mondes, at the restaurant of the *Frères Provençaux*. The two writers were neighbours at table; the conversation commenced most amicably, and on leaving promises were exchanged to see each other again. This was the origin of their *liaison*. In the course of the following week Alfred de Musset paid two or three visits to George Sand.

Three or four months later *Lelia* appeared.

George Sand sent a copy of her work to Musset, accompanied by a letter, which, according to the expression of Mme. Arvede Barine, to whom we owe so much curious information, "marked a progress in the intimacy of the two personages."

We have had the opportunity of seeing the copy of *Lelia* presented by George Sand to Alfred de Musset: Mme. Martelet, formerly house-keeper of the poet † who now has

* M. Mariéton, in his careful and truthful study (*Une histoire d'amour*, G. Sand and A. de Musset) in which he has so skilfully made use of previous publications, asserts that "this reunion is nowhere definitely asserted."

M. Mariéton means to say that the precise date has not been given, for it is well known that it is Paul de Musset who was the first to speak of it in the biography of his brother. This is for us sufficient evidence of the fact itself.

† Mme. Martelet was not admitted to any great extent into the confidence of Musset concerning his connexion with G. Sand. She however remembers hearing the following rather amusing anecdote: In the early days of the *liaison* between the poet and the author of *Lelia*, Planche was an assiduous visitor at the house of G. Sand, of whom he was the faithful watch-dog, or *pétiôt* (drudge). Jealous of the increasing favour of Musset with the lady of the house, he imagined one day a diabolical means of getting rid of him. With a most hypercritical smile, he offered him some chocolate bon-bons: hardly had the poet swallowed two or three of these than he felt

it in her possession. The original edition was in two octavo volumes; on the "end-paper," is the following dedication, which indicates a certain degree of familiarity: "*To my little boy Alfred*, George."

The superscription to the second volume is rather more ceremonious; the dedication is as follows: "*To the Viscount Alfred de Musset*, GEORGE SAND."

A month had not elapsed since the publication of *Lelia* before Musset and George Sand had become the best friends in the world; George Sand announced it, without demanding secrecy, to Sainte-Beuve, whom she had lately chosen as a sort of confessor.*

tormented with the imperative desire... to rejoin the sonnet of Oronte (a).

As the son of a chemist and druggist, Planche had access to all the physic in the paternal shop, and he had offered to Musset purgative bon-bons!.... Whoever would have expected Planche to imitate the example of the Borgias?

Alfred de Musset had taken the same confessor.

One of our friends, M. Maurice Guibert, possesses a letter of de Musset addressed to the critic of the *Lundis* (b) which, on this point, is significant. M. Guibert, having permitted us to take a copy of it, we herewith transcribe it. Although not dated, it relates in all probability to the period of the *liaison* with G. Sand. As for the authenticity of the autograph, there cannot be the slightest doubt: the father of M. Guibert obtained the letter from M. Aug. Lacau-

---

a *Oronte*, a personage of the *Misanthrope* of Molière—the type of a poet in quest of praise, author of a sonnet which he composed in but a few minutes, and alluding to which, in very significative terms, Molière says:

"*Franchement, il n'est bon qu'à mettre au* CABINET!"

(Frankly speaking, it is only worth sending to the closet.)

(*Transl.*)

(b) Sainte-Beuve.

The household worked very well at first." George Sand speaks most enthusiastically of her new friend. "I

sale, formerly secretary to Sainte-Beuve, to whom the latter had given it.

This is the document:

"I no longer go to see you, dear friend. It is because I cannot; ah, my friend, if you have ever suffered the pangs of love, pity me indeed. I would rather have both legs broken.

"It is two days since I have seen her, and who knows when it will be? She shuts herself up—adieu—my head is all in a whirl; be discreet, I am ashamed of myself.

"Yours cordially,

A. de M.

"Wednesday morning."

We at first thought that this letter referred to George Sand, but according to M. Maurice Clouard, it would rather apply to the relations of A. de Musset with another woman. It seems to be of the same date (1828 or 29) as that of another letter which M. Clouard possesses, and which is only dated: *Monday*. "I have passed the evening," says Musset, "with the most beautiful woman I have seen in my life. She is a kept woman, and very well kept . . ." These two letters are addressed to Sainte-Beuve, 10 rue Notre-Dame-des-Champs. But, in 1833, Sainte-Beuve had already been residing for two or three years, Boulevard Montparnasse, No. 1 *ter*, near to Victor Hugo.

* The poet had come to lodge with his friend, on the Quai Malaquais. He could not help meeting there the faithful acolytes of George Sand, her two house-dogs, Boucoiran and Gustave Planche.

It was at this time that Planche fought a duel with Capo de Feuillide, who had conscientiously "pitched into" the author of *Lelia* in two articles published in the *Europe littéraire*.

It was a source of general astonishment that Planche should have appointed himself the *bravo* of Mme Sand, and the minor Press did not fail to make malicious allusions. From that to insinuate that Planche was one of G. Sand's lovers, there was but a step, which was soon taken.

We extract from an unpublished letter of Bixio, then a medical

find in him," she writes to Sainte-Beuve, * "a candour, a loyalty, a tenderness which intoxicate me. It is the love of a youth and the friendship of a comrade ... I am very happy, very happy ... Every day I am more attached to *him*; every day I see disappear from him some slight blemishes which gave me pain." †

It might have been predicted that this association, in which youth and talent were combined, would be for ever indissoluble: it seemed that the two lovers could have nothing better to do than to peacefully enjoy their happiness and revel in its intoxication. But fate decided otherwise.

In reality, never were two more uncongenial beings

student, and afterwards Minister; addressed to "*Monsieur Bocage, artiste dramatique*", the following passage which relates to the above incident:

"You know that the affair between Planche and Dumas has been settled, as it was easy to foresee. Planche has declared in writing that he was not the lover of Mme. Sand (which I consider to be a cowardly falsehood for they live together), upon which Dumas said that he was wrong to have expressed himself as he had done..."

This seems to have been mere malicious scandal, for G. Sand explained the matter to the *director of her conscience* (Sainte Beuve) in terms of the utmost frankness:

"Planche is reputed to have been my lover: this matters but little to me. *He is not.* It now matters very much to me that it be known that he is not my lover, at the same time that it is quite indifferent to me that people may have supposed him to have been so. You understand that I could not live in the intimacy of two men who would pass for having with me relations of the same nature; that would ill suit either of us three." (Letter of 25th August 1833.)

* The first letter of G. Sand to Sainte-Beuve is dated 5th June, 1833.

† Letter of 25th August previously quoted. She had just quitted Prosper Mérimée, whom she had *known* for a week.

coupled together. "These two convicts of Cupid rivetted to the same chain had nothing in common, neither in habits of work, nor in tendencies of mind, nor in dispositions or sentiments; the senses alone had been able to bring them together." Another thing separated them: the difference of age which existed between the two: George Sand was not less than thirty years old, and Musset numbered barely twenty-three when the journey to Italy was proposed.*

* * *

History does not tell us which of the two lovers first conceived the idea of this trip.

Doubtless it was the woman who inspired the idea, and Alfred had but to allow himself to be led. The biographer of de Musset, his brother Paul, relates that it was only through the persistance of George Sand that, in a moment of emotion, the mother of Alfred was brought to consent to his departure.†

On the 22nd of December, 1833, the two lovers, after a brief halt at Lyons, went down the Rhone to Avignon. On the steamer they met Stendhal (Henri Beyle); who was on his way to take possession of his post as consul at Civita-Vecchia.

After remaining a few days at Genoa, where George Sand had an attack of fever, the two lovers proceeded

* We pass rapidly over this period of the amorous existence of the young couple,—their real honeymoon,—because it is to be found related in detail both in *Lui et Elle* and *Elle et Lui*.

† Concerning their departure, see P. de Musset, *Biographie d'Alfred de Musset*, p. 121; and P. de Musset, *Lui et Elle*.

to Leghorn, from thence to Pisa, and finally to Florence.*

From Florence they merely passed through Bologna and Ferrara, and arrived in Venice on the 19th of January, 1834. On the very day of their arrival George Sand was obliged to take to her bed; she had been ailing ever since she left Genoa, and she was now for a fortnight stricken by fever.

On the 28th of January she wrote to her friend Boucoiran that "*she was as well physically as morally.*"

This respite was but of short duration.

A week later George Sand was much tormented, during five days, by dysentery, and informed her correspondent that her companion was also ill. "We have nothing to boast of either of us, for we have in Paris a crowd of enemies who would take delight in saying: they went to Italy for pleasure, and they caught the cholera! What a pleasure for us! They are sick!" †

* * *

It was near the middle of February § that Musset had a severe attack of brain fever. An Italian doctor residing in the neighbourhood was called in. This practitioner summoned at noon had not arrived at four o'clock.

* It was in reading the Florentine chronicles that Alfred de Musset conceived the idea of writing a dramatic piece, the title of which he had not fixed in his mind: this was the origin of *Lorenzaccio* (P. de Musset, *Biographie d'Alfred de Musset*, p. 129).

† Arvède Barine. *Alfred de Musset* (Hachette 1893).

§ Mr. Plauchut is in possession of copies of several unpublished letters addressed by George Sand to Buloz, in the month of February 1834, during the crisis, at a moment when de Musset was at death's door. We will make some extracts which will show, better than

The church-bells were ringing the *Angelus* when at last the *illustrissimo dottore Rebizzo** (*Berizzo*) was pompously

lengthy commentaries, what were the anxieties of the unfortunate woman at this moment:

"4th February.

It is now nearly five days ago since we both fell ill almost together, I, of a dysentery which made me suffer horribly, and of which I am not quite recovered but which has still left me sufficient strength to attend upon him, he, of an inflammatory nervous fever which has made rapid progress, to such a degree that to-day he is very bad and the doctor says that he does not know what to think. I am in despair, overcome with fatigue; in the meantime what is before us? ... Our entire fortune at present is but 60 francs... Alfred is in a fearful state of delirium and agitation. I cannot leave him for a moment. It has taken me nine hours to write this letter. Pity me! Above all, tell no one that Alfred is ill; if his mother should come to know it (and it only requires two persons to divulge a secret to all Paris) she would go mad.

What have I done to God?"

"24th February 1834.

"Alfred is saved. I shall write to his mother. He still talks wildly now and then. For the last eight nights I have not undressed: I sleep on a sofa, and every hour I must be on foot. Nevertheless, I have found time to state that I am no longer anxious about his life, and to write a few pages... You know that to me a debt smarts like a wound. I now pass many sad days here, close to this bed, where the least movement, the slightest noise is to me a source of perpetual anxiety. I spend 20 francs a day in all sorts of drugs. As soon as he gets well he will want to leave, for he has now a horror of Venice and imagines that he shall die here if he remains. I shall take Alfred back to Paris, and then go myself to Berry, there to work like the devil."

* Louise Colet (*L'Italie des Italiens*, t. I, p. 218) declares that the name of the old doctor summoned to attend upon de Musset was Santini; and that she had this information from the landlord of the hotel Danieli.

introduced. He was an old man of eighty years of age, wearing a wig, which had once been black but was reddened by long usage, and seemed the emblem of the decrepitude of the person who wore it. *

After examining the patient, a blood-letting was decided upon, but the poor devil of a doctor, who could not see clearly, had the utmost difficulty in finding out the vein, and finally declared that, not being certain of pricking the proper place, he would prefer to abstain. He promised to send a young fellow who would be able to draw as many pallets of blood as the French *signor* might desire.

The same evening, the young doctor announced, named Pietro Pagello, presented himself at the hotel Danielli, where Alfred de Musset and George Sand were staying.

It was not the first time that Dr. Pagello was in the presence of George Sand; † he had already had occasion, a few days previously, to give her his professional advice; Dr. Pagello has himself related the circumstances.

"It was in February 1834," writes Dr. Pagello, "that I became acquainted with George Sand, and in the following manner. A servant from the hotel Danielli, situated on the *Riva degli Schiavoni* (in Venice), called upon me to visit a French lady who was unwell. I went at once and

Mr. Barbiera, in his articles in the *Illustrazione Italiana*, which appeared in November 1890, articles evidently inspired by the Pagello family, confirms what is said by Mme. Colet.

* *Lui et Elle*, p. 131.

† Pagello is said to have remarked G. Sand while passing below the windows of the *Albergo Danielli* the day before he was called in to see the stranger lady.

found the lady in bed, with a red bandanna round her head. Near the bed was a tall, thin and fair young man who said to me: "This lady is suffering from a severe sick headache from which a bleeding might relieve her.'

"I examined her pulse which was hard and tense.

"I bled her and went away. I saw her again the next day.

"She was better, received me amiably and told me that she felt quite well.

"About a fortnight afterwards the same hotel-servant brought me a note in bad Italian signed: George Sand. From what I could make out it appeared that the French gentleman, whom I had seen in her room, was very ill, that he had a continual delirium, and she requested me to come at once..."

Pagello hastened to obey this summons and at once prescribed an energetic remedy for his patient *.

For more than a week Pagello scarcely quitted the bed-side of his new patient.

* It was not until 1881, nearly half a century after the event, that Pagello for the first time consented to break the silence which he had kept until then. An Italian journal, the *Illustrazione Italiana*, of 1st of May 1881, received his confidences.

Pagello prescribed compresses of iced water and the following calming potion:

Aq. ceras. nigr.	℥ ij.
Laud. liquid. Sydn., gutt.	xx.
Aq. dist. laur. ceras. gutt.	xv.

Dr. Pagello.

(We copy from the original, preserved by Musset): in other terms:

Black cherry water	*2 oz.*
Sydenham's laudanum	*20 drops.*
Distilled cherry-bay water	*15 drops.*

The text is now known of the note or rather the letter in which George Sand requested Dr. Pagello to come and see Musset. We here reproduce it:*

"My dear Mr. Pafello (Pagello). "I beg of you to come as soon as you can with a good physician to consult with him about the sick French gentleman at the Hotel Royal.

"But I must tell you beforehand that I fear more for his reason than for his life. Since he has fallen ill, he has become very weak in his head and often reasons like a child. He is nevertheless a man of energetic character and of powerful imagination. He is a poet greatly admired in France. But the over-excitement of mental labour, wine, pleasure, women and play have greatly fatigued him and have excited his nerves. For the least motive, he becomes as agitated as he might be by an affair of importance.

"Once, about three months ago, after a great anxiety, he was as it were mad for an entire night. He seemed to see phantoms around him, and cried out with fear and horror. At present he is always uneasy, and this morning he hardly knows what he is saying or doing. He sheds tears and complains of an ailment without a name or a cause, asks to return to his country (and) says that he is like to die or to go mad.

* The French translation of this letter, of which important extracts appeared in the *Gazette anecdotique* of 1896 (t. I, p. 272), has been published by Vicomte Spoelberch de Lovenjoul, in a most carefully written study, which appeared in the international the *Cosmopolis* (May–June 1896). It was so closely connected with our subject that we could not omit introducing it into this article.

"I do not know whether it is the result of the fever or of over-excitement of the nerves, or an indication of madness. I think that a bleeding might procure him relief.

"I must beg of you to make all these observations to the physician, and not to allow yourself to be discouraged at the indocile disposition of the patient. This person is the one I love best in the world, and I am in great anguish of mind to see him in this state.

"I trust that you will have for us all the friendship which two strangers may hope for.

"Excuse the miserable Italian that I write.

"George Sand."

* * *

Up to this time the personality of Pagello had remained in the shade and many readers may have been inclined to consider this hero of a real romance only a hero of fiction.

We shall now relate the numerous steps, fortunately crowned with success, which we were obliged to take in order to bring into full day-light his nebulous individuality.

During his last visit to Paris, the Viscount de Lovenjoul, during a call with which he was good enough to favour us, spoke to us at some length of his design to publish the true history of *Elle et Lui* that he had just terminated.

In the course of this conversation, allusion was naturally made to Dr. Pagello who, in this romance of three actors, played a part which at first sight seemed enigmatical.

"So," said we to our interlocutor, "you have been unable to obtain any information concerning this personage, his origin, and manner of life?"

"All that I know of him is this," answered M. de Lovenjoul, "that he is still alive, that he resides in Belluno, that he is very aged, *and that he refuses absolutely to say anything.*" *

A few hours after this conversation, we wrote to a friend, whose kindness we have often put to the test, the Baron Albert Lumbroso, well known for some interesting publications on the Napoleonic bibliography, begging of him to help us in finding out Pagello.

It was nearly a month before the reply came. We were indeed beginning to despair when the important document reached us, so curious from many points of view, which we are fortunate to be first to publish. Professor Vittorio Fontana, of Belluno, doctor of letters, personally intimate with the son of Dr. Pagello, was kind enough to undertake to make the desired enquiries on the spot, and it is the result of his efforts which he had the amiability to have forwarded to us by M. Lumbroso. Needless to say how deeply grateful we are towards MM. Lumbroso and Fontana.

As Professor Fontana writes in most correct French, we have left his text unchanged. We have only modified

* Mr. Barbiera, in his article in the *Illustrazione Italiana* of 15th Nov. 1896, declares that after a conversation with M. de Lovenjoul the *Revue hebdomadaire* decided to institute enquiries at Belluno as to the existence of Dr. Pagello. This is altogether erroneous; the enquiry was spontaneously undertaken by ourselves, as was also later on our journey in Italy, without being charged in any way with a mission by the above review. We write in the *Revue hebdomadaire*, but we do not belong to its editorial staff: this makes a difference.

one expression which might have appeared . . *risky* . . to our unprepared readers.

The following is Doctor Fontana's communication:

"Scarcely had I received your letter of the 14th, than I hastened to make the enquiries with which you had charged me.

"Several inhabitants of Belluno had supplied me with some slight information, but uncertain. I therefore resolved to call upon the Pagello family, and the following is the official information which I obtained from the Dr. Giusto Pagello, first physician to the civil hospital.

"Pietro Pagello was born at Castel-franco Veneto, in 1807.* He went through his surgical studies at the University of Pavia. Having come to Venice, he was there appointed assistant physician to Professor Rima and afterwards first physician to the hospital of that city.†

"Towards 1832 or 1834 (but not later) he was summoned urgently to the bed-side of Alfred de Musset, who was lying ill at the *Hotel Danieli*. An old doctor, who had been called in, was about to bleed the patient when he was stopped by George Sand, because she saw his hand tremble. The old physician then promised to send a younger doctor and it was Pietro Pagello, who thenceforward did not quit his patient. One night, George Sand, after having written three pages of much inspired poetical prose (M. Pagello preserves them, and they are unpublished), took an unaddressed cover into which she inserted the poetical . . . declaration and handed the letter to Dr. Pagello. The

---

* In a letter, addressed to an Italian journal, the *Illustrazione popolare, giornale per le famiglie*, the 25th March 1896, we find the following information furnished by Pietro Pagello himself: "Pietro Pagello, son of Domenico Pagello and of Mme. Maria Cosalini, legally married, born on the 15th June 1807, was baptized in the church of Santa Maria de Pavia at Castelfranco, Venetian territory."

† He first studied at Treviso, followed the medical and surgical lectures at the Faculty of medicine of Padua, afterwards going to Pavia where in surgery he was a pupil of the renowned Professor Scarpa. In 1828 he settled in Venice, where he became an assistant-surgeon at the hospital of that city in the clinical service of Dr. Rima.

letter seeing no address on it, did not or pretended not to understand, and asked G. Sand to whom he was to give it. George Sand then snatched the letter from his hands and wrote the address on it: "to stupid Pagello." From that night there commenced between the two a very intimate . . . relation. Pietro Pagello and G. Sand afterwards quitted Venice together, visited the lakes of Garda and of Lombardy, and finally came to Paris, where young Pagello remained during seven or eight months. Having then ceased all connexion with G. Sand and being short of money, and being recalled by his family as also by his professional duties, he returned to Venice. From there he went to Belluno in 1837 and never quitted that town, where he was head-physician to the civil hospital; which post, when he retired a few years ago, he left to his son, Doctor Guisto Pagello, who occupies it at the present time. It was at Belluno that Pietro Pagello married.* He had several sons; and now, notwithstanding his eighty-nine years, he preserves all the lucidity and serenity of his mind and enjoys excellent health. But one can obtain nothing from him verbally concerning George Sand; he has written a memoir on the subject which is in charge of his eldest daughter, and with regard to the rest remains silent. In his earlier years he had much talent: he used to amuse himself making verses,† and it is known that he

* In 1838, Dr. Pagello married his first wife Margherita Pinzas, who died in 1842; by her he had two children: Giorgio, who died in 1878, and Ada Pagello, now the widow Antonini, who resides alternately at Mogliano and in Venice. In 1849 he married his second wife Margherita Zuliani, who at present notwithstanding her 78 years, enjoys excellent health; by her he had three sons all living: Roberto, Mario and Giusto, the surgeon. The latter has but one child, a little daughter. One of the brothers is married, but has no children.

† Pagello was a poet, and a most distinguished one. What is most remarkable in his case is that none of his verses, which are worthy of universal admiration, have ever been printed.

It would be difficult to give a complete idea of the poetical works of Pagello, thrown to the winds here and there and transformed into legends and popular songs. An incident which occurred in 1887, has enabled us nevertheless to recover some fragments. Molmenti violently reproached the Venetians with busying themselves only with singing love ditties, while Bonaparte was occupying Venice; in

indited a Venetian canzonetta in honour of G. Sand, which was long sung in Venice where it is still remembered.*

Ti xe bela ti xe zovene,
Ti xe fresca come un fior:
Vien per tute le so lagrime, etc.

Some poems by Pagello on marriages and other occasions have been printed. It is known that he furnished the matter for a novel by G. Sand, and assisted her, it would appear, in her *Souvenirs of a* — — .

support of his opinion, he cited the barcarole which we give below. But Pagello loudly claimed the paternity of these verses, adding that he had written them in 1831, for George Sand.

Si in conchigilia i Greci Venere
Se sognava un altro di
Forse visto i avera in gondola
Una bela come ti.

Ti xé bela, ti xé zovene
Ti xé fresca como un fior:
Vien per tuti le so lacrime
Ridi adesso e fa l'amor.

[If the Greeks imagined Venus in a shell, it was perhaps because they had seen in a gondola a woman as lovely as thee.—Thou art beautiful, thou art young, thou art fresh as a flower: the time for tears comes to us all ... but for the present smile on me and make love.]

We know, on the other hand, that among the unpublished papers of George Sand are other pieces of poetry by Pagello, written expressly in honour of her by the poet. There can be no doubt that beside the revelations just made known on the relations between the Venetian poet and the French woman of genius, some of the unknown verses of Pagello will manage to be rescued, for the glory of Venetian letters.

In 1883, the *Intermédiaire des Chercheurs et des Curieux*, published a *Serenade*, composed by Dr. Pagello in 1834, in honour of George Sand.

traveller; he also aided her in some translations she made in Italy at a time when she was short of cash. I saw some other souvenirs with the Pagellos of those erotic times. I particularly remarked a portrait of the young doctor, looking very handsome, painted by Bevilacqua,* precisely at the time when Pietro was most intimate with G. Sand. A very successful photographic reproduction of this portrait has been made for the family, who would make no difficulty in sending it if asked to do so. Pietro Pagello lives now tranquilly in the bosom of his family…."

Wishing to obtain some additional information concerning Dr. Pagello, we then addressed ourselves directly to his son, Dr. Giusto Pagello, now chief-physician of the civil hospital at Belluno.† From his reply we extract what particularly concerns our subject.

"…. My father is in excellent health, and this month (the letter is dated from 9th of June last) he enters his eighty-ninth year.

"Documents and letters are kept in reserve, and I trust that you will be good enough to admit the reasons, as delicate as they are natural, which forbid my father to satisfy public curiosity therewith. I will however endeavour to obtain for you and send you a copy of the letter (a splendid poetical effusion) in which George Sand declared her love for my father, one night, at the hotel Danielli in Venice, *but this will be difficult….*"

At our pressing entreaties Dr. Giusto Pagello, who had succeeded, not without difficulty in overcoming the resistance

* Our colleague Marcel Baudouin, has communicated to us the text of the thesis sustained for the degree of M.D. by Dr. Pagello Jun in 1838.

The title of it is: *La medicazione al deutocloruro di mercurio negli ospitali poveri;* (a) 10 p. in 8vo, Padua, L. Penada.

† It has gone the round of the French and foreign press.

(a) Treatment by deutochloride of mercury in hospitals for the poor. Trans.)

of his father, sent us nevertheless, on the 22nd August, *the promised declaration.*

"I firmly believe," he wrote on this occasion, "that the document has never been published. The original is at Belluno, in an album belonging to an aunt to whom my father gave it half a century ago, with absolute prohibition (*sic*) to allow it to be copied and still less published. But I send and confide it to you, as a testimony of the sympathy with which, as a man of letters and physician, you have inspired me, without forbidding you to publish it, should you think fit sooner or later not to withhold it from the literature of your country. Perhaps this document will be the only one ever published connected with my father's adventure; perhaps is it the only one worthy of being brought to light."

It is therefore, as can be seen, with the full consent of the Pagello family that we give publicity to this admirable page which will no doubt be read and read over again.*

* M. Barbiera believes that he has reason to think that the title *En Morée* "would seem to express a love born in countries inflamed by the sun, a fiery, a furious love. And besides," he adds, "the name of Morea was on the tip of all tongues at that moment. It was barely six years since the expedition to the Morea had taken place, under the command of General Maison. The remembrance of it was still fresh."

For an original explanation, this is a very original one indeed!

M. Barbiera also asserts that the document, which I was the first to make known by publishing it in France, had already appeared, translated into Italian, in a journal destined for young people(!) which was published in Venice. But he has been unable to specify either title or date . . . Strange, strange!!

A man of letters, M. Felix Franck, after seeing our article in the *Revue hebdomadaire*, has sent us the following remarks:

"It seems difficult to admit that George Sand could have written

If we undertook the journey to Belluno, in the first days of September, it was principally to compare the manuscript copy which had been forwarded to us with the letter itself.

The letter, the original of which was placed before our eyes, bore this enigmatical title: *En Morè.* Is it not probable that George Sand had intended to put: *En Amore*, and that in her haste (she wrote this long letter within an hour), and also on account of her imperfect knowledge of Italian, she may have wrongly written the expression, which in her mind, was intended to serve as title to her declaration? But this a mere supposition and on that point we are reduced to conjecture.

Above the autograph, we read the following lines in a different handwriting from that of the autograph itself:

Venezia, 10 Luglio 1834. Pietro Pagello ad Antonietta Segato dona questo manoscritto di Giorgio Sand.

* Pietro Pugello has given this manuscript of George Sand to Antonietta Segato.

such a hybrid motto: *En* (French preposition) and *Amore* (Italian substantive). She could not be ignorant that the French *en* is rendered in Italian by *in*. But it appears to me very simple and logical to read here the old French word: *Enamouré* (enamoured) as it was employed by Jean de Meung, the author of the *Roman de la Rose* and other poets of ancient times."

This explanation has not succeeded in convincing us; it appears to us rather far-fetched.

The original manuscript is cut at this point, as we were able to verify *de visu*; but it had not the appearance of being purposely mutilated.

Here is this master-piece well worthy to appear in future anthologies:

"En Morée.

"Born under different skies, we have neither the same thoughts nor the same language; have we at least similar hearts?

"The cool and hazy climate whence I come has left with me soft and melancholy impressions: the generous sun that has bronzed thy brow, what passions has it given thee? I know how to love and to suffer, and thou, how dost thou love?

"The ardour of thy gaze, the strong embrace of thy arms, the vehemence of thy desire tempt and frighten me. I know neither how to oppose thy passion nor how to share it. We do not love thus in my country; near to thee I am as a pale statue; I gaze upon thee with astonishment, with desire, with trembling.

"I know not whether thou lovest me really. I shall never know. Thou canst barely pronounce a few words in my tongue, and I know not enough of thine to put such subtle questions to thee. Perhaps it would still be impossible for me to make myself understood, did I indeed know to perfection the tongue thou speakest.

"The places where our lives have been passed, the men who have instructed us, are doubtless the cause that we have ideas, sentiments and wants, inexplicable one to the other. My feeble nature and thy fiery temperament must breed very diverse thoughts. Thou must ignore or despise the thousand little miseries which assail me. Thou must laugh at that which makes me cry.

'Perhaps thou knowest not what tears are.

'Wilt thou be to me a support or a master? Will'st thou console me for evils I have suffered before I met thee? Wilt thou know why I am sad? Dost thou know compassion, patience, friendship? Perhaps hast thou been brought up in the conviction that women have no soul. Dost thou know that they have one? Art thou neither Christian, nor Mussulman, nor civilized, nor a savage; art thou a man? What is there in that manly breast, that lion eye, that brow superb? Is there in thee a thought noble and pure? When thou sleepest, dost dream thou flyest towards heaven? When men do thee harm, dost thou hope in God?

'Shall I be thy companion or thy slave? Dost thou desire or dost thou love me? When thy passion shall have been sated, wilt thou know how to thank me? When I shall render thee happy, wilt thou know how to tell it me?

'Dost thou know who I am, and does it trouble thee not to know? Am I to thee else than the unknown which causes thee to seek and to reflect, or am I in thy eyes but a woman like to those that fatten in harems? Thy eye, in which I think I see shining a flash divine, does it express but a desire that such women can appease? Dost thou know that it is the desire of the soul which time can never satisfy, which no human caress can assuage nor fatigue? When thy mistress falls to sleep in thy arms, dost thou remain awake to contemplate her, to pray to God, and to shed tears?

'Do the pleasures of love leave thee panting and stupefied, or do they plunge thee into divine ecstasy? Does thy soul survive thy body, when thou quittest the bosom of thy love!

"Oh! when I shall see thee calm, shall I know if thou art thinking or reposing? When thy glance shall become languishing, will it be from tenderness or from lassitude?

"Perhaps dost thou think that thou knowest me not* . . . , that I know thee not. I know neither thy past life, nor thy character, nor what men who know thee think of thee. Perhaps art thou the first, perhaps the last among them. I love thee without knowing whether thou mayest be worthy of my esteem, I love thee because thou pleasest me; perhaps I may soon be forced to hate thee.

"If thou wert a man of my country, I should question thee and thou wouldst understand me. But I should be still more unhappy for thou wouldst be untrue to me.

"Thou at least wilt not deceive me, thou wilt not make to me vain promises and false vows. Thou wouldst love me as thou knowest how and canst love. That which I have sought in vain in others, I shall perhaps not find it in thee, but I shall always believe that thou possessest it.

"The glances and caresses of love which have always lied to me, thou wilt let me interpret them as I choose without any deceptive words, I shall be able to interpret thy reverie and make thy silence speak eloquently. I shall attribute to thy actions the intention I shall wish to find in thee. When thou wilt look tenderly at me, I will then believe that thy soul is communicating with mine; when

* The incident is related in detail in *Lui et Elle*; in the article by Mr. Clouard on *Alfred de Musset and G. Sand*, published in the *Revue de Paris* (p. 717 and following); and, more completely in the work by Mr. Mariéton.

thou lookest at the sky, I shall believe that thy intelligence is rising again towards the home from which it emanates.

"Let us therefore remain as we are, learn not my tongue, I will not seek in thy words wherewith to tell thee my doubts and my fears. I wish to ignore what are the acts of thy life or what part thou art playing among men. I would wish not to know thy name. Hide from me thy soul that I may always believe it to be beautiful."

This inspired hymn had been improvised in less than an hour, in the presence of the doctor himself, while at their side reposed, in lethargic sleep, the poet, agitated by the convulsions of fever.

* * *

We should liked to have evoked the memory of Doctor Pagello concerning this incident,* with which he was so intimately connected, but we did not then foresee, before going to Belluno, † the difficulties which there awaited us: we could not guess that not only Doctor Pagello could not speak French, but that he was absolutely deaf. §

As some have expressed some doubts about our journey to Belluno, we will state specifically that immediately on arriving we put up at the *Grand Hotel des Alpes*, on Friday, 4th September 1896, at a quarter past three in the afternoon.

† Pagello resided with his brother Roberto (a handsome type of an extravagant fellow) in a modest house at San Fantino, near the "Corte Minelli," not far from the theatre of "La Fenice," then famous throughout Europe for its original performances of Italian music (*Illustrazione Italiana*, 1896, No. 48).

§ The absolute deafness, with which he is afflicted for upwards of 45 years, has not soured his character, as so often happens to others. He himself jokes about it: having been buried for some time

By good luck, his son Dr. Giusto Pagello, the head-physician of the civil hospital of Belluno, was kind enough to serve us as interpreter, seconded by his wife, Mme. Giusto Pagello, who, in these circumstances, was most kind and amiable.

It was at once agreed that we should draw up a list of questions to be transmitted by Dr. Pagello, the son, to his father in an Italian translation. The old man was to answer them in his own language, and these replies were again to be given to me in French by Dr. Giusto Pagello.

It is useless to add, that we had previously had the assurance, that our visit would be received with pleasure by our venerable colleague.

* * *

After waiting a few moments in a tastefully furnished drawing-room, Doctor Giusto Pagello came to inform us that his father "expected" us. Our knowledge of the Latin language, however imperfect, and rather forgotten, enabled us to understand this expression, which at first had somewhat surprised us.

After mounting two or three steps, we found ourselves on a landing, and, after passing through a small room, entered the studio of the aged doctor.

He was quite at the further end of the room, reclining in a comfortable old arm-chair, which had no pretence to elegance, from which he rose at our approach. Very tall, but bent by years, Doctor Pietro Pagello has preserved a

past with pisciculture, he wrote to Mr. Barbiera "that he had chosen for friends the mute denizens of the waters; as that did not oblige him to remember his infirmity." (V. *Illustrazione Italiana*, 1893, No. 15,

freshness in contradiction with his age. But it is not easy to evoke beneath this senile mask, the brilliant cavalier of romantic times.

Doctor Pietro Pagello received us with most exquisite courtesy, and seemed to be flattered at being thus sought after. As we were expressing our thanks, M. Pagello, Jun., reminded us that his father was quite deaf, and that it would be preferable, as it had been arranged, to converse only in writing. We accept this method of interviewing, the novelty of which was far from displeasing us, and seated at a table, we commenced our questions.

Dr. Giusto Pagello translated as we proceeded the answers given by his father to our questions, which we will synthetize, without modifying their bearing.

* * *

"My memory," said the venerable octogenarian, "may perhaps serve me badly; all that is so long ago. You will be good enough to excuse its weaknesses . . .

"It was said that I had recommended the return to France of Alfred de Musset, in order to remain alone with *la Sand*, (Dr. Pagello never designates George Sand otherwise, but we hasten to say that in his mouth the expression has no injurious meaning). This is an absolute error. It was Alfred de Musset himself who insisted, contrary to my advice, supported by the entreaties of George Sand, to set out for France, still incompletely recovered and hardly convalescent from a malady to which he had nearly succumbed. This malady was extremely serious; and you will judge so when I inform you that it was a *typhoidette*, complicated with alcoholic delirism. In my opinion, Alfred de Musset was not epileptic, as some persons have insinuated; the crises which assailed him were those of acute alcoholism; he drank deeply, and his nervous system being much overworked, the abuse of spirituous liquors sufficed to upset him altogether...

"What was the usual life of *la Sand* and I, after the departure of Musset, is what I will endeavour to relate. We almost immediately quitted the hotel Danielli to take an apartment at San Fantino, in the centre of Venice, which we made our home. My brother Robert, who died six years ago in 1890, lived under the same roof.* He,

Pagello frequented the Café Florian, the rendez-vous of the elegant world of Venice, and the apothecary's shop of Ancillo who was reputed to be the greatest scandal-monger in Venetia.

M. Clémenceau has related, in a very curious article published in the *Journal* (1896), that he formerly visited, accompanied by a friend of G. Sand, "Ancillo's pharmacy, on the *Campo San Luca*, where Pagello and his companion had established their headquarters, and the house in the *Corte Minelli* where, between two cries of despair of *Jacques* (a) the novelist would run to the kitchen and prepare those wonderful sauces which her Italian lover so relished."

"I remember," he writes, "a large and very airy apartment part of the Minelli palace, with a vast kitchen, the fire-place of which in itself was as big as a room.

"Ancillo, the father of the present druggist who is himself an octogenarian, was a *[illegible]* of the time of the first Republic. His shop, opposite the *Auberge des trois Roses*, was the most reputed in Venice. He was a frequenter of the latest meetings of the Café Florian, where the literary traditions of the Eighteenth century were carefully preserved. The old gentleman would sit in the day-time ensconced in his mahogany shop, where are still reposing at the back of arched embrasures, the great dusty glass bottles, that have never been opened, I imagine, since the time when George Sand used to drop in to write some letter or chat over the events of the day. In

(a) The novel she was then writing (Tr.).

who was not susceptible of being carried away by the transports of passion, could not understand how I could have fallen in love with *la Sand*, who, at that moment, had become very thin, and who in his opinion was not very seductive. As soon as my father got to hear of my *liaison*, he forbade my brother to remain any longer with us. And yet our life was far from being passed only in pleasure. George Sand worked, and worked a great deal. The only recreation she allowed herself was the cigarette: and even while smoking she continued to write. She always smoked Turkish tobacco and liked to roll her own cigarettes and mine. Perhaps was it for her a source of inspiration, for she would stop her work to follow with her eyes the spirals of the smoke, plunged in reverie.

"It was during our stay in Venice that she wrote on this card-table now before me, her *Lettres d'un voyageur*, and also her novel entitled *Jacques*. On this occasion I may have given her some slight assistance, but my collaboration was but of little importance: I gave her some information relative to the history of Venice, on the manners of the country, and I often accompanied her to reading-rooms and to the Marciana Library.

"She knew our language well, but not sufficiently to

the evening he was once more the jovial companion and merry talker. Sometimes he would perhaps, by his droll tales and genuine gaiety, help the disappointed *amante* of the poet to wait until her handsome Italian, after the style of Leopold Robert, (*a*) gratified her with what *she had not been able to find in others*, as she used to say herself."

In 1834, G. Sand used to have her Paris letters addressed: *A Monsieur Pagello, Pharmacie Ancillo, Piazza Sanluca, pour remettre à Madame Sand.*

a A talented French painter, celebrated for his representations of Italian scenes and types (*Transl.*).

write in Italian magazines. She had enough to do to prepare "copy" for the *Revue des Deux Mondes*, for she never failed to send her manuscript regularly to Mr. Buloz.

"She used to work from six to eight consecutive hours, preferably in the evening; her work was mostly prolonged far into the night; she always wrote without stopping and without making any erasures.

"The dominant points of the character of George Sand were patience and gentleness, an inalterable gentleness: she was seldom vexed and seemed always contented with her lot....

"When we did not dine out, she used herself to prepare the meals. She was besides a most talented cook, and excelled in preparing sauces; she was very fond of fish, and it was a dish that often figured on our table. It may be added that she digested all kinds of food very well, never being ill, except a slight dyspepsia of little importance; I never had to prescribe her any physic....

"I must not omit to mention a particular talent of George Sand: she could use her pencil most admirably: her caricatures were extremely droll; with two strokes of her pencil she could give you the exact portrait of a person: whom she had only once seen. My eldest daughter has preserved some of these drawings which she can show to you....

"George Sand drank a great deal of tea in order to stimulate her to work.

The old doctor, then stooping to a glass cupboard, against which his arm-chair was placed, took from it a cup of a wide, open shape, and a saucer, of unusual depth. The cup presented this peculiarity that it resembled pure tin, whereas the touch shows that the matter composing it was a varnished pottery, one of those earthenwares with stanniferous reflections, which we were afterwards informed are specially manufactured in the neighbourhood of Venice.

After having examined it attentively, we handed it back to M. Pagello, who begged us to keep it in remembrance of our interview.

"Of the entire service," said the old gentleman, who evidently wished to show us the value he attached to his present, "there remain only four cups;" we thanked him, at the same time begging him to enhance the value of his present by a few lines to serve as a certificate of origin.

With a rather trembling hand, doctor Pagello wrote the following lines:

"*All' Egregio Dr. Cabanis,*

"*In memoria della visita che mi faceste, à Belluno, vi offro questa tazza, nella quale molte volte la Sand ha forbito il che quando abitava con me a Venezia.*

"*Belluno, 4 7bre, 1896.*

"*Pietro Pagello.*"

Which is easily translated as follows:

"In remembrance of the visit you have made to me here at Belluno, I offer you this cup, in which many a time *la Sand* drank tea, when she lived with me in Venice.

"Pietro Pagello."

* *

But to return to the narrative of Dr. Pagello:

"On leaving Venice," continued the venerable Doctor, "George Sand and I went to Verona, from there to Lake Garda, to Milan, and thence to Geneva.

"We remained but a short time in these different places, and came to Paris in the early days of August.

"We separated from the moment of our arrival. I would not, under any pretext accept the hospitality that was offered to me.

"I did not much frequent the literary world during my short sojourn in the French capital. Among men of letters, I remember to have seen Gustave Planche, and Buloz. You are surprised that I should not have met with other writers? But it was the time of vacation, and they were nearly all away in the country.

"With regard to Musset, I visited him several times; I always met with a most courteous reception from him, but without the least cordiality; but he was not of a very warm-hearted disposition. I continued some relations with one Frenchman only, a friend of Musset, M. Alfred Tattet, * a very strange person if there ever was one, a great amateur of Cyprus wine, of which he used every year to have a small barrel sent to him from Italy: a *bon-vivant* as you say in France. We exchanged a pretty good number of letters, but I should be puzzled to say in what corner they may be to-day; I don't know even whether I have preserved them.

"In Paris I resided in the rue des Petits Augustins, at the Hôtel d'Orleans. My mornings were passed in the hospitals, where I followed the clinical courses of Lisfranc, Amussat, and Broussais, who at that time was extraordinarily in vogue . . .

* We may obtain some definite information as to the ties of friendship which existed between Pagello and M. Tattet, by reading a letter from G. Sand to the friend of Alfred de Musset; reproduced by M. Maurice Clouard in the *Revue de Paris, loc. cit.* pp. 721—724.

"I hardly ever saw Mme. Sand; she caused me to be invited by M. Boucoiran, the tutor of her children, to pass a few days at Nohant. I refused the invitation and preferred to return to Italy ...*"

"Since my return to my country I have never received the slightest news of *la Sand*. I know of her literary successes by the newspapers, and that was all ...

* Pagello lodged in Paris in a little room on a fourth floor, and used to take his meals at a table-d'hôte kept by a certain Venetian of the name of Bambarela, who had kept an hotel in Paris for the last thirty three years ...

He used sometimes to go to the *Jardin des Plantes* to satisfy his hunger with a penny loaf and some fruit, after following the clinical lectures of Velpeau and other illustrious physicians and surgeons of Paris, to whom G. Sand had recommended him in order to get rid of him politely. Who can imagine what dark days the poor Venetian surgeon must have undergone in this cosmopolitan bachelor-room, so foreign to him, ignorant of the language, of the people, without money, and under the bitter humiliation of being abandoned by the woman he had loved. On the 18th of August, disheartened, he wrote to his father: "I seem like a strange bird thrown into the storm;" and again: "If any one has every reason to cast himself into the Seine, it is I!"

But the hour for bidding farewell to the loved one had come. The adieux were made. "I pressed her hand, without daring to raise my eyes to hers. She appeared to be embarrassed. I kissed her children and went."

Pagello returned to Italy. Thanks to a learned Venetian gentleman, Mr. Paolo Zanaini, he modestly entered the hospital of Belluno as surgeon and was there sufficiently esteemed. He married Margherita Piazza, who went out of her mind, and by whom he had a daughter, Ada, still living, and a son, who went into business, and died at the age of 36 years. His wife having died, he married a second time a Belluno lady, another Margherita ... by whom he had three sons, of whom one is the surgeon Giusto Pagello (*Illustrazione Bellunese, loc. cit.*).

"It was quite by chance that I heard of her death, but I was not directly informed of it ..."

* *

"I was quite a young man," said in his turn, Doctor Pagello, Jun., "when the newspapers announced the death of Mme. Sand. I remember that my father received the news with the utmost indifference. He spoke to us of the family about this woman as if he had scarcely known her: half a century had elapsed without a letter, without a greeting. It was the news of the death of a *bohémienne* (sic), that our father related to us of the family ... The past was long since dead, long indeed before the death of George Sand!

"But let us leave this subject of conversation ... Will you allow me to show you some objects of curiosity which we possess ... Before quitting this room, I must show you an object which has a character, which I may call historical. It is a cup in Sèvres china, which has a rather curious origin which I will tell you.

"The Prince of Rohan was camping with the Austrians on an estate belonging to my grandfather, two miles from Castelfranco, when Massena came up with his troops.

"The Austrians had but just time to retreat, without carrying away their camp equipage. The next day, a peasant in the employ of my grandfather brought him this cup, which he had found in the tent of the Prince, and which still contained the rest of the chocolate he was drinking when he was surprised by the arrival of the troops of Massena.

"These paintings that you see are also of some value:

here is a picture by Tempesta, two aquarelles by Bisson, a head by Schidone and a series of 24 drawings by Callot.

"As we are on this subject, I shall feel obliged if you will assist me to destroy a false legend: in one of the letters of G. Sand to Alfred de Musset, published in the *Revue de Paris*, the novelist pretends that she had submitted to the appreciation of an expert the paintings which my father had brought with him to France; that according to the expert these paintings *were of no value*, but she had nevertheless offered my father two thousand francs for them, *adding that it was a manner of con-

* Pagello, in a conversation with Mr. Barbiera, asserts that at the time when the event occurred, "he was not handsome, but healthy and robust", and that it was the chase which had developed his vigour. He added, "when I was in Paris I expected to be challenged to fight some duels. Inexpert in fencing, but skilful with the gun as a hunter, I practised with the pistol and soon became very expert, but had no occasion to use my skill."

Mr. R. Paulucci di Calboli writes in the *Revue des Revues* (1896, p. 372): Dr. Pagello was quite a young man to whom might have been well applied the verse of Dante in which he describes Conradin: "*Biondo era e bello e di gentile aspetto.*" (a) His features and manners denoted his descent from an ancient Venetian family ennobled by Pope Paul II. He had a fine and delicate wit, a woman's heart, and the intelligence of an artist. His conversation was charming, always gay and bright, he was very elegant in appearance, and the favourite of the Venetian salons and the spoiled child of the ladies. Although very young, he had a good reputation as surgeon, having published some pamphlets which gave evidence of the serious nature of his experiments and observations. Is it then astonishing that George Sand should have found him worthy of her love? He was neither used up by pleasure, nor disabused by experience. Pagello was as generous and romantic as she was herself; he had the true soul of a poet!

(a) Fair he was and handsome, and of pleasing aspect. (*Transl.*)

cealing a pecuniary *assistance*." My father protested as soon as this came to his knowledge, and we shall not cease to protest every time it is repeated. I was informed by my late uncle that these paintings though not exactly Raphaels were far from being ordinary. They were signed by a master, the painter Ortesiti. Besides, my father much frequented the artistic world, where his taste had been developed, and he was reputed to be a connoisseur. Under such circumstances you may be sure that he had been careful not to take along with him mere daubs of which he could not have disposed.

"He came back ruined, his practice was gone, he had to begin life over again, these were indeed misfortunes enough!"

"Be persuaded," continued Mr. Giusto Pagello, "that the connection of my father with George Sand was but an episode in his life and nothing more. George Sand, tired of the strange vicious habits of Alfred de Musset, had abandoned herself unreservedly to my father, who was young, with broad shoulders, a really handsome, brave and right good fellow, who as far as I know, was by no means at his first love.* My father loved the pretty stranger for her genius, for her goodness, and, *without*

* At the moment that he became acquainted with George Sand, Pagello was beloved "by a woman lovely as are the madonnas of Paul Veronese, with a splendid figure and wavy golden hair. She bore the romantic name of Arpalice." George Sand was of an esthetic type forming the most complete contrast to that of Arpalice.

"Her short raven hair, her large eyes swimming beneath dark lashes, her wide-spread sensual lips, her little hands and feet, her decided gestures, and above all the halo of her European fame, subjugated Pagello." (*Illustrazione Italiana*, 1896. No. 47.)

placing her among the stars, he was much enamoured of her. But all that was soon forgotten. Once returned to Italy, my father resumed his professional occupations. He soon got his practice again around him. His skill, particularly as a surgeon was already long established: as a former pupil of the celebrated Scarpa and of Rima the surgeon, former chief-surgeon of Napoleon's great army, he had been in a good school.

"My father was the first to introduce lithotrity into Italy, as he had seen it performed by Lisfranc, and perineal cystotomy; he acquired also a genuine reputation as accoucheur. *

"It is not more than eight years ago that my father gave up practice. Until then he used to attend to his service at the Belluno hospital with the most scrupulous regularity. He has never ceased to interest himself in the progress of science, and in the rare hours of leisure that this practice left him, he occupied himself with geology, palaeontology, conchology and pisciculture. But he has always had a marked predilection for literature. Even now he takes care to know all that is being published and passes several hours every day reading reviews, newspapers and new books. And, notwithstanding his ninety years, he reads without spectacles!

"He writes less than formerly, although he still commits his reflexions and thoughts to paper. Formerly he composed a memoir, a sort of act of contrition of *the deep repentance of a good fellow* (*sic.*), who deplores the sins of his youth. But neither the events, nor the persons therein alluded to are in any way specified.

* The *Histoire de la Chirurgie et de l'Obstétrique* by Corradi enumerates his professional merits. (*Illustrazione Italiana, loc. cit.*)

"We also preserve a manuscript-work by my father, containing numerous poems, moral tales, travelling reminiscences, social sketches, domestic economy, etc. This work is dedicated to his sons and nephews; not a fragment of it is to be published during his lifetime.

"I was one day glancing through the pages of this voluminous manuscript, when a paper dropped from it to the ground which I hastened to pick up. It was a portrait of George Sand, admirably done. I have never been able to find it again, notwithstanding the searches I have made . . . ."

The name of George Sand having turned up again in the conversation, we profited by it to ask a question which our lips had long been burning to put: does there exist a correspondence of George Sand with Pietro Pagello? Does this correspondence consist of many letters? When and by whom are they to be published?

"It is certain," answered Dr. Giusto Pagello, "that a good many letters were exchanged between my father and Mme. Sand, but my father *has always assured us that he had burned them all except three*, which are indeed the most interesting. It is an Italian man of letters, a friend of my father, Mr. Antonio Caniamiga, and not Mr. Zanardelli, as has been asserted, who is charged with the posthumous publication, for *my father insists that they are not to be published during his lifetime*. We are quite determined to respect his wishes in this matter.

"Besides these three letters, there is the declaration of love addressed by George Sand to my father, at the hotel Danielli, and which I have communicated to you."

At the present time the letters of George Sand to Alfred de Musset have been made public; those of Alfred to George have appeared almost entirely;* Dr. Pagello alone has hitherto resisted all solicitations.

After having been the least unhappy of the three, he has remained, in spite of all that may have been said, the most discreet.

When the moment shall have come to bring before the tribunal of posterity the passionate pleadings of the *lovers of Venice*, we hope that he will receive some credit for the reserve and decorum he has always shown.

* M. de Lovenjoul has published in *Cosmopolis*, a great many of the letters of G. Sand to Sainte-Beuve; the *Revue de Paris* has also given a good number.

Mme. Lardin de Musset has communicated several of her brother's letters to Mr. Maurice Clouard (*Revue de Paris*), and also to M. Mariéton who published them in his recent work. Lastly we have had the letters of G. Sand to A. de Musset, the publication of which had been confided to the care of M. Aucante (*Revue de Paris*, 1896): the letter of George Sand to Abbé Rochet (*Nouvelle Revue* 1896) and we are not sure of not having omitted some others!

It is nevertheless rather amusing that Mme. Clésinger wanted to oppose the publication of her mother's letters, and particularly those addressed to Pagello, whereas another member of the family, Mme. Lina Sand, had, a few years ago, begged of an Italian writer to use his influence to induce Dr. Pagello to consent to give up to publicity the correspondence which he possessed. (Vide *Illustrazione Italiana*, 1896, No. 18.)

It is not with less surprise, that one reads the astounding interview with Mme. Clésinger, in which that lady asserted, as seriously as possible, that if her mother had several lovers, it was because *she had a horror of solitude!!*

INDEX

to the Names of Persons, Places, and Subjects mentioned.

Il y a présent une inquisition sévère sur les livres; mais un ministre, en défendant un livre, l'accrédite. Le vrai secret serait de le faire réfuter par un auteur sage et homme de bien.

Un livre défendu est un feu sur lequel on veut marcher et qui jette au nez des étincelles.

INDEX

The references marked "F" refer to the article on "FLAGELLATION IN FRANCE", *which is given away gratuitously with the present volume.*

A.

D.

G.

H.

I.

J.

K.

L.

N.

Q

T.

Y.

Z.

List of Mr. CARRINGTON's Recent

Medical and Philosophical Publications

Criminal Ethnography, being a Treatise on the Development of Crimes peculiar to the Inhabitants, native and civilized, of the French Colonies of Indo-China, by Dr. Corre.

The Dangers of Debauchery, with especial reference to the Intellectual and Physical Faculties, its Influence on the Health and Human Life, by Dr. Virey.

Anthropological Studies of the Esoteric Habits and Customs of Antiquity, translated into English, by Alfred Allinson M.A., from the Seventh German Edition of Dr. Julius Rosenbaum.

Polygamia Triumphatrix; the History and Philosophy of Polygamy, based on the work of Th. Alethaeus (*XVI Century*) with the Scriptural and Medical arguments used by the Advocates and Adversaries of this Doctrine.

The Morbid Manifestations of the Sexual Instinct, from the double standpoint of Jurisprudence and Psychology, by Dr. B. Tarnowsky, Professor at the Imperial Medical Academy of St. Petersburg.

Medical Studies of the Latin Poets, translated from the French of Dr. P. Ménière, together with considerable additions and textual illustrations.

Curious Bypaths of History, being Medico-Historical researches, by Dr. Cabanès, with a copper-plate frontispiece after the original of Daniel Vierge, edition limited to 500 numbered copies.

Lectures on the Origin, Progress and Elimination of Syphilis, with special chapters on the cerebral developments of this disease, and its bearings on Marriage and Divorce, by Paul Robertson M.D. (*Edin.*).

La Jeunesse rendue aux Vieillards:—traduction faite sur les M.S.S. arabes (1068 de l'Hégire) dans la Bibliothèque Nationale à Paris. Suivie d'un Supplément traitant de la Nature et Efficacité des Aphrodisiaques.

www.ingramcontent.com/pod-product-compliance
Lightning Source LLC
Chambersburg PA
CBHW032025220426
43664CB00006B/369

* 9 7 8 3 7 4 2 8 2 7 1 0 4 *